OCEAN LINERS

An Illustrated History

OCEAN LINERS

An Illustrated History

Peter Newall

Foreword by Stephen Payne

Seaforth
PUBLISHING

Half title page photo: Cunard Line's *Ivernia*, see page 166.

Title page photo: *Guglielmo Marconi*, see page 151.

First published in Great Britain in 2018 by
Seaforth Publishing,
A division of Pen & Sword Books Ltd,
47 Church Street,
Barnsley S70 2AS

www.seaforthpublishing.com

British Library Cataloguing in Publication Data
A catalogue record for this book is available from the British Library

ISBN 978 1 5267 2316 1 (hardback)
ISBN 978 1 5267 2317 8 (epub)
ISBN 978 1 5267 2318 5 (kindle)

Pen & Sword Books Limited incorporates the imprints of Atlas, Archaeology, Aviation, Discovery, Family History, Fiction, History, Maritime, Military, Military Classics, Politics, Select, Transport, True Crime, Air World, Frontline Publishing, Leo Cooper, Remember When, Seaforth Publishing, The Praetorian Press, Wharncliffe Local History, Wharncliffe Transport, Wharncliffe True Crime and White Owl.

Typeset and designed by Stephen Dent
Printed and bound in China by 1010 Printing International Ltd

Contents

Foreword

Apart from a few isolated exceptions, the passenger ship is singularly the most social of the modes of transport. Social in that passenger ships, depending on their size, can be seen as small villages, small towns or even small cities – some maybe even as large cities. Within their confines, the whole experience of life can be seen to be played out; sleeping, dining, dancing, sports, watching films etc.; in fact, all the social interactions that occur on land, but in the passenger ships' case, the village, town or city moves from place to place. Behind the scenes, just as on land, fresh water has to be produced, sewage collected and disposed of, electricity for numerous consumers generated, food prepared etc. Indeed, the list of activities is too long to enumerate here.

Apart from the short-sea passenger ferry, passenger ships can be described as passenger liners or cruise ships. The latter are specifically designed to cater for the leisure or holiday trade, whereas the passenger liner was a scheduled means of getting from one place to another. As the late and lamented John Maxtone-Graham described, passenger ships were in many cases, 'The Only Way to Cross'. As such, the passenger liner holds an even more elevated place than the cruise ship, as this mode of transport fulfilled an altogether different and important function. In their heyday, passenger liners took diplomats and civil servants overseas to important appointments, business people travelled to far-off lands to sell their goods and wares to foreign markets, friends and relatives were brought together for reunions and special events, and crucially, these ships fuelled the hopes, dreams and aspirations of thousands of people looking for salvation or a new life elsewhere from the lands of their origin. Undeniably, before the aeroplane stole her thunder, the passenger liner was the iconic mode of transport, coincidentally for many years also being the largest moving object made by man. What a miraculous creation she was.

Some passenger liners were quite humble, quietly and faithfully serving their passengers on the sea routes around the world without undue publicity, whereas others were grand 'ships of state' financed and forged by nationalistic pride. Some ships were slow and sailed at a leisurely pace, whilst others vied with each other for speed records and fame. Many passenger liners not only operated in peacetime, but went to war in the service of their nations as troopships or armed merchant cruisers – and in some cases even as full warships following hasty conversions. The history of the passenger liner is surely wide and immeasurably varied.

Who better to provide us with a definitive history of the passenger liner than the noted maritime author Peter Newall. With a string of successful books behind him, this new volume *Ocean Liners* provides a very informative voyage through the history of many of the ships, the advancing technologies that drove innovation and the companies that operated them. Think of yourself as a passenger travelling through the pages of the book. Many of the ships featured are naturally old favourites, but some lesser-known ships are at anchor amongst the pages here too. It is a fascinating read, brought in a relaxed easy style that is sure to inform and keep the passenger interest.

So, present your ticket at the gangway, step aboard, find your cabin and then quickly make your way up top – for soon the whistle will blow and you wouldn't want to miss the spectacle of departure.

Bon Voyage!

Dr Stephen M Payne OBE RDI MNM FREng FRINA FRSA FSNAME HFIE CEng
Past President, The Royal Institution of Naval Architects
Designer, Cunard Line RMS *Queen Mary 2*

Introduction

Ocean liners are essentially people carriers and, unlike cargo ships, most of the innovations happen internally. Even now the key passenger-ship developments are in engine types and size of vessel. However, before the advent of the jet age, the ocean liner played a pivotal role in the transportation of people around the world. From humble beginnings in the 1830s, liner services grew rapidly. This growth was driven not only by political changes and developments in marine technology and design but also by increased competition as new companies were established to meet the demands of travellers.

Most liner books tend to be focussed on the transatlantic routes, whilst those written in this country are usually Britocentric. What I have tried to achieve with this book is a balanced coverage of the 100-year history of ocean liners from the early years of the nineteenth century until their demise in the 1970s. This meant having a global coverage with the inclusion of many lesser-known routes and ships. A key goal of the book was also to produce a work which not only has high-quality images but is also an informative read and as a result I have avoided featuring the entire history of each ship's career as that tends to spoil the flow of the narrative.

Although many company histories were consulted, original contemporary source material was used as the main source of information for the book wherever possible. This included press releases and articles/information in the following key shipping journals and registers

Engineer
Fairplay
Journal of Commerce
Lloyd's List
Marine News
Rhodes Directory of Passenger Steamers
Sea Breezes
Shipbuilding and Shipping Record
The Journal of Commerce
The Motorship
The Shipbuilder
The Shipbuilder and Marine Engine-Builder
The Times

Lloyd's Register of Shipping
Mercantile Navy List
Miramar Ship Index
Starke-Schell Registers

Acknowledgements

I would like to thank my publishers for their patience and faith in this project which turned out to be more complicated and time-consuming than originally planned. The book would also not have been possible without the support and encouragement of my wife Julie. My dear friends Andrew Bell, Bruce Peter and Luis Miguel Correia also kindly read the text and offered many useful suggestions. Finally, a big thank-you must go to Stephen Payne for his wonderful foreword to the book.

Chapter 1
Nineteenth-Century Liners

For most of the nineteenth century people were on the move in the greatest migration ever seen. Many were escaping poverty in their home countries whilst others were seeking their fortune in the gold rushes of North America, Australia and South Africa. Communications around the world were also rapidly improving with the introduction of railways, the opening of the Suez Canal, a universal postal system and, most importantly, the laying of undersea telegraph cables. Tourism as we know it took off in the 1870s and 1880s. For the first time in many years there was peace in Europe with the ending of the Franco-Prussian War between France and Germany. Italy and Germany became unified nations in 1861 and 1871 respectively. This was also a time of colonial expansion which would see Britain establishing the world's largest empire. To meet the demand, passenger ships became increasingly important throughout this period with great advances being made not only in ship design but also marine engineering.

The first steamship line on the North Atlantic

The first steamship line to be established on the North Atlantic was not Cunard Line. It was the British and American Steam Navigation Company which had been formed in 1835 by an ambitious London-based American entrepreneur, John Junius. He saw that the future of Atlantic travel lay not in sail but in steam-powered ships which could halve the average westbound crossing time of over a month. A 1,862gt paddle steamer was ordered from the London shipyard, Curling & Young. Laid down as *Royal Victoria*, her maiden voyage in 1838 was delayed because the engine builders went bankrupt. With the imminent arrival of Isambard Kingdom Brunel's 1,320gt *Great Western*, British & American was determined to be the first into New York and chartered the small Irish Sea passenger ship *Sirius* (1837/703gt), shown below. Despite rough weather and limited coal supplies, *Sirius* arrived in New York on the morning of 23 April 1838, a few hours before *Great Western*. This event had a profound impact and one commentator wrote 'there can be little doubt that ere long the Atlantic will be aswarm with these sea monsters and that a complete revolution will be wrought in the navigation of the ocean, as has already been witnessed on the rivers and inland seas'. How right he was. Within two years, the British postal system had been revolutionised with the introduction of the Uniform Penny Post and more importantly, the awarding by the Admiralty of subsidised mail contracts. These led to the formation of Britain's leading shipping lines, including P&O, Royal Mail Line, Pacific Steam and Cunard Line. At a stroke, the world had become a smaller place with a faster and reliable postal service. Instead of months waiting for the mails, they would arrive in a matter of weeks.

Brunel's 'Greats'

Although *Great Western* was the first steamer constructed for service on the North Atlantic she was, like all three of Brunel's ships, a one-off. His second ship, the 3,270gt *Great Britain*, below, was completed in 1843. She was not only the first screw-propelled passenger ship but also the first built of iron to cross the Atlantic. The largest ship in the world at that time, she was built at Bristol by Messrs William Patterson and Sons. With accommodation for 252 passengers, she was fitted with six masts and carried around 1,700 square yards of sail. Unfortunately this innovative vessel was a failure as she did not have a running mate so operating a regular service was problematic. Samuel Cunard, on the other hand, took a more cautious approach for his Liverpool to Halifax passenger-mail service with his fleet of four small, 1,100gt wooden paddle ships. The company's first iron-hulled, screw-driven ship, *Andes* (1,275gt), only appeared in 1852. Meanwhile *Great Britain* stranded on the coast of Ireland in 1846 but was refloated the following year. She was subsequently sold and operated as an emigrant ship to Australia. She eventually became a sailing ship and in 1886 arrived at Port Stanley in the Falkland Islands where she was used as a coal hulk. In 1970 she was returned to Bristol aboard a large floating barge. She has now been fully restored to her former glory as a museum ship.

Brunel's third ship was even more astonishing than his earlier ships. The 18,915gt *Great Eastern* was five times the size of any ship built to that date. Her record tonnage was not exceeded for another forty-three years. Designed for the Indian and Australian passenger and cargo trade she was completed on the Thames by John Scott Russell and Co. in 1858. Her four-year construction was a logistical nightmare and contributed to Brunel's early death. She was also unique in the fact that she used both paddle wheels and screw propulsion and was able to do 14 knots. She had five funnels, six masts with sails and could accommodate 800 first, 2,000 second and 1,200 third class passengers. First class was sumptuous, with rich wall hangings and mirrored bulkheads. The 63ft long, 47ft wide and 14ft high Grand Saloon had a balcony and gas-lit chandeliers. Some of the cabins also had baths with hot and cold running water. Although a failure as a passenger ship *Great Eastern* revolutionised the world in July 1866 when she successfully laid the first transatlantic telegraph cable. She was sold for scrap on the Mersey in 1888.

The last Atlantic paddle steamers

On the North Atlantic, where speed was very important, paddle power had the edge over propeller-driven ships. However, they were expensive to operate with a daily coal consumption double that of a screw steamer. Despite this, Cunard was determined to have the fastest ships on the Atlantic so prestige took precedence over cost. In 1862, the Robert Napier shipyard completed the 3,871gt *Scotia*, Cunard's last paddle steamer. She was one of the finest ships built for the company up to that date, not only in terms of looks but also passenger comfort. In 1863 she made the fastest-ever Atlantic crossing in both directions. Her record from Queenstown to New York (eight days, three hours), averaging 14.5 knots, remained unbroken until 1872 whilst her New York–Queenstown record (eight days, five hours and forty-two minutes), averaging 14.2 knots, remained in place until 1867. She had space for 1,400 tons of cargo, 573 cabin passengers and 1,500 troops in case of war. She was only withdrawn from service in 1878. She later became a cable ship and was wrecked in Guam in 1904.

The newly-formed Compagnie Générale Transatlantique (French Line) was also committed to a fast transatlantic service and ordered nine paddle steamers for its new routes to the Caribbean, Mexico and North America. Three were built at Greenock by John Scott and Company. The first to be delivered in 1864 was the 3,204gt, 13-knot *Washington*, below, which inaugurated the Le Havre to New York service in June of that year. She was followed by *Lafayette* and *Impératrice Eugénie*. Impressive-looking ships with two tall funnels and twin masts, they each carried 330 passengers and 1,000 tons of cargo. However, their careers as paddle steamers were short lived as it soon became apparent that paddle propulsion was no longer a viable option. In 1867 *Washington* was converted to twin-screw propulsion and became the first Atlantic liner to be fitted with twin-screws. The remaining CGT paddlers also had their paddle power replaced with screw propulsion. *Washington* remained with French Line for thirty-six years and was only broken up in 1899.

Compound engines

The development of the compound engine for screw-driven ships in the 1850s was one of the great advances in nineteenth century marine engineering. Although the single-cylinder expansion engine was easy to operate, it was a very inefficient use of steam power. The compound engine, on the other hand, allowed the steam to be passed from two cylinders of differing sizes without much loss of temperature and this not only provided better power, it also saved on the amount of coal used. Although coal was cheap and in plentiful supply, lower coal consumption meant smaller coal bunkers and thus more space for revenue-earning cargo. On longer routes operational costs were significantly reduced because they were not only able to travel further but also used less coal. Among the first companies to use these new engines was the Peninsular and Oriental Steam Navigation Company (P&O) which in 1840 had been awarded the mail contract to carry the mails between Southampton to Alexandria in Egypt and between Suez and Calcutta. This was later extended to Singapore, Hong Kong, Shanghai, Australia and Japan. *Mooltan* (1861/2,257gt) was the first to be fitted with an early type of compound engine which produced a speed of 12 knots. She was used on the Southampton to Alexandra service and carried 112 first and 37 second class passengers. In 1884 she was sold and reduced to a sailing ship and disappeared in 1891 whilst on a voyage from Newcastle upon Tyne to Valparaiso.

The first ship to cross the North Atlantic with a compound engine was the small 764gt steamer *Brandon* in 1854 whilst the first compound-engine passenger liner to operate on the Atlantic was Anchor Line's 2,290gt *India* in 1869. Powerful compound engines also played a key role in the phenomenal success of Thomas Ismay's Oceanic Steam Navigation Company Limited, commonly known as White Star Line, which commenced its service between Liverpool and New York in 1871 with the 3,707gt *Oceanic*, the first of a quartet of elegant 14-knot ships built at Belfast by Harland and Wolff. These four-masted ships were a revolution on the Atlantic with their extreme length and accommodation extended to the full width of the hull instead of the traditional narrow amidships deck-house. The main dining salon was also placed amidships where there was least motion and noise from the propellers. From the start, White Star Line's main focus was passenger comfort in first class with larger cabins, steam heating, electric bells, taps for water, individual dining chairs instead of fixed, armless swivel chairs, and a dedicated smoking room. *Oceanic* carried 160 first and 1,000 steerage class passengers. The new White Star liners soon broke the Atlantic crossing records and during 1873, the average time for a Cunard Liverpool to New York voyage was almost a day slower than White Star. *Oceanic*'s name was passed to another White Star innovative liner in 1899, three years after the original pioneer ship was broken up.

The Suez Canal and the threat to P&O

The opening of the Suez Canal on 17 November 1869 was not only one of the most significant events in P&O's history, it also posed a great threat. Although it was now able to operate ships all the way between Britain, India and the Far East, the canal also allowed foreign competitors to enter the market.

During the 1870s P&O upgraded its fleet and the most significant ship of that decade was the single-screw, iron-hull *Kaisar-i-Hind* built at Greenock by Caird and Co Ltd Not only was she P&O's first ship over 4,000gt, she was also the first in the fleet fitted with refrigerating machinery. Nicknamed the 'Bridge to India' because of the comfortable accommodation for 176 first and 64 second class passengers, she made her maiden voyage from London to Bombay in September 1878. Her Indian name, which means 'Emperor/Empress of India', celebrated Queen Victoria's adoption of that title the previous year. Her 15-knot service speed also made her the fastest ship in the P&O fleet. Here she is passing through the Suez Canal. Note that most of her ports are open to help with ventilation in the stifling heat. Within a few years she was superseded by more impressive steel-hulled ships, P&O's first steel vessel was the 3,340gt *Ravenna* of 1880. *Kaisar-i-Hind* lasted until 1897 when she was sold to breakers in Bombay.

The first Castle liners on the Cape route

With opening of the Suez Canal in 1869, many people in the Cape Colony were concerned about the impact on trade as many ships bound for Australasia went via the Cape. However, this worry was short-lived after the discovery of diamonds in the northern Cape earlier that year. Diamond fever broke out with mining equipment and people pouring into the Cape Colony. Needless to say, shipping companies had a field day, with a number of new lines emerging. The failure of one of these allowed the wolf through the door. He was the ambitious Donald Currie, who would eventually swallow up Union Line which had been operating the Southampton to Southern Africa mail contract since 1857. *Edinburgh Castle* (1872/2,678gt), below, was one of four ships ordered by Currie for the London to Calcutta run but which were transferred to the new Castle Packets passenger-mail service which offered twice monthly sailings to Cape Town from London, via Dartmouth. These tiny vessels were the first of the famous Castle mailships which sailed between Britain and Southern Africa for over a hundred years. *Edinburgh Castle* was sold to Spanish owners in 1889 and was broken up in 1898.

First steel passenger ships

The inventions of Sir Henry Bessemer and Sir William Siemens transformed the making of steel in the mid-nineteenth century. Their methods made it easier to produce large quantities of steel much cheaper than before. Steel is not only lighter than iron it is also stronger and is therefore an ideal material for use in ships. The first steel ocean-going ship was the William Denny-built *Rotomahana* (1,727gt), right, of 1879. This good-looking vessel, with a long clipper stem surmounted by a figurehead depicting a Maori princess, was designed for the Union Steam Ship Company of New Zealand's passenger-mail service between Wellington and Sydney. She originally carried 105 first class and 69 second class passengers and had a service speed of just over 15 knots. When she was sold for scrap in 1925 her steel hull was still in remarkably good condition.

The first steel ship to operate on the North Atlantic was Allan Line's 4,000gt *Buenos Ayrean*, shown below. She was also built at Dumbarton by William Denny and at the time of her completion in 1879, four months after *Rotomahana*, she was the largest steel ship in the world with the largest steel engines. She had a bridge deck which extended for most of her length and was designed as a cattle vessel for both the Canadian and River Plate routes. She was subsequently used on the Glasgow-Montreal service mainly as an emigrant carrier and was broken up in 1911.

Also in 1879, Cunard Line announced that it had placed an order with J and G Thomson, for a 'screw steamship, the size of which will only be exceeded by *Great Eastern*, while the speed will be greater than that of any ocean steamship afloat'. In November 1881 it took delivery of the 7,392gt *Servia*. Not only was she a major break with the past, she was Cunard's first ship built of steel. Like the Belfast-built White Star liners, *Servia* was a long, narrow ship. She also had a long, full-height forecastle in place of the usual transatlantic turtleback forecastle and was the first Cunarder to have electric lighting and remote-controlled watertight doors. However, although she was a relatively fast ship (16.7 knots), she was not a record-breaker and with her tall twin funnels, looked somewhat ungainly, certainly in comparison with White Star's crack ships. She had a single screw, triple-expansion engines and carried 404 cabin class and 750 steerage passengers. Within a few years she was outclassed by newer and faster Cunard liners. She was withdrawn in 1901 and sold to breakers the following year.

The battle for the Atlantic speed record intensified in the early 1880s with the decision to build large, fast ships by two companies usually associated with the emigrant trade, Guion Line and National Line. Guion's *Alaska* (1881/6,950gt) was the first ship to cross the Atlantic in less than a week whilst the magnificent, 18.5-knot, 7,374gt *Oregon* of 1883 further reduced the crossing times. However, the cost of *Oregon*'s building was too great and she was sold to Cunard Line. National also had similar problems with its record-breaker, the 5,528gt *America* of

1884, shown here. She was built of steel by J and G Thompson, Clydebank and fitted with large three-cylinder compound engines which produced an average speed of 18 knots. She had a striking profile with two masts, a clipper bow and two large elliptical funnels. Her passenger capacity was 300 first and 700 third class. The finest room on the ship was undoubtedly the 51ft long Grand Saloon which was situated forward of the bridge. It extended the full width of the ship and was surmounted by a large barrel-vaulted glass dome which rose to a height of 19ft and which was supported by large carved pillars. However, without a running mate she was too expensive to operate and was sold to the Italian Government. She was used in various roles including as the Italian Royal Yacht and was only sold for demolition in 1925.

Orient Line

In 1878 P&O faced major competition to Australia from the newly-formed Orient Steam Navigation Co Ltd, which had started a new monthly passenger-cargo and emigrant joint service between London and Australia with the Pacific Steam Navigation Company (PSNC). The ships went outbound via the Cape, returning through the Suez Canal. It initially used chartered PSNC steamers but in 1879 took delivery of its first newly-built ship. The 5,365gt *Orient* was constructed by John Elder and Co and at the time was the largest ship in the world after the *Great Eastern*. She was also the first ship to be built to Admiralty standards for service as an armed merchant cruiser in time of war and carried 120 first, 130 second and 300 third class passengers. With her four tall masts and pair of raked funnels, *Orient* set the style for the first generation of handsome Orient and PSNC Australian liners. With a 16-knot service speed she broke all the existing records to Australia and South Africa and the South African record remained unbroken for ten years. Here she is off Tilbury in the late 1880s or early 1890s. Her yards were later removed and in 1898 she was given new triple-expansion engines and the two funnels were replaced by one tall funnel whilst the main and mizzen masts were removed. She was scrapped in 1910 after a career of almost thirty years. After being awarded the New South Wales mail contract in 1883, the Cape route was abandoned and the service ran via the Suez Canal. From 1888 the Australian mail contract was shared between Orient Line and P&O and the fortunes of the two companies became inextricably linked. In 1918 P&O took a controlling interest in Orient Line although the two companies continued to exist as separate entities until 1960 when P&O-Orient Lines was formed.

P&O passenger-mail services to India and Australia

P&O was awarded its first mail contract in 1837, the same year Queen Victoria ascended to the throne. Fifty years later the company celebrated its fiftieth anniversary whilst the Queen was feted with numerous Golden Jubilee celebrations. In honour of both these events, P&O ordered four new passenger ships, the 'Jubilee' class, for its Australian and Indian routes. The 6,500gt, 16-knot *Victoria*, *Britannia*, *Oceana* and *Arcadia* were the largest built to that date for the company. The first pair were constructed by Caird and Co Ltd in 1887, whilst the slightly larger second pair came from Harland and Wolff, Belfast the following year. They had a distinctive profile with four tall masts and two slim, closely-spaced, raked funnels. *Victoria*, shown here coaling at Port Said, was the first to be delivered. She had a large cargo capacity and carried 230 passengers in first class and 156 in second. Her maiden voyage to Bombay was delayed so that she could take part in the Jubilee Naval Review at Spithead, near Portsmouth. She and her sisters were also designed and subsidised for conversion when necessary under the Admiralty's Auxiliary Cruiser Agreement of 1887. In the 1890s she was chartered, like many of P&O's ships, as an Indian troopship. Modernised in 1904, she was sold with her sister *Britannia* to a Genoese ship breaker in 1909.

The P&O Express Service

Brindisi, situated at the heel of Italy was an important port for the embarkation of the mails to India, Australia and the Far East. Passengers and mails left London a week after the departure of the main line steamer from London and boarded a special train at Calais, bound for Brindisi. To speed up this service P&O ordered a pair of 1,728gt, two-funnelled ships from Caird and Co Ltd *Isis* and *Osiris* were completed in 1898 and with twin screws and triple-expansion engines, their service speed was 20 knots and they usually completed the express crossing between Brindisi and Port Said in two days, thus enabling their seventy-eight first class passengers to reach Egypt in four days from London instead of twelve days by the all-sea route. Most of the crew were Italian but with British officers. *Isis* is shown here at Port Said with a Royal Mail pennant and a large Blue Peter flag. After the outbreak of war she became the Admiralty fleet messenger HMS *Isonzo*. She was sold in 1920 to M H Bland and Co Ltd, Gibraltar and was renamed *Gibel Sarsar*. She was broken up in 1926, four years after her sister went to the breakers. After the First World War, the P&O Express Service went by train from London to Marseilles instead of Brindisi.

British India Line

One of P&O's greatest competitors on the India run was the British India Steam Navigation Company (BI) which started a fortnightly passenger and cargo service from London in 1869, the same year in which the Suez Canal was opened. For fifteen years the 6,037gt, 13-knot *Golconda* of 1888 was the largest in the BI fleet. The biggest ship built on the River Wear to that date by William Doxford & Sons, she had been constructed by the builders on speculation to show off its skills at shipbuilding. The gamble paid off and established Doxford's as one of the leading British shipbuilders. With four tall masts and two raked funnels, her design was similar to P&O's 'Jubilee' class. She also had a large cargo capacity and considerable deck space for 102 cabin passengers and offered a great improvement for BI on the London route, which until then had been operated by ships of more modest tonnage. Launched as *Transpacific*, she was bought by British India soon after completion and renamed *Golconda*. She became popular among passengers and was known by rival shipowners as the 'Calcutta thief' because of her large cargo capacity. Here she is coaling, probably in the Hooghly River, Calcutta. Note the extreme sheer and turtle-back forecastle. She was chartered as a transport during the Boer War and carried ammunition. In 1913 she was transferred to the East Africa service. On 3 June 1916 she struck a mine off Aldeburgh and sank with the loss of nineteen lives.

The Royal Mail Steam Packet Company and the last days of sail

Established in 1839 with a Royal Charter to operate to North and South America and the West Indies, the Royal Mail Steam Packet Company was, like Cunard Line, a very conservative company during its first half-century of operation. Its last paddle steamer was only sold in 1883 whilst many of its ships were sail rigged. A turning point for the company came in 1886 with the completion by Caird and Company of the 4,572gt *Orinoco* which had been designed for the Southampton to the West Indies service. Not only was she the largest ship in the Royal Mail fleet to that date she was also the last of its passenger-cargo ships with cross yards and a flush upper deck with wooden deckhouses. Other firsts included a steel hull, triple-expansion engines and electric lighting. She was the forerunner of a series of five beautifully-proportioned Royal Mail ships. She carried 257 first and 26 second class passengers and had four hatches for working cargo. In 1897 she took part in the Diamond Jubilee Naval Review and around the turn of the century her yards were removed. Overtaken by increasingly larger ships she was sold for demolition in 1909.

ORINOCO

The west coast of South America

For over eighty years Royal Mail's associate, the Pacific Steam Navigation Company, had a virtual monopoly of the coastal trade between Chile and Panama and was sometimes known as the 'South American Railway'. By 1873 it had become the largest steamship company in the world with a fleet of fifty-seven ships, of which thirty-one were used on the Pacific coast service. The 3,227gt, twin-screw, 12.5-knot *Guatemala* was typical of PSNC's passenger-cargo coastal ships of the latter part of the nineteenth century. A three-class vessel, she had two tall masts and a large funnel set slightly aft of amidships. Her superstructure also extended almost to the bow whilst much of the promenade decks offered covered shelter from the extreme heat and heavy rain. She and her sister *Colombia* were built at Greenock by Caird and Company in 1899. However, *Colombia*, like so many of the coastal ships, was wrecked on the treacherous coast of Peru in 1907. In 1922 the Chilean Government passed a new cabotage law which restricted foreign companies from operating between ports in Chile. The following year PSNC closed its coastal service and sold the remaining ships to local companies. *Guatemala* was bought by R W James and Cia and renamed *Fresia*. She foundered at Valparaiso in 1949.

The opening up of Japan and new routes to United States

On 8 July 1853 a squadron of four United States Navy warships under the command of Commodore Perry sailed into Tokyo Bay with a demand from the United States Government that Japan open its ports for trade. The arrival of these 'Black Ships' brought to an end over 220 years of isolation and was the catalyst for Japan's transformation from a feudal state into a modern nation. A dozen years later, the United States Congress agreed to subsidise a steamship line between the United States, China and Japan. The Pacific Mail Steamship Company's paddle steamer *Colorado* (1865/3,357gt) inaugurated the first regular passenger service from San Francisco to Hong Kong and Yokohama in 1867. Despite competition, Pacific Mail was the premier line between the United States and the Far East for most of the nineteenth century. In 1889 it took delivery of one of its most impressive ships, the 5,060gt *China*. At the time she was the largest and fastest (19 knots maximum) ship on the route and reduced the Yokohama–San Francisco record by 17 hours. Unusually, she was constructed on the Clyde by Fairfield and was very similar to Orient Line's *Ormuz* which came from the same yard three years earlier. She carried 120 cabin passengers and 1,000 in steerage. In 1915 Pacific Mail withdrew from the trans-Pacific services because a law was passed by Congress which significantly reduced the number of Orientals serving on US ships and *China* was sold to a new company, China Mail Steamship Company. She was eventually broken up in 1925 at the end of a 36-year career.

Further expansion in Southern Africa

The discovery of gold on the Witwatersrand in the Transvaal in 1886 had a tremendous impact on both the trade and the political environment of Southern Africa. However, it was only in the early 1890s when local harbours were able to accommodate larger liners. Although they had shared the weekly mail contract between England and South Africa since 1876, the Union Steamship Company Ltd and Castle Packets Company Ltd were great rivals in the battle for supremacy in the last decade of the nineteenth century. In 1891 the magnificent 6,844gt, Denny-built *Scot* was completed for Union Line. The first twin-screw Cape liner and the largest ship to that date on the route, *Scot* was an outstanding vessel. Her March 1893 Southampton–Cape Town record of fourteen days, eighteen hours and fifty-seven minutes remained unbroken until the arrival of *Stirling Castle* in 1936. Her triple-expansion engines produced a top speed of almost 19 knots. Despite lengthening in 1896, which considerably enhanced her appearance, she remained a failure because of her high operating cost and limited cargo capacity. She carried over 400 passengers in three classes and was sold in 1905 to HAPAG. She survived the war and became a Spanish liner until her demolition in 1927.

Both the Southampton-based Union Line and London-based Castle Packets had intermediate ships which operated on an ad hoc basis between the mail contract sailings. These smaller, slower, 'extra' ships called at a wider range of ports and were often used by migrants seeking a new life in South Africa. The 11-knot *Harlech Castle* (1894/3,264gt), seen here in the Thames, was typical of the type. She had considerable cargo space and carried 44 first and 250 third class passengers. She was used extensively during the Second Boer War as a troopship before being sold in 1904. She was broken up in 1934.

German mail service to Australia and the Far East

In the years following the unification of Germany in 1871 the country had its eye on global power and established various colonies in Africa, the Pacific Ocean and China. In 1885 Norddeutscher Lloyd entered into an agreement with the Imperial German Government to operate a subsidised passenger-mail service to the Far East and Australia, which also included three feeder lines and involved a fleet of sixteen steamers. Many of these mail ships also operated on the North Atlantic and were painted white. One of the finest liners on the monthly service between Bremerhaven to Sydney via Southampton was the triple-expansion, 16-knot *Kaiser Wilhelm II* (1889/6,990gt). Built at Stettin by AG Vulcan she was designed to compete with the best ships of Orient Line and P&O, and carried 180 first and 84 second class passengers in superior accommodation. The dining saloons, smoking rooms, ladies' cabin and music room were all situated on the upper deck whilst first class cabins had tables and wardrobes. With her four tall pole masts, buff funnels and white hull, *Kaiser Wilhelm II* had the appearance of a royal yacht. In 1900 she was rebuilt. Reduced to two masts, she was renamed *Hohenzollern* as her name was required for a new 19,361gt *Kaiser Wilhelm II*. She was sold for demolition at Genoa in 1908.

The 'All-Red Route' to the Far East

In 1886, Granville in British Columbia was chosen as the terminus for the first trans-Canadian railway, the Canadian Pacific Railway (CPR). This small town renamed Vancouver was to be the focal point for a great expansion plan which provided Britain with an 'All-Red Route' to the Far East. Worried about Russian influence in northern Asia, the British Government wished to see an increased British presence in the region, especially because of the strategic importance of Hong Kong. The new railway, linked with a trans-Pacific sea service, offered a more direct connection than the Suez Canal, and also allowed a speedier military response in times of crisis and an improved mail service. After a trial period on the Vancouver–Far East service using chartered tonnage, CPR ordered three beautifully-proportioned twin-screw liners of just under 6,000gt from the Naval Construction and Armament Company, Barrow-in-Furness. *Empress of India*, shown here, *Empress of Japan* and *Empress of China* were delivered in 1891. Operating at a service speed of just under 17 knots, they had yacht-like profiles with raked tall pole masts, twin funnels, overhanging stern and clipper bow with a figurehead. First class accommodation was of the highest standard, with a typical layout of the period i.e. dining saloon with long tables on the upper deck, the library on the deck above, its plush seats surrounding the domed roof of the dining saloon, and a smoking room aft. With few connecting corridors, many of the cabins opened onto the deck. The white 'Empresses' were record-breakers and proved to be very reliable with no sailing missed in fifteen years. In 1911 a pair of 17,000gt liners, *Empress of Russia* and *Empress of Asia*, were ordered as replacements for the original CPR trio. In the same year *Empress of China* was wrecked in Japan and in 1914, the Maharajah of Gwalior bought *Empress of India* for use as the hospital ship *Loyalty*. Later owned by Scindia she was the first ship to sail internationally under Indian ownership. *Empress of Japan* was laid up in 1922 and scrapped in 1926.

LEWIS'S
TAILORING

The first twin-screw express Atlantic liners

With the development of reliable triple-expansion engines and the introduction of twin screws, liners finally dispensed with sail. Up to that point, auxiliary sail was always carried because of constant problems with engine breakdowns and broken propeller shafts. Now if one engine failed, the ship could still continue with the remaining one. On the Atlantic run, the first twin-screw express liners were Inman Line's 10,499gt *City of New York*, below, and *City of Paris* which were delivered by J and G Thomson, Glasgow in 1888 and 1889 respectively. Designed to carry 450 first, 200 second and 1,000 steerage class passengers, they featured many innovations. Subsidised by the Admiralty for use as auxiliary cruisers, the ships also had unique safety features which included a continuous double bottom, the engines and boilers contained within separate watertight bulkheads which extended to the saloon deck, a centreline bulkhead which divided the two engine rooms; a semi-balanced rudder situated well below the waterline, and lifeboats able to accommodate all on board. They were also the first Atlantic liners to be fitted with a forced draught system to improve the performance of the boilers, and anti-rolling tanks which were an early form of stabiliser. Numerous other technological improvements included lifts to bring food from the sealed galleys to the pantries, and the most comprehensive hydraulic system yet fitted which powered the steering gear, winches and capstans. Externally, they were beautifully proportioned with three closely-spaced raked funnels situated amidships and balanced by three tall pole masts. Passengers were accommodated on four decks, with first class amidships and the principal public rooms on the saloon and promenade decks. The highlight of the interior was undoubtedly the main dining room which was situated well forward on the saloon deck. Entered through large glass doors, this wood-panelled room on the *City of New York* was surmounted by a huge barrel-shaped glass dome which rose 20ft above the deck, its base supported by sculptures of mythical sea creatures. Electric lighting was fitted throughout, and for the first time on any vessel, electric motors were used to ventilate the ship. At the time of their completion they were not only the most luxurious ships afloat but also the largest and fastest liners in the world. In 1889 they became the first to complete a transatlantic crossing in less than six days. In 1893, they were transferred to the United States flagged American Line and renamed *New York* and *Paris*. Operations were also moved from Liverpool to Southampton. They survived the First World War and at the end of long and eventful careers were broken up at Genoa in 1923.

Cunard's record-breakers of the 1890s

Cunard Line's response to the Inman pair was the 12,952gt *Campania* and *Lucania* built on the Clyde by Fairfield Shipbuilding and Engineering Company Ltd. These powerful ships were record-breakers in terms of speed and size. They also looked the part with two large funnels atop a relatively low superstructure. The funnels were widely spaced because the first class drawing room and dining saloon were situated between the uptakes. Their five-cylinder 47ft-high triple-expansion engines, another first for Cunard, were so immense that the cylinder tops reached the promenade deck. As the first Cunarders to be built to Admiralty specifications under the armed auxiliary cruiser scheme, many safety features were incorporated into their design. The accommodation, especially for the 600 first class passengers, was superb, with red velvet curtains and rich mahogany panelling much in evidence. There was also a fully-stocked library, an impressive three-deck-high dining saloon and for the first time on a Cunard ship, large suites with a parlour and attached bedroom. With an average speed of over 21 knots they both set new Atlantic crossing records. However, their reign at the top was short lived. Within five years they were superseded by faster and larger ships. *Lucania* was destroyed by fire in 1909 whilst *Campania* remained in service until 1914. She was sold to the Admiralty for conversion into a seaplane carrier. She sank in 1918.

Germany flexes its muscles on the Atlantic

In the latter part of the nineteenth century Germany began to flex its muscles on the international stage, especially on the North Atlantic where the German rivals Hamburg-Amerika Linie and Norddeutscher Lloyd introduced increasingly larger and faster ships. In 1898 Norddeutscher Lloyd's *Kaiser Wilhelm der Grosse* became the first German ship to capture the record for the fastest Atlantic crossing at an average speed of over 22 knots. This triple expansion, twin-screw, 14,349gt liner, which was built at Stettin by AG Vulcan, was the first transatlantic liner, apart from *Great Eastern*, to have four funnels. The gap between the pairs of funnels became a characteristic of the large four-funnelled German liners at the turn of the nineteenth century. This allowed space for a vertical well from which the main public rooms could radiate. A skylight at the top of the well provided natural light for the rooms below and enabled dining saloons to have multi deck high ceilings. *Kaiser Wilhelm der Grosse*'s grandiose neo-Baroque gilded interiors were designed by the well-known architect Johann Poppe. The 558 first class passengers enjoyed a single sitting dining saloon, wide sheltered promenade deck and cabins which were the equivalent of the best hotels ashore. She also carried 338 second and over 1,000 steerage class passengers. Until the arrival of Cunard's *Lusitania* in 1907, Germany and its four-funnelled liners dominated the transatlantic speed record in both directions. Not long after the outbreak of the First World War *Kaiser Wilhelm der Grosse* was requisitioned as a German armed merchant cruiser but was scuttled by her crew after she was discovered by a British cruiser whilst bunkering off the coast of West Africa.

White Star giants

Although it had also joined in the race for record-breaking ships with the 19-knot *Teutonic* (1889/9,984gt) and *Majestic* (1890/9,861gt), White Star Line decided to concentrate its effort on large liners with high quality passenger accommodation. In the space of two years it introduced two Harland and Wolff, Belfast-built ships which were the first vessels to exceed the dimensions of *Great Eastern*. In 1899, the 17,274gt *Oceanic* entered service as the world's largest ship. With a length of over 700ft, she was the first to exceed the length of *Great Eastern*, which had been broken up in 1889. *Oceanic* was a beautifully-proportioned liner with three tall masts, two funnels and a narrow beam. To accommodate her, the world's largest dry dock, the Canada graving dock, was constructed at Liverpool. Designed as a floating hotel, her décor by the leading British architect Richard Norman Shaw was more constrained than the exuberance of the German liners of that time. The 360-seater, domed dining saloon was particularly noteworthy not just for its size but also for its rich design. The four sides of the well under the dome each contained an allegorical female figure representing Great Britain, America, New York and Liverpool. The side walls of the saloon were also fitted with luxurious sofas upholstered in Genoa crimson velvet. Many of the staterooms on the upper decks were suites with bathrooms. Her passenger capacity was 410 first, 300 second and 1,000 in steerage. As she had to operate a schedule with the other express liners she had twin-screws driven by triple-expansion engines which produced a maximum speed of 21 knots. The last purpose-built White Star express liner, her end came in September 1914 when she ran aground in fog in the Shetlands whilst on duty as an auxiliary cruiser.

CHAPTER 2
The Early Years of the Twentieth Century

The Edwardian Era between the turn of the century and the start of the First World War was a time of both great luxury and extreme poverty, when size of ship mattered for the leading shipping lines. It also saw the introduction of the steam turbine and the diesel engine, two inventions which transformed the design of the passenger liner.

White Star's Big Four

Oceanic was the world's largest ship until the arrival of White Star's 20,904gt *Celtic* in 1901. The first vessel over 20,000gt and the first to exceed the tonnage of *Great Eastern*, she was also the first of a new class of intermediate liners known as the 'Big Four'. Although slightly shorter than *Oceanic* she had a greater beam. Fitted with twin-screws and quadruple-expansion engines she was not designed for speed. She had a large cargo capacity, 677,820ft^3, and a mean speed of only 16 knots. Although less lavish than Cunard's express liners, *Celtic*'s 347 first class passengers had facilities of a high standard which, for the first time, included single-berth cabins. She also carried 160 in second class whilst the 2,352 steerage passengers were accommodated in cabins or dormitories on the lower decks. Married couples and single women in steerage were housed aft and single men forward. The bridge and officers' quarters was also separated from the passenger accommodation. The success of *Celtic* led to the order for three more increasingly larger ships. The 21,035gt *Cedric* in 1903, 23,884gt *Baltic* in 1904 and 24,541gt *Adriatic* in 1907. These profitable ships became the backbone for the White Star fleet. *Celtic* was stranded in a storm at Cobh in 1928 whilst the remaining three liners were sold for demolition in the early 1930s.

The formation of the Union-Castle Line

For the 1900 mail contract the Cape Government withdrew the requirement which forbade a merger between Union Line and Castle Packets. As a result, the two lines decided to amalgamate into a new company, the Union-Castle Steamship Company Ltd in March 1900. The first new mail ship to be delivered to the new company was the 12,385gt, twin-screw, 17.5-knot *Saxon*. This beautifully-balanced liner was the third in a series of two-funnelled liners built for Union Line at Belfast by Harland and Wolff. The first ship, *Norman* (1894/7,537gt) was a smaller version of Harland's elegant White Star Atlantic liners. The shipyard had a long association with Union-Castle Line right up to *Pendennis Castle* in 1958. *Saxon* carried 310 first, 203 second and 286 third class passengers. She remained in the fleet until 1935 when she was sold for scrap.

The first modern liner of the twentieth century

The large liners of the early 1900s saw the introduction of the main public rooms being situated on a single deck, usually the boat deck with its long unbroken promenade space. The first truly modern liner of the twentieth century, however, was Hamburg-America Line's 22,622gt *Amerika* of 1905 which not only had the first electric passenger lifts but also the first à la carte restaurant on a passenger ship. Run by chefs from the famous hotel group, the Ritz-Carlton restaurant on *Amerika* offered those in first class even greater exclusivity. For a premium, passengers could eat in a separate à la carte dining room. The success of this concept prompted White Star to include a similar restaurant in *Olympic* and her sister-ship, *Titanic*. *Amerika* was constructed at Belfast by Harland and Wolff as a faster and more luxurious version of White Star's *Celtic*-class. Designed for the Hamburg to New York route, her twin-screws were driven by quadruple-expansion engines which produced a service speed of 18 knots. She carried four classes of passengers: 388 first, 150 second, 222 third and 1,750 in steerage accommodation. The interiors of her stylish first class public rooms were the work of Charles Mewès (1860–1914) who designed César Ritz's hotels in Paris, London and Madrid. In 1906 she was joined by her larger Stettin-built sister, the 24,581gt *Kaiserin Auguste Victoria* and together the two liners offered the most luxurious service across the Atlantic. Requisitioned by the US Government in 1917, *Amerika* became the troopship *America*. After the war returned to the North Atlantic initially as part of the US Mail Line fleet which was taken over by United States Line. Handed back to the Government in 1931 she was rebuilt as the single-funnel army transport *Edmund B. Alexander*. She was eventually scrapped in 1958.

The first purpose-built deep-sea cruise ship

After the end of the Franco-Prussian War in 1871 and the unification of Italy and Germany, tourism in Europe and the Mediterranean took off. The first passenger ship dedicated to cruising was *Ceylon* (1,858/2,110gt), a former P&O liner. She was converted into a 'cruising yacht' and in 1882 made her first cruise to the North Cape for the Ocean Steam Yachting Company. The romance of visiting the Norwegian fjords and the Arctic Circle by sea soon attracted other companies such as the North of Scotland, Orkney and Shetland Shipping Company. This line introduced regular ten-day cruises to Norway in 1886 and the success of these led to the order of the first purpose-built cruise ship, *St. Sunniva* (1887/864gt). In 1901, Hamburg-Amerika Linie, which had been in the cruising business since 1891, introduced the world's first purpose-built deep-sea cruise ship, the 4,419gt, twin-screw, 15-knot *Prinzessin Victoria Luise*. This beautiful all-white vessel only carried 180 passengers in luxurious accommodation. With her twin funnels and clipper bow she looked like a royal yacht. Included in her facilities was a gymnastic hall, where 'the passenger who desires to keep himself in form has all the facilities for so doing'. Unfortunately her career ended in 1906 when she was wrecked on an uncharted reef near Jamaica.

Government troopships

In 1865 the British Government ordered five iron screw-driven troopships, the *Euphrates* class, to transport troops and their families to India. By the 1890s these Royal Navy-operated vessels were showing their age and required replacing. Instead of building new ships the Admiralty invited tenders for troopships which could be hired by the Government. The first contract was awarded to P&O in 1894 when two of the 'Jubilee' class liners were selected for service. British India and Bibby Line were also heavily involved in trooping. However, P&O was the first private British company to order purpose-built troopships. Three ships were constructed at Greenock by Caird and Co Ltd, *Assaye* (1899/7,367gt), *Sobraon* (1900/7,382gt) and *Plassy* (1901/7,342gt). Used as intermediate ships, their prime role was as a troopship. *Plassy*, shown here at Southampton probably on Boer War service, was used almost exclusively as a trooper and hospital ship. Usually laid up in Southampton Water between trips she became a hospital ship during the First World War and was present at the Battle of Jutland in May 1916. As a liner she carried 114 first and 57 second class passengers. She had triple-expansion engines, a service speed of 16 knots and was sold to Italian breakers in 1924.

PLASSY.
Nº3

The first large Scandinavian liners

The arrival of thousands of Scandinavian immigrants transformed the American Midwest during the nineteenth century and the first quarter of the twentieth century. Although most came from Sweden and Norway a fair number also arrived from Denmark. It was the Danes who first introduced large passenger ships to ,carry these immigrants direct from Scandinavia instead of via German or British ports. In 1898 the Scandinavien-Amerika Linien was founded by the long-established Danish company Det Forenede Dampskibs-Selskab (DFDS) which had bought Thingvalla Line, operators of a passenger line between Copenhagen and New York. An order was placed with the Clyde shipyard Alexander Stephen and Sons Ltd. for three new twin-screw liners which would be the largest Danish ships to that date. The first ship, the 10,012gt *Oscar II*, seen here, was completed in 1902. She was named after the then King of Sweden and Norway. The two countries were a unified kingdom until 1905. An impressive-looking ship for her size, she carried 123 first, 133 second and 843 third class passengers. Her triple-expansion engines produced a service speed of 15.5 knots. She was followed in 1903 by *Hellig Olav* and *United States*. This trio operated from Copenhagen to New York via Christiana (Oslo) and Christiansand. Although they initially benefitted from Denmark's neutrality during the First World War, in the face of increasing danger from U-boat attacks on the North Atlantic, they were laid up for the last two years of the war. Badly hit by the restricted United States immigrant quotas and the onset of the Great Depression, they were sold for demolition in the 1930s.

The resurgence of Royal Mail Line

Owen Cosby Philipps, later Lord Kylsant, took control of the Royal Mail Steam Packet Company in 1903. Under his dynamic leadership the company regained much of its lost pre-eminence through the construction for the Southampton–Brazil–River Plate service of a new design of ship, the 'A' class. These liners were not only luxurious but also had sufficient space to carry large quantities of chilled beef as well as many emigrants. Between 1905 and 1915, with a progressive increase in size, nine 'A'-class liners were built for Royal Mail. With one exception, *Araguaya* (1906/10,530gt), all were constructed at Belfast by Harland and Wolff. The first to appear in 1905 was the 16.5-knot, 9,588gt *Aragon*, below. With a passenger capacity of 305 first, 66 second and 600 third class, she was considerably bigger than anything previously owned by the company and was its first twin-screw ship. She had quadruple-expansion engines producing a service speed of 16.5 knots. At the time, her profile was unusual with two tall raked masts, a large single funnel situated just forward of the centreline and a split superstructure separating the bridge and the officers' quarters from the passenger accommodation. To cater for wealthy South American passengers her first class accommodation was sumptuous whilst the best cabins had a separate bathroom, bedroom and a large sitting room. There was a large gymnasium and children had their own nursery, but facilities for the emigrants picked up en route in Spain and Portugal were very basic with iron beds, portable tables and chairs which could be easily dismantled for the homeward journey when much of this space was required for cargo. On all the A-class liners, there was considerable cargo space, much of it refrigerated – the bulk of the Argentinean beef destined for Britain was chilled and had to be eaten within forty days so speed was of the essence, hence the five holds, all served by cranes. Coal fired, her bunker capacity was also sufficient for the entire round trip. The final 'A'-class ship, *Almanzora* (16,034gt), was delivered in 1915. *Aragon* was torpedoed and sunk off Alexandria in December 1917.

Since 1841 Royal Mail Line had also been operating the British Government inter-island passenger, cargo and mail contract in the West Indies. In 1907 it secured a new contract and ordered two new, 2,379gt, twin-screw, quadruple expansion 13-knot steamers for the service. *Berbice* (shown here) and *Balantia* were delivered by Harland and Wolff in 1909. They looked like mini-versions of the 'A'-class ships and had accommodation for a large number of first and second class passengers and provision for deck passengers. The bridge deck was used by those in first class and had a lounge at the forward end and a veranda at the after end. They were also fitted with hydraulic cranes and refrigerated space. Used as hospital ships during the First World War, their return to service was short lived. In 1920 the British Government withdrew the subsidy for the West Indies service and both ships were sold for further trading. *Berbice* was wrecked in 1929 as United Baltic's *Baltara* whilst *Balantia* operated in the eastern Mediterranean until 1935 as Khedivial Mail Line's *Boulac*.

Spanish competition to South America

In 1887 the Spanish shipping line Compañía Transatlántica was awarded a Spanish Government contract to carry mail and passengers between Barcelona and Buenos Aires. For the next twenty years it operated this service with a number of mainly second-hand ships. In 1908 Pinillos, Izquierdo y Compañía started a rival emigrant service on the route with brand-new tonnage. Four years later Pinillos Line introduced the first of a handsome pair of twin-screw, quadruple expansion, 15-knot liners built on the Clyde by Russell & Co. The 8,182gt *Infanta Isabel* (seen here) carried 120 first, 150 second and 1,750 steerage class passengers. The arrival of Pinillos also forced Compañía Transatlántica to order a pair of new liners of just over 10,000gt for delivery in 1913. In 1914, just before the outbreak of the First World War, *Infanta Isabel*'s sister-ship *Principe de Asturias* entered service. Unfortunately she was wrecked near Santos, Brazil in March 1916 with the loss of 415 lives in one of Spain's worst maritime disasters. Worse was to follow in September 1919 when another Pinillos steamer foundered in the Caribbean and all 488 passengers and crew perished. In 1925 *Infanta Isabel* was purchased by another Spanish company which sold her a year later to Osaka Shosen Kaisha (OSK). Renamed *Midzuho Maru*, she was placed on the Osaka–Keelung route where she remained until 1937 when she became a Japanese Army hospital ship. She was torpedoed and sunk by a US submarine in September 1944 with the loss of 1,294 troops and crew.

British liners on the New York to South America route

Another important British operator to Argentina and Brazil was the Liverpool-based Lamport and Holt. It also had a long link with New York going back to 1869 when *Halley* (1865/1,637gt) became the first iron steamship to transport Brazilian coffee to New York. In 1902 the company started a regular passenger service between New York, Brazil and the River Plate. Five passenger-cargo liners, all with 'V' names, were built for the route between 1906 and 1909. The last of these was the 15-knot, quadruple expansion 10,117gt *Vasari*. A three-class ship, her first class accommodation was of a very high standard and included special suites and a sheltered open-air veranda café aft. Her success led to an order with the Belfast shipyard Workman, Clark for a further three slightly larger twin-screw versions, *Vandyck* (1911/10,328gt), *Vauban* (1912/10,660gt) and *Vestris* (1912/10,494gt). This trio had been designed for the Liverpool-South America run. However, following the acquisition of the company by Royal Mail in 1911, they were placed on the New York service. During the First World War three of the 'V'-class liners were lost and were replaced by another pair from Workman, Clark. The geared turbine *Vandyck* (1921/13,233gt) and *Voltaire* (1923/13,248gt) were the largest Lamport and Holt liners. They also had a similar profile to the earlier ships with a long forecastle and a tall raked funnel with the distinctive black, white and blue bands. With the introduction of these ships the Lamport and Holt service became very popular. Unfortunately, shortly after leaving New York in November 1928 *Vasari* sank in heavy weather with the loss of 112 lives. This disaster brought to a close Lamport and Holt's New York passenger service in September 1930 and all the liners were laid up. *Vauban*, seen here, was sold to the breakers in 1932, the same year *Vandyck* and *Voltaire* were transformed into full time cruise ships. Both sisters were sunk during the war whilst serving as armed merchant cruisers.

Dutch services to South America

Although Holland America Line briefly operated a service to South America from 1888 to 1890, it was Koninklijke Hollandsche Lloyd (Royal Holland Lloyd) which became the premier Dutch line on the route until the mid-1930s. Its origins went back to 1899 when Zuid Amerika Lijn was founded to carry cattle and cargo between Holland and South America. With an upsurge in emigration from Holland and neighbouring countries to South America, the company was restructured in 1908 into Koninklijke Hollandsche Lloyd and new orders were placed for a trio of passenger-cargo ships with considerable steerage space. These were followed in 1913 and 1914 by two 13,900gt, quadruple expansion, twin-screw liners, *Gelria*, shown here, and *Tubantia*. Built by Alexander Stephen and Sons Ltd, not only were they the company's finest liners but also they were the fastest. On trials *Gelria* achieved 17.5 knots. She carried 250 first, 230 intermediate, 140 special third and 900 third class passengers. The exquisitely-panelled first class accommodation was outstanding, so much so that *The Shipbuilder* magazine made special mention of its 'spaciousness, architectural dignity and lavishness'. The smoking room was a deck and a half high whilst the height from the centre of the dining saloon to the glass dome over the well in the centre of the lounge on the deck above was 40ft. All first class staterooms had telephones and bedsteads or cot berths whilst a number also had private facilities. Unusually for that time, the ship's name in large enamelled letters was situated between the funnels. It was illuminated at night, red on the port side and green on the starboard side. Most of the lifeboats were housed in a stacked system so that one set of davits could deal with two lifeboats. The ship could also carry sufficient coal for both the outward and return voyages. As Holland was neutral during the First World War Koninklijke Hollandsche Lloyd initially benefited from the withdrawal of British and French lines on the route. However, in March 1916 *Tubantia* was torpedoed and sunk by a German submarine off the coast of Holland despite her illuminated name and clear markings of neutrality. Fortunately, all crew and passengers were rescued. *Gelria* was laid up and did not return to service until 1919. Converted to oil-firing in 1928, she was laid up in 1931 and following the company decision to withdraw from passenger services in 1935 was sold to the Italian Government. Managed by Lloyd Triestino, she was renamed *Gradisca* and was seized as a British war prize in 1944. After grounding in 1946 she was later salvaged and laid up in Venice where she was broken up in 1950.

French South American services

Messageries Maritimes had been operating passenger services from Bordeaux to South America since 1860. In 1911 the mail contract was awarded to Societe D'Etudes De Navigation, a new concern formed by leading French shipowners and two banks. Renamed Compagnie de Navigation Sud-Atlantique in 1912, it ordered four 15,000gt, 20-knot, French-built liners for the fortnightly service between Bordeaux and Buenos Aires. The first pair delivered in 1913 were the quadruple-screw 14,783gt *Lutetia*, seen here, and her slightly larger, triple-screw sister *Gallia*. Driven by a combination of triple-expansion engines and turbines, at the time they were the fastest liners on the South American run. Quirky-looking ships with the forward funnel almost atop the bridge, their first class accommodation was outstanding, with all cabins outboard. With the outbreak of war, they were fitted out as auxiliary troopships whilst construction of the third ship *Massilia* was suspended and the order for the fourth vessel was cancelled. In 1916 the management of the mail service was transferred to Chargeurs Reunis and Sud-Atlantique later became a subsidiary of Chargeurs. *Gallia* was lost during the war and *Lutetia* returned to service in 1920 alongside the newly-completed *Massilia*. In the late 1920s both ships were converted to oil-firing whilst the accommodation was restyled from eighteenth-century period style to modern art deco. However, with the arrival of *L'Atlantique* in 1931, *Lutetia* was laid up and was scrapped seven years later.

US competition for the Canadian Pacific Railway

Across the western Canadian border the Great Northern Railway was completed in 1893. Running from St. Paul, Minnesota to Seattle, Great Northern was the first US transcontinental built without public money. Its owner James Hill also wished to start a new steamship line, the Great Northern Steamship Co., from Seattle to the Far East which would compete directly with CPR's 'Empress' liners. He ordered two immense 20,700gt ships from the Eastern Shipbuilding Co, New London, Connecticut, which had never built a ship before. The largest ships operating in the Pacific region, *Dakota* and *Minnesota* of 1905, were handsome ships with magnificent first class passenger accommodation and a 200-capacity dining saloon. They also had space for 2,400 in steerage which included an opium den for Chinese travellers. Considerably slower than the CPR ships, they also struggled to find sufficient cargo to fill their immense holds. Unfortunately *Dakota* was wrecked near Yokohama in 1907 and became the largest and most expensive merchant ship loss to that date. In 1916 *Minnesota* was sold to Atlantic Transport Line and from 1920 until her sale to breakers in 1923 operated on the Atlantic as a cargo-only ship.

The 'All-Red Route' extended to New Zealand and Australia

The completion of the trans-Canada railway also encouraged the opening of another 'Imperial' route, this time to New Zealand and Australia. The Canadian-Australian Steamship Company commenced services in 1893. Operated initially by the Australian-based Huddart, Parker Ltd, the route was taken over by the Union Steam Ship Co. of New Zealand (USSNZ) in 1901 when it bought a share in the line which it purchased outright in 1910. USSNZ, which had run a mail service from San Francisco to New Zealand and Australia since 1885, ordered some impressive, fast liners for the Vancouver route, including *Makura* (1908/8,075gt), the first purpose-built liner on the Vancouver to Sydney route and the triple-screw, 13,415gt *Niagara* (above). Built on the Clyde by John Brown & Co Ltd., *Niagara* was the first passenger vessel to use oil fuel under a British Board of Trade certificate. She had two sets of triple-expansion engines, each driving an outer screw with a low-pressure exhaust turbine driving the central screw. This combination machinery produced a service speed of 16.5 knots. She carried 278 first, 224 second and 191 third class passengers whilst she also had space for 209,000ft^3 of cargo, 80,000ft^3 of which was insulated for fruit, meat and dairy produce. At the time of her delivery in 1913 she was one of the finest liners operating in the Pacific. Her success led to an order for an 18-knot, 14,744gt running mate with twin screws and geared turbines. *Aotearoa* was completed in 1915 but was sunk as an armed merchant cruiser in 1917. Despite two world wars *Niagara* ran continuously on the Sydney–Vancouver route until June 1940 when, outbound from Auckland, she sank after striking a mine laid by the German auxiliary cruiser *Orion* (1930/7,021gt).

The rise in Australian immigration and trade

On 1 January 1901 the Commonwealth of Australia was formed as a dominion of the British Empire and during the first quarter of the twentieth century the population almost doubled to six million, with over 10,000 assisted migrants entering the country each year. One of the immigrant carriers was Blue Anchor Line which was operated by William Lund and Sons. Its association with the Australian trade went back to 1869 and by the early 1900s it had established itself as a major cargo and passenger line on the routes between London and Australia via the Cape. Unfortunately in July 1909 its 9,339gt flagship *Waratah* vanished between Durban and Cape Town on her second homeward voyage with the loss of 211 passengers and crew. The company never recovered from this loss and its ships and goodwill were bought by P&O in 1910. Although it initially retained the distinctive blue anchor funnel marking the new owner renamed the line the P&O Branch Service and ordered five new, twin-screw, quadruple expansion, 15-knot, 11,120gt emigrant ships from the Scottish yard Caird & Co. Delivered between 1911 and 1914 these rather plain, unattractive ships were all given Australian names beginning with B. *Ballarat*, seen here off Tilbury, was the first to be completed in November 1911. She carried 1,100 third class passengers in very basic accommodation although there was a large dining saloon, a smoking room with veranda and a music room. She also had insulated space for the carriage of meat and fruit cargoes. All five ships became troopships during the First World War although *Ballarat* became the only casualty when she was torpedoed and sunk by a U-boat in April 1917, fortunately with no loss of life.

The new country also attracted new investment and shipowners were quick to respond to this great business opportunity. One of these was White Star Line which ordered a new class of five 12,000gt cargo-passenger ships from Harland & Wolff for the Australian route. Amongst the largest cargo carriers of their day, the *Medic*-class also carried some 350 cabin class passengers and were delivered between 1899 and 1901. Around the same time, Harland & Wolff also built three slightly larger, 12,234gt, 13-knot, twin-screw ships for White Star's London to New Zealand service which it operated jointly with Shaw Savill and Albion Co Ltd Shaw, Savill and Albion was a pioneer in the transportation of frozen meat from New Zealand when its sailing ship *Dunedin* (1874/1,310gt) carried the first consignment of frozen lamb to Britain in 1882. *Athenic* (1901), seen here, *Corinthic* (1902) and *Ionic* (1902) revolutionised the New Zealand trade. With a single tall funnel and four masts these flush-decked liners were virtually identical in all respects including the quadruple-expansion engines. They carried a large amount of refrigerated cargo and around 400 passengers in three classes. Passengers not only enjoyed comfortable accommodation but also a larger-than-average area of deck space. Whilst her sisters were broken up in the 1930s *Athenic*, the first of the trio, had an extraordinarily long career. She was sold in 1928 to the Tønsberg firm Bruun & von der Lippe and was converted into the Norwegian whale factory ship *Pelagos*. In January 1941, she was captured by the German auxiliary cruiser *Pinguin* and subsequently used as a U-boat depot ship in Norwegian waters. Returned to her owners in 1945, she was rebuilt with an extended superstructure, and broken up at Hamburg in June 1962.

In 1910 Alfred Holt and Company, better known as Blue Funnel Line, also entered the Australian passenger trade with *Aeneas* (10,049gt), the first of three purpose-built passenger-cargo liners. The success of these 'A'-class ships led to an order for an enlarged pair of ships. The 15,501gt *Nestor* and 14,499gt *Ulysses*, shown here, delivered in 1913, were built at Belfast by Workman, Clark and Company. Not only were they the largest ships built to that date for the Australian service, they were also the largest vessels on the South African service and 1,000 tons greater than the biggest Union-Castle Line mailship. They carried 350 first class passengers in accommodation described in promotional literature as 'without any magnificence but with the good solid comfort which is essential to the enjoyment of a long voyage'. With only one class, passengers had access to most of the ship and although the decoration was conservative, the facilities were very cosy and without the stuffiness found in first class aboard ships crossing the Atlantic. They also had a considerable cargo capacity (682,000ft^3) including refrigerated space for frozen meat, dairy produce and fruit. Cargo was handled by twenty-nine derricks working seven holds and the power for the ships was provided by two triple-expansion engines which gave a service speed of 14 knots. The overall design was by the company naval architect Henry Bell Wortley and although their profile was rather stiff because of the lack of rake to the masts and funnel, the ships were very distinctive with an enormous funnel rising 75ft above the boat deck. Following their completion, Blue Funnel was able to offer monthly sailings to Australia via the Cape and an order for a pair of 20,000gt ships was placed but with the advent of war, this was cancelled. Although *Nestor* survived both world wars and was only demolished in 1950, *Ulysses* was torpedoed and sunk by a U-boat off the United States coast in April 1942.

The Australian mail service in the early 1900s

The carriage of mail and passengers to Australia was a vital part of P&O and Orient Line's operation. The two companies shared the mail contract which in 1898 required a reduction in the journey time between London and Melbourne to just over thirty-one days. To meet the exacting demands of this contract and a new one in 1908, P&O ordered ten passenger-mail ships, the twin-funnel 'M' class, which were built over a period of eight years. Starting with the 9,500gt *Moldavia* in 1903, they were based on the same design which gradually increased in size as improvements were introduced. The final ship in the series, the 12,350gt *Medina*, was delivered in 1911. The first twin-screw P&O mail steamers, with one exception, *Morea* (1908/10,890gt), they were built by either Caird and Co Ltd or Harland and Wolff. *Morea*, seen here at Gravesend, was constructed at Glasgow by Barclay, Curle and Co Ltd and with slightly wider funnels was arguably the most attractive of this distinctive class of ship. Like the other ships her navigation bridge was more lofty than normal whilst she had hydraulic cranes so that her cargo could be worked at night without disturbing her passengers. She also had a bullion room and large post office for sorting the mails. She carried 407 first and 200 second class passengers with all the well-ventilated rooms situated above the upper deck. The rather old-fashioned first class interiors were the work of P&O's preferred designer Thomas Edward Collcut. The first class dining saloon had long tables and an open well which extended through three decks. Although her service speed was 16 knots on her trials her quadruple-expansion engines produced a top speed of 18 knots. The 'M' class suffered heavy losses during the First World War with only four survivors Including *Morea*. A new series of 'M' ships were built and *Morea* was transferred to the Far East routes. She was sold to Chinese breakers in 1935.

The 1908 mail contract was worth £170,000 per annum in subsidies and the managers of Orient Line were determined that they could maintain the fortnightly mail service independently. Unable to raise sufficient capital to finance the building of five 12,000gt ships, the largest ever seen in Australia, the managers gave personal guarantees to the shipbuilders for the initial money. Favourable repayment terms were also negotiated and the order was spread over a number of yards, with three built on the Clyde and two at Workman Clark in Belfast. The new vessels were delivered between May and November 1909. The first to arrive was *Orsova* and with her twin funnels and Admiralty cowls, she became the template for the next generation of Orient liners, which culminated in *Orontes* of 1929. The new vessels also had five cargo holds and carried over 1,000 passengers. To confirm its independence, the OSNCo letters were dropped from the Orient Line flag and this became the house flag until 1966. *Orama*, the final ship of the pre-war fleet, was completed in 1911 as a replacement for *Ormuz*, the last of the four-masters which, despite her age, was sold on to Cie de Navigation Sud Atlantique and was only scrapped in 1922. Although she looked similar to the earlier five ships, the slightly larger *Orama* was unique. She was the sole Orient liner with triple-screws and also the first to use a turbine, albeit in combination with two four-cylinder triple-expansion engines.

The giant British India Line

At the outbreak of the First World War British India (BI) Line owned 126 ships and was one of the largest shipping companies in the world. In 1914 it merged with P&O but continued to trade as a separate entity, its vast network spread across the eastern oceans including the east coast of Africa where it had been since 1872. BI's founder Sir William Mackinnon played a major role in the development of this region. The first purpose-built ships for the Bombay–East Africa–Durban service were the three 'K'-class ships which were built on the Tyne by Swan, Hunter & Wigham Richardson and delivered between 1915 and 1917. The first in the series was the 7,117gt *Karoa* and her cruiser stern introduced a new style for BI ships which until then had counter sterns. Her passenger capacity was 64 first, 64 second and 1,471 deck passengers. Taken up as an ambulance and troop transport during the war she remained on the East Africa run until the arrival of larger ships in 1932. She was then transferred to the Calcutta–Singapore route and like her sisters survived the 1939–45 conflict and was scrapped in 1950.

In 1913 BI embarked on its largest group of passenger-cargo ships, the 'M' class, which were designed to be the backbone of the India to London service. Twin-screwed, they were three-island types with a large centre castle, open promenade decks and a tall raked funnel amidships. They operated at a moderate service speed (13 knots), carried around 150 passengers in two classes and had 1,000ft^3 of refrigerated space. Nine 8,200gt ships in the first group were delivered between 1913 and 1917. The next series of eight completed between 1920 and 1922, were slightly larger. The last six of these also had cruiser sterns whilst a further two 'M'-class ships were completed as BI's first passenger motor ships, *Domala* and *Dumana*, then the largest passenger motor ships in the world. Whilst the pre-war 'M'-class ships had triple-expansion engines, all but one of the post-war ships were given more fuel-efficient geared steam turbines. The 8,975gt *Madura* entered service in 1921 and remained in the fleet for thirty-two years. She was the first of the 'M' class with a cruiser stern and in 1933 her accommodation became single class. She was used principally on the London to Mombasa route and in 1942 survived an attack from Japanese bombers in which six lives were lost. She was scrapped in 1953.

The turbine revolution

The origins of the modern steam turbine came about in 1884 when the English engineer Charles Algernon Parsons patented a reaction marine turbine which consisted of a series of fixed and rotary disks fitted with rings of blades. Twelve years later this revolutionary machinery was installed in *Turbinia*, Parson's small experimental steamship. On 26 June 1897, *Lucania* (1893/12,952gt), Cunard Line's transatlantic record-breaker and the world's largest ship, took part in the Diamond Jubilee Fleet Review at Spithead, the stretch of water between Portsmouth and the Isle of Wight. This grand occasion was held to celebrate the sixtieth year of Queen Victoria's reign. As the Royal Yacht *Victoria and Albert* led the way through the fleet, with Edward Prince of Wales, aboard, the occasion was interrupted by an uninvited guest, *Turbinia*, dashing through the line of ships at over 30 knots. In one fell swoop Charles Parson demonstrated to the world the superiority of his new turbine-driven marine engine.

The first ocean-going turbine ships

For operators of passenger ships, apart from the obvious speed advantage, turbines were less noisy. compared with reciprocating engines. The first turbine-powered merchant ships were constructed at Dumbarton by William Denny & Bros. Denny in 1901 built not only the first turbine-powered merchant ship, the Clyde steamer *King Edward*, but also in 1904, Union Steam Ship Company of New Zealand Ltd.'s *Loongana*, the first ocean-going turbine passenger liner and the first turbine steamer to operate in the southern hemisphere. The 18-knot, 2,448gt *Loongana*, right, had been ordered because Union had won, with Huddart, Parker, the express passenger-mail contract across the Bass Strait between Melbourne and Launceston, Tasmania. Apart from the raised forecastle, her design was similar to other Denny-built Irish and English cross-Channel ferries. Triple-screwed with three-shaft turbines manufactured by Parsons she managed over 20 knots on trials. For the nine-hour overnight voyage 200 first class and 100 second class passengers were accommodated in cabins. *Loongana* remained on the route until 1935 and was sold to Japanese breakers a year later.

British India Line was also a pioneer in the use of turbine-driven passenger steamers. For the 1904 Indian Government mail contracts, it ordered four 2,171gt, twin-funnelled ships from Denny, two for the Bombay to Karachi service and two for the Calcutta–Rangoon run. The first turbine ships in eastern waters, this handsome quartet had triple screws and recorded top speeds on trials of over 18 knots. They each carried 22 passengers in first class, 22 in second and 1,200 on deck. *Linga*, shown here, was delivered in 1904 and like her sisters, *Lhasa*, *Lama* and *Lunka*, set new standards on the premier mail runs to Karachi and Rangoon. She was requisitioned for war service during the First World War and in 1925 was sold with one of her sisters for demolition at Bombay.

Union Steam Ship Company of New Zealand's experience with *Loongana* led to the order in 1904 with William Denny for a 16-knot, 5,282gt, triple-screw, direct-drive turbine liner for its Australia–Tasmania–New Zealand intercolonial and coastal services. *Maheno* was delivered in 1905 and soon established a reputation for herself as a record-breaker. She carried 231 first class, 120 second class and 67 third class passengers. Her accommodation was also excellent and included a Bechstein grand piano in first class. In 1906 she became the first turbine-driven ship to cross the Pacific when she operated briefly on the prestigious service between Sydney and Vancouver known as the 'All-Red Route'. In 1914 because of heavy coal consumption she was fitted with twin-screws and geared turbines. The following year she became the first New Zealand liner to be converted into a hospital ship, a role she continued until 1919. She was withdrawn from service in 1935 and sold to Japanese breakers. Whilst under tow to Japan she ran aground on Ocean Island, Queensland where her remains can still be seen.

First transatlantic turbine liners

Meanwhile in the North Atlantic, Allan Line, which had monopolised the mail contract between Liverpool and Canada for almost fifty years, faced a major challenge in 1903 when the Canadian Pacific Railway decided to start services across the Atlantic following its purchase of the ships and goodwill of the Beaver Line from Elder Dempster. As it was inevitable that Canadian Pacific would build new liners, Allan Line took the initiative and ordered two 11,000grt ships, *Victorian*, shown here, and *Virginian*, from the Belfast firm, Workman, Clark & Co. With reciprocating engines, these vessels were designed to be the finest on run between Canada and Europe. Work had already began on *Victorian* when Allan Line decided that both ships would be powered by turbines. Not only were they the first turbine-driven transatlantic liners, they were also the first to have triple screws. Interestingly, the first turbine passenger ship to cross the Atlantic was the 2,000-capacity Great Lakes steamer *Turbinia* (1904/1,065gt) which had been completed on the Tyne in May 1904 by Hawthorne, Leslie and Company for The Turbine Steamship Company Ltd. Nothing of this magnitude had been attempted before, which is why a contemporary publication stated that 'Messrs. Allan must be congratulated on their pluck and enterprise in installing this method of propulsion in a vessel of this size'. With such a high-profile order, Workman, Clark decided that it would be unable to build both ships, so *Virginian* was constructed on the Clyde by Alexander Stephen & Sons. The three direct-drive turbines for each ship were built by Parsons. They were nicely-balanced ships, with a large raked funnel, situated just aft of the centre line. The accommodation for first and second class passengers amidships was typically Edwardian with polished mahogany panelling and dining saloons still using long tables. Almost a thousand emigrants were housed in the poop and 'tween decks fore and aft. All areas were heated and ventilated by the Thermotank system. They were had considerable cargo space including 23,000ft^3 for refrigerated cargo. The two ships were completed weeks apart in March 1905 with the 10,635gt *Victorian*, the first to sail for Canada. She had accommodation for 346 first and 344 second class passengers. Although Allan Line was eventually bought by Canadian Pacific, both liners were considered to be a great success. *Victorian* was scrapped in 1929 whilst *Virginian* only went to the breakers in 1955 after a long and varied career.

Japanese turbine liners

The Parsons Marine Steam Turbine Company played an important role in the early development of the ship-building industry in Japan. In 1904 it entered into a licence agreement with the Mitsubishi Company to build both marine and land turbines. This led to an order from Toyo Kisen Kaisha for two triple-screw, turbine-driven, 13,454gt liners, *Tenyo Maru* and *Chiyo Maru*, for its prestigious Hong Kong, Shanghai, Nagasaki, Kobe, Yokohama, Honolulu and San Francisco route. The largest ships built in Japan to that date and the first Japanese-built merchant ships with turbines, they were designed to compete with Pacific Mail's similar sized-vessels. The turbines were direct drive and produced a maximum speed of over 20 knots, making the ships the fastest liners on the Pacific. Completed in April and November 1908 respectively, they carried 275 first, 54 second and 800 third class passengers. *Tenyo Maru* was noted for her Japanese silk drapery and art nouveau-style first class interiors. She was also the first Japanese ship to be fitted with Telefunken wireless communication equipment. This pair was joined by a third sister, *Shinyo Maru*, in 1911, right. *Chiyo Maru* was wrecked near Hong Kong in 1916 and faced with severe competition from both Canadian Pacific and Dollar Line in the early 1920s, the company was taken over by NYK in 1926. *Tenyo Maru* was sold for scrap on 1933 followed by *Shinyo Maru* in 1936.

CARMANIA

The largest and fastest liners in the world

During the first decade of the twentieth century Cunard Line was also under pressure to build new ships especially after the formation of the International Mercantile Marine Corporation of New Jersey in 1902 by John Pierpoint Morgan, the American financier. It was created to take over a number of key transatlantic lines including White Star Line. With national prestige at stake, the British Government loaned Cunard Line £2.6 million to build two of the largest, fastest and most luxurious liners ever seen. In May 1903 John Brown & Company Ltd., Clydebank, formerly J and G Thomson, and the Newcastle-based Swan, Hunter and Wigham Richardson Ltd. were awarded the contracts to build, respectively, *Lusitania* and *Mauretania*. Having initially turned down the use of this relatively untried type of engine, Cunard set up a committee of marine professionals to look at its possible use on the new liners. The relative merits of turbines and reciprocating engines were investigated in a series of trials using the turbine-driven cross-Channel ferry *Brighton* and the similarly-designed *Arundel*, which had reciprocating engines. In 1904 it was decided that turbines should be used on the new express liners. In order to gain some experience of these new engines, Cunard asked John Brown to fit turbines on *Carmania*, left, the second of a pair of 19,500gt intermediate liners under construction at the yard. *Carmania* was completed in 1905 and this gave Cunard almost two years of experience before the introduction of their new super-liners in 1907. The 31,550gt *Lusitania*, above, made her maiden voyage in September 1907 and was followed by the slightly larger *Mauretania* two months later. By far the largest ships in the world, these vessels were the first over 30,000gt, the first on the Atlantic with quadruple screws and the first British liners with four funnels. They were fast ships and soon reduced the crossing time to less than five days in each direction. *Mauretania's* average speed was over 25 knots and her transatlantic record remained unbroken for twenty years. They also offered 50 per cent more light, air, space and deck promenade per passenger than any other liner afloat. The accommodation for the first class passengers was indeed spacious and no expense was spared in the decoration and panelling of their magnificent public rooms. On *Mauretania*, just under a quarter of a million square feet of fancy hardwoods was used to fit out her interiors. During the First World War *Mauretania* was used initially as a hospital ship and later as a troopship. *Lusitania* continued to operate the transatlantic service until her sinking in May 1915 by a German submarine which resulted in the loss of 1,198 lives. *Mauretania* was withdrawn from service in 1934 and was sold for demolition at Rosyth the following year.

The first ocean-going passenger liner with engines aft

Matson Line's long association with Hawaii came about in 1882 when the Swedish-born Captain William Matson arrived in Hilo Bay in his schooner *Emma Claudina* to load coconuts, hides, tropical fruits and sugar. By the turn of the century, Matson had a sizeable sailing fleet operating primarily on the 2,100-mile run between Hawaii and San Francisco. Hawaii was annexed by the United States in 1898 and four years later Matson bought his first steamship. He also recognised the advantages of oil over coal and was a pioneer user of the new fuel in his ships. In 1908 he took delivery of the world's first ocean-going passenger ship with engines aft. The 6,572gt *Lurline* was the first in an extraordinary group of combination cargo and passenger ships of this type which were designed to provide greater cargo capacity and improved passenger comfort. With passenger space amidships there was less vibration from the engines. The largest of these liners were *Matsonia* (1913/9,402gt), seen here, and *Maui* (1917/9,801gt). The latter was twin-screwed and driven by geared turbines, the first on the Pacific, she carried 240 passengers in comfortable accommodation which included single-seating dining and staterooms with private baths.

New Canadian Pacific 'Empresses'

In 1911 the Canadian Pacific Steamship Company placed an order with the Fairfield shipyard, Govan for a pair of fast 17,000gt liners to replace its twenty-year-old trio of liners on the service between Vancouver and the Far East. Completed in 1913, the quadruple-screw, turbine-driven *Empress of Russia* and *Empress of Asia* (seen here), marked a turning point in the company's history. Not only were they its largest ships to that date but also they were record-breakers on the Pacific run. These three-funnelled ships had a maximum speed of over 21 knots. Each ship had two large spaces for bales of silk. At the time Vancouver was one of the world's major silk terminals and because of high insurance premiums involved in transporting silk, speed played a major role in their success in the silk trade. The first large liners to have a cruiser stern, they were also coal burners and remained so for the rest of their careers at a time when many ships were starting to use oil fuel. Interestingly, cruiser sterns first appeared in western Canada in 1910 with the arrival of The Grand Trunk Pacific Railway's *Prince Rupert* (1910/3,379gt) and *Prince George* (1910/3,372gt). As built, each of the new 'Empresses' carried 200 first class, 100 Asiatic second class and 808 Asiatic steerage class passengers. The first class accommodation was very fine and included a number of de-luxe suites. The large panelled first class lounge situated between the first and second funnels was similar to the one on *Mauretania* whilst the elegant two-deck-high dining saloon had seating for all first class passengers. At the opposite end of the spectrum many of the Asiatic steerage passengers were housed in cramped portable accommodation. The pair had very successful careers and became troopships in both World Wars. *Empress of Asia* was lost during a Japanese aerial attack off Singapore in April 1942 whilst *Empress of Russia* was destroyed by fire in September 1945 when undergoing repairs in Barrow,

French Indo-China

France's association with South East Asia goes back to the seventeenth century. Between 1887 and 1954 France ruled over Vietnam, Laos and Cambodia, the three countries which formed French Indo-China. During this period Saigon grew into a major trading port rivalling both Singapore and Hong Kong. At the same time, Marseilles-based Messageries Maritimes (MM) became the leading French shipping line in the Asia-Pacific and Indian Ocean region area. MM's beginnings started, like P&O, during the 1850s and rapidly expanded after the opening of the Suez Canal. In the early years of the twentieth century the company ordered a series of liners to replace older ships. The most significant of these were built at the MM-owned yard at La Ciotat for the Marseilles–China and Japan service. *Paul Lecat* (1912/12,550gt) and her larger sister *Andre Lebon* (1915/14,368gt), seen here, were not only the largest ships owned by MM, they were also the most luxurious liners yet seen on the Far East trades. Twin-screwed, 15-knot ships, they had quadruple-expansion engines and carried about 500 passengers in three classes. First class was sumptuous and on *Paul Lecat* the large public rooms were decorated in the style of Louis XVI. There was a passenger lift, veranda café, single-seating dining room, eight de-luxe suites and a separate children's playroom which included a marionette theatre. Although *Andre Lebon* survived both wars and was only demolished in 1952, her sister was burnt out in a fire in 1928.

France's first turbine-driven passenger ship

Algeria was France's oldest colony and the route between Marseilles and Algiers was vitally important to the French state. Speed and comfort on the 467-mile crossing to Algiers was always key and Compagnie Générale Transatlantique (CGT) usually had the edge over its main competitor Compagnie de Navigation Mixte. In 1909 CGT introduced the 18-knot, 4,451gt *Charles Roux* on the route. She was France's first turbine-driven passenger ship and was built by Chantier de l'Atlantique, St-Nazaire (Penhoët). Manufactured under licence, the three direct-drive Parsons-type turbines were placed further aft than usual. Named after CGT's president, *Charles Roux* was painted white with two short black funnels and looked like a mini-transatlantic liner. However, her attractive profile changed after her funnels were raised and she was given a black hull. She originally carried 205 first, 70 second and 54 third class passengers in excellent accommodation. The first class drawing room was decorated in Louis XVI style in white and gold whilst the *apartment de luxe* consisted of a drawing room, bedroom and en-suite bathroom. She carried cars and was among the first ships plying the Mediterranean to have wireless telegraphy. During the First World War she was used as a troopship, hospital ship and armed merchant cruiser. In a major refit during the 1929 and 1930 winter months she was transformed into a twin-screw, oil-fired, turbine-driven, 14-knot ship. She was sold to breakers at Dunkirk in 1936.

The express de-luxe service between Marseilles and Alexandria

Another pair of direct-driven turbine Mediterranean liners of note during the first decade of the twentieth century were the triple-screw *Heliopolis* (1907/10,897gt), right, and *Cairo* (1908/10,864gt). At the time of their completion they were the largest, fastest and most luxuriously-equipped passenger liners on the Mediterranean. They were ordered from Fairfield Shipbuilding and Engineering Co Ltd, Govan by The Egyptian Mail Steamship Co. of London for an express de-luxe service between Marseilles and Alexandria, via Naples, in direct competition with P&O, Messageries Maritimes and Norddeutscher Lloyd. Parsons-type turbines, one high pressure for the centre shaft and two low pressure ones for the outer shafts produced 18,000shp and top speeds of almost 21 knots. They reduced the journey time between Marseilles and Alexandria via Naples by a day and a half to only three days. The great Italian composer Giacomo Puccini travelled on *Heliopolis* and considered her to be 'magnificent'. The ships, which carried 550 first and 280 second class passengers, were a model of Edwardian elegance. Much of the wood panelling in the first class public rooms was painted white, with colour provided by the pastel shades in the carpeting, curtains and fabrics. The Ritz Café on the boat deck had its own kitchen and was oak panelled in Louis XVI style, while the main 256-capacity first class dining room took up the whole width of the ship. There was also a separate children's nursery and *suites de luxe* for 'travelling millionaires.' The five passenger decks were serviced by an electric lift whilst some of the interconnecting staterooms were arranged so that families could be accommodated in 'flats' of their own. However, despite their critical acclaim, the operation was a commercial failure and after only a year, the ships were taken over by the shipbuilders and laid up at Marseilles in 1909. A year later they were bought by the Canadian Northern Steamship Co., Toronto for service between Avonmouth and Canada. Converted into three class ships they were heavily modified for the Atlantic and were renamed *Royal George* (*Heliopolis*) and *Royal Edward* (*Cairo*). Whilst the latter was torpedoed and sunk in 1915 the former survived the war under Cunard ownership and was broken up in 1922.

Geared turbines

High installation and operating costs meant that, for vessels of lower speeds, direct-drive turbines were an uneconomical proposition. The solution lay in the use of mechanical gearing between the turbine and the screw shaft. In 1909 the freighter *Eastern Prince* (1887/2,147gt) was purchased by Charles Parsons. Renamed *Vespasian* she was fitted with experimental geared turbines which proved to be a great success. The first large transatlantic liner fitted with geared turbines was Cunard Line's *Transylvania* (1914/14,315gt), the first of two handsome ships ordered for a joint Cunard-Anchor Mediterranean service to New York. Anchor Line had been operating on this route since 1870. Designed by Leonard Peskett, Cunard's senior naval architect, the 16.5-knot *Transylvania* carried 263 first, 260 second and 1,858 third class passengers. The latter were mainly housed in dormitories on 'E' and 'F' decks. The first class public rooms were situated on the promenade deck and consisted of a writing room, lounge, smoking room, veranda café and gymnasium. The stylish, elegant and classical first class interiors were designed by the architect Robert Frank Atkinson who was also responsible for the design of Liverpool's famous Adelphi Hotel. *Transylvania* was propelled by twin-screws, each driven by Parsons-type geared turbines. She and her sister *Tuscania* (1914/14,348gt) were both sunk during the First World War.

The birth of Norwegian America Line

In 1905 the union between Norway and Sweden was dissolved and for the first time in centuries Norway was once again an independent state. Five years later the Norkske Amerikalinje (Norwegian America Line) was formed with its livery featuring the colours of the Norwegian flag. Two 11,000gt, two-funnelled, twin-screw, 17-knot liners were ordered from Cammell Laird and Co Ltd, Birkenhead for a new, government-subsidised service between Kristiana (Oslo) and New York via Bergen. Both ships were delivered in 1913 and the first to be completed was the 10,699gt *Kristianiafjord*, shown here. These handsome ships were the first Norwegian-flagged deep-sea passenger liners. Although they carried 105 first and 216 second class passengers, they were principally emigrant ships with space for 700 in portable cabins. The 106ft-long forecastle had lavatories and a deck saloon for emigrants. Although *Kristianiafjord* was only four years old when she was wrecked off the coast of Newfoundland, her sister *Bergensfjord* had a long career and was only broken up in 1959.

Enter the Russians

Although it is an immense country covering two continents, much of Russia's coastline is very inhospitable, apart from the Black Sea and the Baltic. Before the Russian Revolution the country was isolated and behind the times, both commercially and industrially. Most of the merchant fleet was in private hands whilst there were few passenger liners. The largest Russian shipping line was the Odessa-based Russian Steam Navigation and Trading Company, founded in 1857, which at the turn of the twentieth century owned seventy-two steamers. In 1912 it signed an order for four handsome Clyde-built, 15-knot, twin-screw, 5,556gt passenger liners, all named after members of the Russian royal family. Two of the ships were built on Clydebank by John Brown whilst the other two came from the William Denny yard at Dumbarton. Completed in 1913, they were designed for the passenger and cargo service between Odessa and Alexandria. They carried 82 first, 54 second and 300 third class passengers. First class was luxurious and included a veranda café. Relatively slow ships, the main machinery consisted of two sets of triple-expansion engines. After the fall of the Tsar in 1917 many of the Russian Steam Navigation and Trading Company assets were transferred to France. Whilst two of the ships were subsequently sold to Messageries Maritimes, the John Brown-built *Imperatritsa Ekaterina* (Empress Catherine), shown here, was sunk by a German submarine in 1918. The only one of the quartet to remain in Soviet hands was *Imperator Petr Velikiy* (Emperor Peter the Great). She had an extraordinary career and lasted until 1987 when she foundered in Busan, Korea after being sold for scrap.

Early twentieth century emigrant ships

Russian migration

Because of extreme poverty, disease and discrimination, tens of thousands of Russians sought a better way of life abroad during the early part of the twentieth century.

Between 1901 and 1914 around two and a half million migrated to the United States. The Russian American Line was founded by A/S Det Østasiatiske Kompagni (Danish East Asiatic), Copenhagen and HAPAG in 1906 to offer a direct Russia service from Libau (Liepāja in modern-day Latvia) to New York. Prior to then, emigrants had to travel to Holland or German for their transatlantic crossings. Danish East Asiatic had a Russian subsidiary, the Russian East Asiatic Steam Ship Co Ltd, St. Petersburg which operated a passenger-cargo service between St Petersburg and the Far East. After the defeat of Russia by Japan in 1905 the company turned its attention to the transatlantic trade and after it bought HAPAG's shares in Russian American Line, it ordered the first of four 15-knot liners from Barclay Curle and Co Ltd, Whiteinch. The triple-expansion, four-masted *Russia* (1908/8,595gt), shown here, was followed by the smaller quadruple-expansion, two-masted *Kursk* 1910/7,869gt), *Czar* (1912/6,516gt) and *Czaritza* (1915/6,598gt). This handsome quartet carried mainly emigrants. *Russia* had space for 54 first, 204 second and 1,368 steerage passengers. The New York operation came to an end in 1914 with the outbreak of the First World War. The three smaller ships were later chartered by The Shipping Controller, London and managed by Cunard Line as troopships. All four were renamed and reverted to the Libau-New York service in 1921. By then Latvia had become free of Russian domination. *Russia* was sold to Japanese buyers in 1923 whilst the remaining sisters were bought by Gydnia-Amerika Line in 1930.

The first Greek emigrant liners

Between 1896 and 1921 415,000 Greeks, more than 8 per cent of the total population, left their homeland, many bound for the United States. As they tended to sail on German, French, Austrian and British ships, this was an opportunity for Greece to establish its own passenger-ship line. The first Greek-owned ocean liner was the 6,045gt, British-built *Moraitis* which was completed for the Hellenic Transatlantic Steam Navigation Company in 1907. Unfortunately the company went bankrupt after only a year and its two ships were bought in 1908 by the newly-formed National Steam Navigation Company of Greece which was operated by Embiricos Brothers. This company ordered a number of emigrant ships from British yards, the largest of these being the twin-screw *Vasilefs Constantinos* (1914/9,272gt) which was built at Birkenhead by Cammell, Laird and Company Limited. Although the upper and main decks were used to accommodate 1,800 emigrants, she also carried 60 first and 450 second class passengers. An unusual feature of the ship was a Greek chapel on the shelter deck with a stained-glass dome framed in polished brass and surmounted with a cross. In 1923 she was renamed *Byron*, shown here. By now the company was struggling because of increasingly stricter United States emigrant quotas. In 1935 her owners ceased trading and she was withdrawn from service. Two years later she was scrapped at La Spezia.

Fabre Line

One of the most important emigrant lines in the first quarter of the twentieth century was the Compagnie Française de Navigation à Vapeur Cyprien Fabre & Compagnie (Fabre Line) which had been operating regular service between Marseilles and New York since 1882. Calls were made in Naples and Palermo to pick up Italian migrants and from 1911 Lisbon and the Azores were added to the schedule after it was awarded the Lisbon–New York mail contract. In 1905 Fabre took delivery of the twin-screw, 16-knot *Madonna* built by Swan, Hunter and Wigham Richardson and seen here on the Tyne flying the British flag. Although she was only 5,537gt she had two funnels and carried 1,650 steerage passengers in addition to 54 in first class. In April 1911 she made Fabre's first call at Providence, Rhode Island and between then and 1934, Fabre carried over 80,000 southern and eastern European emigrants to the port. Because of the Depression and emigrant restrictions Fabre withdrew from the trade in the early 1930s. *Madonna* was scrapped in 1934.

Cunard Hungarian-American Line

Anchor Line had been operating on the Mediterranean to New York route since 1870, mainly as an emigrant carrier. In the early part of the twentieth century emigration from southern and eastern Europe to the United States experienced a huge expansion and in 1903 Cunard Line started a new service between Fiume, Trieste, Palermo, Naples and New York called the Cunard Hungarian-American Line. The recently-completed, 16-knot, twin-screw *Carpathia* (1902/13,555gt) was placed on the new service which also provided Cunard with its first venture into the Mediterranean cruise market. Although *Carpathia* had a large third class capacity (2,250) she also carried 100 first and 200 second class passengers. Famous as the ship which rescued 703 passengers from the doomed *Titanic* in 1912, she was torpedoed and sunk by a German submarine in July 1918.

Giant ships and combination machinery

Although direct-drive turbines were deemed a success for record-breakers such as *Lusitania* and *Mauretania*, many shipowners still felt reciprocating engines to be superior to direct-drive turbines for larger liners. However, as turbines were highly efficient, Parsons invented a system which made use of reciprocating engines and turbines. This combination system was first used in a merchant ship when it was installed on New Zealand Shipping Company's refrigerated steamer *Otaki* (1908/7,420gt). Built by Denny she had two sets of triple-expansion engines, one for each outer shaft, with a low-pressure turbine driving the central shaft. The steam from the outer engines exhausted into the turbine whilst the outer engines were also used for going astern.

As Cunard's main competitor, White Star Line, considered that comfort aboard its ships was more important than speed, the combination system provided an ideal solution not only in terms of costs but also efficiency. Harland and Wolff, White Star's main shipbuilder, had no experience of turbines and turned to help from John Brown, the yard which had constructed *Lusitania*. The first large liner with combination machinery was the 16-knot *Laurentic* (1909/14,892gt), shown below. She and her sister *Megantic* (1909/14,878g) were built for the White

Star-Dominion Line service between Liverpool and Canada. They were the largest liners on the Canadian trade and inaugurated White Star's entry into this lucrative market. Whilst the twin-screw *Megantic* was fitted with conventional quadruple-expansion engines, the triple-screw *Laurentic* had two triple-expansion engines either side of a low-pressure turbine built by John Brown. This gave White Star the opportunity to compare the performance of the two engine types before a decision was made about the machinery for its giant *Olympic*-class ships on order from Harland and Wolff. The results showed that not only did the combination machinery produce a 20 per cent increase in power for a lower weight it also significantly reduced the amount of coal used. *Laurentic* had a large single funnel and bore a strong resemblance to the Royal Mail 'A'-class liners. She was a three-class ship with accommodation for 260 first, 430 second and over 1,000 in third class. The rather traditional style in first class included stained glass effigies of poets, painters and dramatists in the well-stocked library. There were also en suite staterooms and a barber. She became an armed merchant cruiser during the war and in January 1917 struck a mine off the coast and Ireland and sank with a large loss of life.

The success of the combination engines on *Laurentic* convinced White Star Line to install this type of machinery in its three *Olympic*-class ships. These giant liners were ordered in 1908 from Harland and Wolff as White Star's response to Cunard's record-breakers *Mauretania* and *Lusitania*. They were designed not only as floating palaces for the super-rich, but also they would also carry over 1,000 passengers in steerage class. The 45,323gt, triple-screw *Olympic* (above), the first in the series, took almost two and a half years to build and was handed over on 31 May 1911, the same day that her sister *Titanic* was launched. She was a revelation with magnificent public rooms, the likes of which had never been seen before. Not only did she have an à la carte restaurant in addition to her first class dining saloon, she also boasted a gymnasium, plunge pool, Turkish bath and a squash court. The first class staterooms were outstanding with cot beds and decorated in various designs from French Empire to Adam style. In 1907, White Star Line moved its main transatlantic mail service from Liverpool to Southampton and to cope with its 852ft trio, a new dock was built at Southampton. *Olympic*'s passenger capacity was 1,054 first, 510 second and 1,020 in third class. Although her two triple-expansion engines and low-pressure turbine produced an average speed of 21 knots, four knots less than *Mauretania* and *Lusitania*, her passenger facilities were considered superior to her Cunard rivals. *Olympic* also suffered two major collisions at both ends of her career but unlike *Titanic* (1912/46,329gt) she survived until 1935 before being broken up. She also carried thousands of troops during the First World War thus earning the title of the 'Old Reliable'. The last in the trio, *Britannic* (1915/48,158gt) was completed in 1915 but never carried commercial passengers since she was requisitioned as a hospital ship and hit a mine and sank the following year.

SOLAS

In 1893 the largest ships in the world were Cunard's *Campania* and *Lucania*. They were 13,000gt and carried around 2,000 passengers. By 1907, with the arrival of *Mauretania* and *Lusitania*, the size of the world's largest ships had increased to 32,000gt, with a passenger capacity of over 2,300. Despite this massive increase in size, the number of lifeboats (sixteen) required by the Board of Trade to be carried on the new ships was four fewer than those carried on the 1893 liners. This was because it was inconceivable at the time that these ships could ever sink, given their many safety features such as watertight doors and safety compartments. Lifeboats also cluttered the top decks and restricted the amount of open deck space available for first class passengers. In a competitive environment such as the North Atlantic, passenger safety was as paramount for all the major shipping lines in the early 1900s, as it is for the cruise industry of today. The *Titanic* disaster in April 1912, when 1,503 passengers and crew perished, has often been portrayed as the result of greed being put over safety. This is not true, however, as it was the result of a series of unfortunate incidents which ended in catastrophe. Despite the recent introduction of wireless technology, the annual loss of British ships alone was around 800. The British Government set up an international conference in November 1913, attended by representatives from thirteen countries, to examine these issues. On 20 January 1914, the Safety of Lives at Sea (SOLAS) conference, as it became known, agreed a series of internationally-binding changes, which would come into effect in July 1915. These included improved life-saving and fire-fighting equipment, the provision of watertight and fire-resistant bulkheads and the carriage of radio telegraphic equipment for ships carrying more than fifty people.

Another catalyst for change occurred a month before the start of the 1913 international conference when the twin-screw, British emigrant ship *Volturno* (1906/3,586gt), owned by Uranium Line, caught fire mid-Atlantic with the loss of 134 lives. The fire started in the forward hold which was loaded with a potentially lethal mix of cargo including chemicals, peat-moss, cocoa husks, tar oil and straw mats. Although most of the fatalities happened during the launching of the lifeboats in extremely rough weather, the fact that a passenger ship could also carry such a dangerous cargo caused great concern. However, it was also a fine example of co-ordinated efforts by the eleven ships which answered *Volturno*'s wireless distress call and successfully rescued the remaining 520 passengers and crew.

The glory of France

The first large passenger liner to be fitted with triple-expansion, direct-drive turbines was in fact Compagnie Générale Transatlantique's quadruple-screw, 24-knot, 23,666gt *France* of 1912. Often overlooked, she was designed as a statement of French prestige on the North Atlantic and at the time of her completion was also the fastest vessel on the trade apart from *Mauretania* and *Lusitania*. Delayed by a fire, her construction by Chantiers de l'Atlantique took three years and she sailed from Le Havre on her maiden voyage to New York on 20 April 1912, five days after the sinking of *Titanic*. Her passenger capacity was 534 first, 442 second and 950 in third class. Her first class interiors were based on the grandeur and opulence of Louis XIV's Versailles with antiques and huge oil paintings. The three deck high dining saloon was very impressive with its elegant grand staircase and painted ceiling. She also had a Moorish-style lounge, Salon Mauresque, with an iced water marble fountain and attendants dressed in fezes and baggy pantaloons serving coffee. Another unusual feature was a bowling alley on the games deck. *France* was also the only French-built passenger liner with four funnels, the largest to be constructed in France to that date and the first large French liner with turbine engines. Her success led to the order for an even larger running mate, the three-funnelled, 34,569gt *Paris*. Laid down in 1913 she was only completed in 1921. Meanwhile, *France* spent much of the First World War as a troopship and returned to service in 1919. By the late 1920s she was looking very dated certainly in comparison with the art deco-style *Ile de France* (1927/43,153gt). Following the Wall Street Crash and the onset of the Great Depression French Line suffered huge losses and *France* was laid up in 1932 and sold to the breakers two years later.

Size matters

Size of ship now became the new mantra and in 1910, Hamburg-Amerikanische-Packetfahrt-Actien-Gesellschaft (HAPAG), led by the dynamic Albert Ballin, ordered three giant ships for delivery between 1913 and 1915. The quadruple-screw, 22.5-knot *Imperator* (1913/52,117gt), the first in the class, was constructed at Hamburg by Vulcan-Werke. She carried 908 first, 972 second, 942 third and 1,772 steerage passengers. The machinery considered to be most suitable for such a large ship was direct drive Parsons-type turbines used in a triple expansion configuration. These consisted of four ahead and four astern units which produced ahead power of 61,000shp and 35,500shp astern. These engines were more effective for reversing than White Star's combination machinery where only the reciprocating engines had astern capabilities. Completed a year after the sinking of *Titanic*, *Imperator* also featured many new safety features including watertight bulkheads and a double skin which extended above the load waterline. The eighty-three lifeboats, including two motor boats, gave easy access for all four classes of passengers whilst the first class accommodation, arranged on six decks amidships, was equal in luxury to the finest hotels ashore. The interiors of the vast public rooms on 'B' deck were created by Charles Mewès who was responsible for the interiors of *Amerika* and *Kaiserin Auguste Victoria*. Mewès also designed *Imperator*'s grandiose Pompeian-style indoor swimming pool, the first full-size swimming pool at sea, which was based on his designs for the pool in London's RAC Club. Unfortunately all this excess, which included marble bathrooms and a giant eagle on her bow, made *Imperator* top heavy and she had to be returned to her builders for alterations to improve her stability. The next two ships, *Vaterland* (1914/54,282gt) and *Bismarck* (1921/56,551gt), were built by Blohm & Voss and featured variations of the original design. The most significant was the division of the engine room smoke uptakes for the forward two funnels (the aft funnel was a dummy) into two narrow spaces, some distance apart, rising for five decks and joining again above the boat deck. This allowed the designers to produce a virtually unbroken sequence of wide public rooms in first class. However, the downside of this was that the passenger accommodation on the lower decks became a maze of corridors. Unfortunately because of the intervention of war Ballin's dream ended in ruins. The three ships were eventually handed over as war reparations to the allies. *Imperator* went to Cunard Line as *Berengaria*, *Vaterland* as *Leviathan* for United States Lines and *Bismarck* to White Star Line as *Majestic*. These ships remained the world's largest until 1935.

The elegant *Aquitania*

Across the Channel, Cunard Line's answer to White Star's *Olympic* trio was the 45,646gt, quadruple-screw *Aquitania* which entered service not long before the start of the First World War. Larger than the White Star ships, she also had four funnels and was designed as a running mate to *Mauretania* and *Lusitania*. Although her 24-knot service speed was not as fast as the record-breaking sisters, her arrival enabled Cunard to offer a weekly, three-ship express service between Liverpool and New York. She carried 618 first class, 614 second and 1,998 third class passengers. She had triple expansion, direct-drive turbines which produced a total power output of 60,000shp, *Aquitania* was undoubtedly one of Cunard's finest ships. She also signalled the end of an era with her grand period-style interiors designed by Arthur Davis, who was a close associate of Charles Mewès. These ranged from the first class Louis XVI dining saloon to the Adam-style drawing room and included a number of new Cunard Line features such as the 132ft Long Gallery and two large enclosed winter garden lounges with sea views. To reduce rolling she was fitted with Frahm anti-rolling tanks. The first large ships to have these tanks, which were also used on the *Imperator* class, were the HAPAG passenger-cargo liners *Corcovado* and *Ypiranga* (1908/8,103gt) in 1910. The only Cunard liner to serve in both World Wars, *Aquitania* was sold to breakers in 1949.

Germany and South America

Founded in 1871, the Hamburg-Südamerikanische Dampfschiffahrts-Gesellschaft was the third most important German shipping company after HAPAG and Norddeutscher Lloyd. Faced with increased competition from the new Sud-Atlantique liners and Royal Mail Line's impressive 'A' class, Hamburg Süd ordered a trio of new passenger ships which were delivered between 1911 and 1915. The first to enter service was the twin-screw, 16-knot *Cap Finisterre* (1911/14,503gt). This rather unattractive ship with two slender, closely spaced funnels was a remarkable vessel which set the scene for the company's next two ships, which were at the time, the largest and most luxurious ships built for the South American run. The second ship the 18,805gt, 17-knot, triple-screw *Cap Trafalgar*, shown here, was completed four months before the outbreak of the First World War. Not only did she have three funnels, she was also the first German ship to be driven by combination machinery. *Cap Trafalgar* carried 400 first class passengers, 276 in second and 913 in third. Like *Cap Finisterre* she had an impressive two deck-high first class dining room forward on the bridge deck with large windows which can be clearly seen in the photograph. Above the dining room were two winter gardens with marble walls, stained-glass dome and enormous potted plants. On the same deck was a gymnasium and a 34ft by 23ft open-air swimming pool. The pool was situated between the forward and second funnel and had changing rooms and a yellow-glass roof for protection against the sun's rays. The third in the series, the 20,576gt *Cap Polonio* was completed in 1915. She was initially confiscated after the war by the Allies but was returned to Hamburg Süd in 1921. Meanwhile *Cap Trafalgar* was converted into an armed merchant cruiser and was sunk off the Brazilian coast in September 1914 by HMS *Carmania* (1905/19,524gt), the Cunard liner which had also become an armed merchant cruiser.

The venerable Österreichischer Lloyd

Trieste had been part of the Austro-Hungarian Empire for over 500 years. Not only was it the Empire's main trading port and shipbuilding centre, it was also its fourth largest city after Vienna, Budapest and Prague. Its main shipping line, Österreichischer Lloyd, founded in 1836, was older than both Cunard and P&O and was one of the largest shipping companies in the world. Its routes extended across the Mediterranean and to India and the Far East. By 1913 it had a fleet of 64 ships and carried 527,841 passengers. Two years earlier, it took delivery of the first of a pair of 7,367gt, twin-screw 18-knot steamers for the express Trieste–Brindisi–Alexandria service. *Vienna* and *Helouan* were sleek, racy-looking ships with two widely-spaced funnels. These were followed by two slower, similar-looking, but larger ships which were designed for the mail, passenger and cargo service from Trieste to Bombay. At 8,448gt, *Gablonz* of 1912 and *Marienbad* of 1913 were the biggest ships built for Österreichischer Lloyd and their striking appearance made P&O's 'M'-class liners look rather staid and stolid. Built at Trieste by Cantiere San Rocco, *Gablonz* was the first to be completed. She carried 150 first, 30 second and 100 third class passengers who were accommodated above the main deck in cabins with portholes. All first class passengers could be seated in the oak-panelled dining room whilst the main music room and lounge on the promenade deck was surmounted by a large glass dome. There was also a fully-fitted gymnasium at the aft end of the boat deck. Her twin-screws were driven by a set of quadruple-expansion engines which produced a service speed of 16 knots. Whilst both ships survived the war, *Marienbad* was seized by France in 1918 and later became CGT's *Pellerin de Latouche*. However, for the Austro-Hungarian Empire the First World War was a disaster. Not only did it see the collapse of the empire, but Austria became landlocked with the annexation of Trieste by the Kingdom of Italy. Österreichischer Lloyd was reconstituted in 1918 under Italian ownership and became Lloyd Triestino. *Gablonz* returned to the Bombay service and in 1921 was renamed *Tevere*, shown here with yellow funnels, white hull with blue ribbon and green boot-topping. In the mid-1930s she was used during the Italian-Abyssinian war to bring back Italian wounded and during the Second World War she became a hospital ship. Her end came in 1943 at Tripoli when she was scuttled as a blockship having suffered severe damage during an air raid.

The first ocean-going motor ship

The East Asiatic Company (EAC) was Denmark's most prestigious shipping line. It was also a pioneer in the development of the motor ship. On 22 February 1912, the 4,964gt, 11-knot, twin-screw *Selandia*, the world's first ocean-going motor ship, sailed from Copenhagen on her maiden voyage to Bangkok. Whilst the sinking of *Titanic* a few months later had a dramatic impact on safety at sea, the arrival of *Selandia*, shown here, was probably one of the most significant events in marine engineering of the past 100 years. Her eight-cylinder, single acting engines, situated aft between the third and fourth holds, were built by the Danish engineering company Burmeister & Wain which had been given the rights to develop Rudolf Diesel's revolutionary internal combustion engine. She was the first of three passenger-cargo liners ordered by EAC. She had no funnel and three tall masts, two of which concealed exhaust fumes from the galley and engines. The German Kaiser was so impressed with her that, not long after her delivery, *Fiona* (1912/4,964gt) the second of the EAC ships, was bought by HAPAG and became *Christian X*, Germany's first ocean-going motor ship. *Selandia*'s twenty-two passengers enjoyed beautifully-fitted accommodation forward and well away from the engines. The deck above the elegant dining room and lounge was raised by 4ft to give the sense of being in a mansion ashore. Known as the 'ship without funnels' she was the template for future generations of EAC motor ships. She was sold in 1936 and ended her career as a Japanese coastal trader in 1942 when she was wrecked between Nagoya and Yokohama.

CHAPTER 3
Post-War Reconstruction and the Rise of the Passenger Motor Ship

The First World War had a devastating impact on the world's merchant shipping fleet, with thousands of ships lost in submarine attacks whilst the Treaty of Versailles imposed incredible hardship on the German nation and destroyed its once-great merchant navy. However, the post-war reconstruction in the 1920s was also a period of great development in passenger ship design and increased use of the diesel engine.

Germany rises from the ashes

Before the outbreak of the First World War, Hamburg-America Line (HAPAG) was the largest shipping line in the world, with a fleet of 190 ships, whilst Norddeutscher Lloyd (NDL) had 116 vessels. Hamburg had also become the world's fourth largest port after London, Rotterdam and New York. At the end of the war, all vessels over 1,600gt were handed to the victorious powers including HAPAG's giants which became Cunard Line's *Berengaria* (ex-*Imperator*), White Star's *Majestic* (ex-*Bismarck*) and the newly-established United States Line's *Leviathan* (ex-*Vaterland*). HAPAG and NDL also lost all their property abroad, including the piers at New York. With his fleet in ruins, Albert Ballin, the architect of HAPAG's great resurgence, committed suicide in 1918, a sad end for one of the fiercest opponents of the war. The only large liner left in German hands was the former cruise ship *Victoria Luise* which was in such a state that even the Allies had no desire for her. Converted into *Hansa*, a high-density emigrant ship, she became a stopgap on the New York service for HAPAG until the arrival of a new series of 21,000gt passenger liners which it was hoped would re-establish the company's reputation on the North Atlantic, the *Albert Ballin* class. *Albert Ballin*, *Deutschland*, *Hamburg* and *New York* reflected the new ethos of the company which was to carry passengers in comfort rather than statements of national prestige or extreme luxury. These four, twin-screw, turbine-driven ships were built at Hamburg by Blohm & Voss between 1923 and 1926. They were also the first German ships with a cruiser stern and the first liners to boast a cinema. The first to be delivered, *Albert Ballin* and *Deutschland*, had four masts whilst the final pair only had two. They carried a sizeable amount of cargo and passengers in three classes and were fitted with anti-rolling tanks. First class had spacious public rooms with high ceilings and contemporary décor whilst the comfortable and unpretentious accommodation in second and third attracted many American and British passengers. As built, they had a service speed of 16 knots. In 1930 they were fitted with new turbines which increased their speed to 19.5 knots. In 1933 and 1934 they were further modernised with a lengthened forepart – note this photo of *Albert Ballin* – which not only increased their service speed to over 20 knots but made a considerable saving in fuel costs. Although Germany once again reigned supreme across the Atlantic, NDL, like its rival HAPAG, experienced great financial difficulties in the early 1930s. Both companies had managed to regain their former glory across the globe but had been burdened with debt in the process. In 1933 the National Socialists were swept into power and the party faithful soon infiltrated all walks of German life including the boardrooms of the two great lines. The state also took control of German shipping and because of Ballin's Jewish origin *Albert Ballin*'s name was changed to *Hansa* in 1935. After the war his memory was reinstated with the naming of HAPAG's headquarters, Ballindam. Although all four ships were sunk during the war, two, *Hansa* and *Hamburg*, were raised and had long careers as Soviet ships.

The German return to Africa

The Woermann and Deutsche Ost-Afrika Lines (DOAL) of Hamburg were also hit hard at the end of the war. Not only did they lose almost their entire fleet of seventy-two ships, the equivalent to over a quarter of a million gross tons, but their main destinations and reason for being, the German colonies in Africa, were handed over to France and Britain as League of Nations' mandates. However, in 1920, the unique funnel markings of these two companies reappeared in African waters after an absence of six years. Shortly afterwards a new building programme started which saw between 1921 and 1928 a dozen new, turbine-driven liners of less than 10,000gt appearing on the routes. These fine vessels soon re-established the pre-war eminence of Woermann and DOAL as the major competitors for British companies operating on the African trades. Although evolutions of pre-war designs, they looked impressive for their size. Their flush decks, which enhanced their sheer, gave them a distinctive appearance. They also had a yard just above the cross tree on each mast which was used for additional lighting as many of the ports had no harbour facilities to speak of. DOAL's 12-knot *Usambara* (8,690gt), completed in 1923, carried 108 first, 57 second and 120 third class passengers and had ample cargo space in four holds. Used as a German Navy accommodation ship during the war, she was burnt out in 1944 during an air raid on Stettin. A year later she sank after another air attack.

Cunard post-war intermediate liners

The attrition rate for Cunard Line's intermediate ships during the 1914–18 war was very high. To replace war losses in 1919 Cunard embarked on an ambitious replacement programme for the intermediate service. This included five 20,000gt liners for the New York and Boston service, and six 14,000gt liners for the Canadian route. However, the construction of these new ships soon became embroiled in major problems with the shipyards, which faced spiralling cost increases through labour disputes and shortages of steel. Cunard also saw its third class traffic fall by a quarter in 1922, the first year after the new United States' emigrant quota scheme was introduced. In the same year, the first of the new class of large intermediates entered service. She was the twin-screw, turbine-driven, 16-knot, 19,730gt *Scythia*. She and her four sisters, *Samaria*, *Laconia*, *Franconia* and *Carinthia*, were single-funnel, enlarged but slower versions of the pre-war *Franconia* (1911/18,150gt) and *Laconia* (1912/18,099gt). They became very popular ships, especially among US tourists and students bound for Europe, and were used extensively for cruising. In the winter of 1922/23 the brand-new *Laconia* made the first-ever world cruise by a passenger liner whilst the last in the series, *Carinthia* and *Franconia*, were the first in the Cunard fleet designed for worldwide cruising. They were also fitted with a 'sports arena', consisting of a swimming pool, gymnasium and squash court. Because *Franconia*'s design was modified during construction, *Carinthia* became Cunard's first specially-designed dual-purpose transatlantic liner and worldwide cruise ship. Cruises were usually made during the winter months when they operated as single-class ships. During the summer they sailed on the Liverpool to New York route in a three-class configuration. *Carinthia*, shown here painted white on a cruise, carried 331 first, 473 second, and 806 third class passengers. The first class accommodation was comfortable but not ornate. The main lounge and baronial-hall-style smoking room was described in a contemporary brochure as having 'an air of informal luxury which is reminiscent of a rambling country house'. There was also a garden lounge which was transformed at night into a dance area. Within a year of the outbreak of war in 1939 the five ships of the *Scythia* class were requisitioned for war duty. *Laconia* and *Carinthia* became armed merchant cruisers. Unfortunately, both these ships became war losses, *Carinthia* was sunk by a German submarine in 1940 whilst on patrol off the coast of Ireland, with the loss of four lives, whilst 1,658 *Laconia* passengers and crew were killed during the infamous '*Laconia*-order' attack in September 1942.

The last four-funnelled liners

On the subsidised mail service to South Africa, Union-Castle Line, which had become part of the Royal Mail Group in 1912, restarted its fleet modernisation programme which had been interrupted by the war. *Arundel Castle*, the first of two 19,000gt, twin-screw, 16-knot liners ordered in 1913, had been laid down in 1915 but work was suspended until 1919. Although *Arundel Castle* and *Windsor Castle* were 50 per cent larger than earlier Union-Castle mailships and the largest Cape liners built to that date, they were coal-fired, with an outdated profile for the early 1920s. They were also the last four-funnelled liners ever constructed and the only ones with a cruiser stern. The uptakes for the four small funnels created immense problems for the layout of the public rooms. However, despite their old-fashioned design, they were Union-Castle Line's first turbine-driven liners and the first with a cruiser stern. *Arundel Castle* (shown here) carried 234 first, 362 second and 274 third class passengers. Although the first class accommodation was a considerable improvement on earlier Union-Castle ships, it still featured period décor. Only first class had an elevator. Most first class cabins had compactum-type, folding washbasins instead of hot and cold running water basins. There was also a gap at the top of the bulkheads for better air flow which in fact allowed in light and noise from adjoining cabins. Two features which were a first on the South African run were the enclosed swimming pool on the boat deck in first class and the large gantry davit situated at the after end of the fourth funnel. *Arundel Castle* and *Windsor Castle* were completed in 1921 and 1922 respectively. Within a few years they were superseded by a series of impressive motor ships starting with the 20,063gt *Carnarvon Castle* in 1926. In the late 1930s, because of increased completion and a more demanding mail contract, both ships were extensively rebuilt. With new oil-fired engines and boilers, a raked bow and two large streamlined funnels they were transformed into a pair of very handsome, 19-knot ships. Improvements to the passenger accommodation included the provision of hot and cold water in all cabins whilst the gravity davits were also removed. *Windsor Castle* was torpedoed and sunk during an air attack near Algiers in 1941 whilst *Arundel Castle*, right, returned to service after the war and was only withdrawn in 1958.

The first motor ship passenger liner

Danish East Asiatic's *Jutlandia* (4,874gt), the first British-built ocean-going motor ship, was the third of *Selandia*'s sisters. She was constructed in 1912 at Glasgow by Barclay, Curle & Company as were her Burmeister & Wain (B&W) type engines. In the same year, Harland and Wolff became the sole licensee of B&W engines in the United Kingdom. This meant that when, in 1918, Barclay, Curle delivered Glen Line's 14-knot, twin-screw *Glenapp* (7,374gt), the largest and most powerful motor ship yet built, her B&W engines came from Harland and Wolff. *Glenapp* was sold to Elder Dempster Line two years later and was reconstructed by Harland and Wolff into *Aba*, the world's first motor ship passenger liner. She entered service in 1921 with a passenger capacity of 225 in first class, 105 in second and 35 in third. At the time she was described as the 'most-perfectly equipped liner engaged on the West African run'. Her two-deck-high first class dining saloon had white panelling and could seat all first class passengers. She also carried sufficient oil fuel to enable the ship to make the round trip from Liverpool to West Africa and back without bunkering. *Aba* was the template for the next three Elder Dempster passenger liner motor ships, *Adda* (1922/7,816gt), *Accra* (1926/9,337gt) and *Apapa* (1927/9,333gt) which were all built by Harland and Wolff. During the Second World War *Aba* became a hospital ship. In 1947 she returned to her owners and was sold but unfortunately capsized at Birkenhead soon afterwards during the removal of ballast.

Australian emigrant ships

In 1920 and 1921 five 13,900gt passenger-cargo ships were delivered to the Australian state-owned Commonwealth Government Line. Twin-screw, 15-knot ships, they were designed to carry immigrants to Australia and were ordered at the peak of the post-war ship-building boom, thus costing the Australian taxpayers over £6 million. *Jervis Bay*, below, was the last to be completed and carried a nominal number (12) in first class whilst the 700 in third class were accommodated in two-, four- and six-berth cabins. Public rooms were austere with no attempts to hide pipes or steel bulkheads. Four of the six holds were insulated for refrigerated cargoes. By 1928 losses incurred by the line were extensive and the five ships were sold to White Star Line, which was then part of the giant Kylsant group. The Commonwealth Line was eventually amalgamated with the well-known Aberdeen Line, forming the Aberdeen and Commonwealth Line. They were painted in Aberdeen colours with a green hulls and a buff funnel. After the collapse of Kylsant in 1931 the ships were managed by Shaw, Savill and Albion who eventually took full control of the company. They were also modified into single-class ships with reduced capacity but more comfortable accommodation which also included a veranda café. Because of their relatively unsophisticated style they appealed to the egalitarian Australians. At the beginning of hostilities in 1939 the five ships, one of which had been transferred to Shaw, Savill, were converted into armed merchant cruisers. HMS *Jervis Bay* was sunk by the German 'pocket battleship' *Admiral Scheer* whilst defending an Atlantic convoy in November 1940. Extensively refitted after the war the remaining 'Bays' remained in service until the mid-1950s by which time they were not only old but also totally outdated.

Aorangi, the world's largest and fastest motor ship

The Union Steam Ship Co. of New Zealand was persuaded by Professor Percy Hillhouse, chief naval architect at the Fairfield Shipbuilding and Engineering Company, to fit diesel engines in the replacement for *Aotearoa*, the running mate of *Niagara* on the Sydney–Vancouver route, which never saw commercial service and was lost during the war. Professor Hillhouse produced designs for a motor vessel which would consume half the weight of fuel of *Niagara* and would carry 200 more passengers. The result was the quadruple-screw, 17,491gt *Aorangi*. She was an impressive-looking ship with a green hull (later painted white) with a buff hull band, two tall, raked steamship-type funnels and a cruiser stern. When she was delivered in December 1924 she was not only the world's largest motor ship but also the fastest. Her four Sulzer engines were arranged alongside one another and produced a top speed of over 18 knots whilst her large oil storage capacity allowed her to do a round voyage from Sydney to Vancouver and back without bunkering. She also carried 436 first, 284 second and 227 third class passengers and had 225,000ft^3 of general cargo space and 90,000ft^3 of insulated space for fruit, meat and dairy produce. First class was outstanding and included a two-deck-high lounge and eight suites, each decorated in a different period-style. Passengers in the suites also ate in a private dining saloon. Operating with Canadian Pacific Railway's rail and sea service, she sailed between Vancouver, Fiji, Honolulu, Auckland and Sydney and offered the quickest service from the United Kingdom to New Zealand and

Australia. However, within a few years this rather old-fashioned liner faced serious competition from the San Francisco-based Matson Line and in 1931 a jointly-owned company, Canadian-Australian Line Ltd, was formed with CPR to meet these new challenges. Seven years later shipyards were invited to tender for a pair of 22-knot, geared-steam turbine, 30,000gt. liners. With the outbreak of war the project was cancelled and although *Aorangi* survived the war she was sold for scrap in 1953 after the loss-making route was closed.

First transatlantic motor ship

Taking full advantage of Sweden's neutrality, the Svenska Amerika Linien (Swedish American Line) started transatlantic services in 1915 with *Stockholm* (1900/12,606gt) a former Holland America liner. Another second-hand ship was bought in 1920 and the success of the operation led to an order with the Tyne shipyard Armstrong, Whitworth and Co Ltd for Swedish American's first purpose-built liner. The twin-screw, 17,993gt *Gripsholm* was not only the largest Scandinavian ship at that time but she was also the first motor-driven passenger liner on the North Atlantic. Her Burmeister & Wain diesels produced a top speed of 17 knots. She had unusually high sides which were perfect for the tough northern route across the Atlantic. However, her overall appearance was spoilt by two slim funnels which were relatively close together. She carried 127 first and 482 second plus 948 third class passengers accommodated in the shelter deck space. The public rooms in both second and first class were fitted to a very high standard. First class was sumptuous and included a two-deck-high lounge and extensive library, a large swimming pool and an elegant dining room. The chosen style for a number of the public rooms was late eighteenth century Gustavian which had been used extensively in the decoration of the Swedish royal palaces. The large second class lounge was also based on the Hall of State at Gripsholm Castle near Stockholm. *Gripsholm*'s maiden voyage from Gothenburg to New York took place in November 1925. At the time she was the world's largest motor ship. From 1927 she was employed during the winter months as a cruise ship and in the early 1930s was painted white, the colour which became synonymous with Swedish American liners. In 1928 she was joined by a larger running mate, the 20,223gt *Kungsholm*, which was also used extensively for cruising. With Sweden again neutral during the Second World War, *Gripsholm* was used for diplomatic and repatriation duties and on International Red Cross missions under guaranteed safe passage agreements. With her name and a large Swedish flag painted amidships she undertook these roles between 1940 and 1946. In 1949 she was extensively rebuilt which included full air-conditioning, a new raked stem and two larger, raked funnels. Initially placed on the Gothenburg to New York route, in 1954 she was transferred to the Bremen-American Line, a joint venture between Swedish American Line and Norddeutscher Lloyd. The following year Norddeutscher Lloyd took over the running of the ship and renamed her *Berlin*. Swedish American Line retained part ownership of the liner until 1959. In 1966 she was sold for demolition at La Spezia.

Germany's first ocean-going motor ship

The 3,693gt, engines aft *Monte Penedo* was Germany's first ocean-going motor ship. Completed for Hamburg Süd in August 1912. Her engines were built by Sulzer, the Swiss engineering firm, founded in 1834. A dozen years later Hamburg Süd took delivery of its first diesel-powered passenger-cargo ship. The two-funnelled, twin-screw 13,625gt *Monte Sarmiento* was the lead ship of five similar liners which were built between 1924 and 1931. Two-class ships, they were designed principally as emigrant ships. They also carried coffee-pickers from Northern Spain to Brazil. *Monte Sarmiento* was the first large German passenger motor ship and among the first oil-engined ships to have two engines geared to one shaft. This arrangement ensured that machinery was installed as low in the ship as possible so that the maximum amount of 'tween-deck space could be used for emigrants. At the time of her delivery in November 1924 she was the world's largest motor ship. She carried 1,328 passengers in third class and 1,200 in steerage and was joined by a sister *Monte Olivia* in 1925. They were followed by the slightly larger *Monte Cervantes* in 1928 and *Monte Pascoal* and *Monte Rosa* in 1931. With a decline in emigrant traffic, the 'Monte' ships were ideally suited for low-cost, single class cruising and were used extensively as cruise ships in the 1920s and 1930s. *Monte Sarmiento* was sunk by Allied aircraft at Kiel in 1942. Only *Monte Rosa* remained at the end of the Second World War and she became the British troopship *Empire Windrush*, famous for bringing the first West Indian immigrants to Britain in 1948.

Cruising to the Canaries

The seven Spanish-owned islands off the coast of north-west Africa which make up the Canary Islands have played an important role on the trade routes between Europe, South America and Africa. Alfred Jones, founder of Elder Dempster, took a keen interest in the Canaries and in the latter part of the nineteenth century he started importing bananas into Britain. In 1900 the Liverpool-based fruit importers Yeoward Brothers bought its first ship to carry fruit and bananas direct to Britain. This second-hand vessel had three tall masts and a funnel two-thirds aft. This distinctive profile became the hallmark for all new Yeoward Line passenger-cargo ships starting with the 1,414gt *Ardeola* in 1904. They had superior first class accommodation and offered cruises to the Canaries under the slogan 'Sunward by Yeoward'. All these ships, which had names starting and ending with the letter A, were built at Dundee by the Caledon Shipbuilding and Engineering Company. The final three Yeoward liners were delivered between 1922 and 1927. The first of these was the single-screw, 13-knot, triple-expansion, 3,445gt *Alondra*, shown here. Like her sisters she shared the same Yeoward profile which had barely changed in almost a quarter of a century. However, what they also had was very fine accommodation for 120 first class passengers which was spread over three decks with considerable promenade deck space. All staterooms were outboard rooms and had beds with sprung mattresses. The Yeoward cruises were very popular especially as they operated weekly from Liverpool during the winter months. However, with the downturn of trade during the Spanish Civil War, *Alondra* was sold to the Chilean State Railways in 1938 for use on the Chilean coastal trade. With her name unchanged she joined her former running mate *Andorinha* (1911/2,548gt) which had been renamed *Vina del Mar*. Although *Alondra* was broken up in 1961, the remarkable remains of *Vina del Mar* exist on the shore of Puerto Chacabuco in southern Chile, where she ran aground in 1963.

The rebirth of Compañía Transatlántica

At the start of the 1920s Compañía Transatlántica, Spain's leading shipping line, commenced a new building programme to replace much of its fleet of older and smaller ships with fewer and larger liners. For the first time, the company also decided to have the ships built at Spanish yards instead of British ones. The northern coast of Spain was starting to be industrialised and the lead ship of the new fleet, the 10,551gt *Alfonso XIII*, was the first ship to be constructed at Bilbao by Sociedad Española de Construcción Naval, Spain's leading shipyard firm which was mainly owned by the British yards John Brown and Vickers-Armstrong. She and her slightly larger sister *Cristóbal Colón* were not only the largest liners built for Compañía Transatlántica but also they were the largest ships to that date constructed in Spain. Designed for the Bilboa to Cuba route, the pair were well-balanced ships with two tall masts, a single tall funnel and cruiser stern. They had twin-screws and were driven by geared turbines which produced a service speed of 16 knots. On trials, *Alfonso XIII* managed 19.5 knots. Despite their relatively plain exteriors, the pair had very impressive first class public rooms. The two-deck-high lounge on *Alfonso XIII* was based on a Moorish design and included a bronze statue of King Alfonso XIII who was then the ruler of Spain. The first class dining saloon featured several reproductions of Goya tapestries whilst the winter garden was decorated in a Spanish Renaissance style. Her passenger capacity was 245 first, 82 second, 148 third with space for 1,589 emigrants or troops. Unfortunately, soon after her launch in September 1920 much of the ship was destroyed in a fire which delayed her completion until 1923, the year *Cristóbal Colón* was delivered. After four years on the Central America run both ships included homeward-bound calls at New York in 1927. In 1931 *Alfonso XIII* was renamed *Habana*, left, following the abdication of King Alfonso XIII and the formation of the Spanish Republic which was followed in 1936 by the outbreak of the Spanish Civil War. This caused havoc with Spanish shipping. *Alfonso XIII* was laid up in Bordeaux whilst *Cristóbal Colón*, which had been seized by supporters of General Franco, was wrecked at Bermuda in October 1936. At the conclusion of the war *Alfonso XIII* returned to Bilbao in June 1939 for a refit by her builders. Unfortunately three months later her entire passenger accommodation was destroyed in a fire. She was subsequently converted into an 8,279gt cargo ship, shown here, and returned to service in 1942. In 1946 she underwent a six-month conversion at the Todd Shipyard in New York. The work included accommodation for 101 first class passengers, all berthed in outboard cabins, a dining saloon seating sixty, a forward-facing cocktail lounge on the boat deck and a small chapel. In April 1947 she sailed from New York to Bilbao, her tonnage modified to 10,069gt. In 1962 when she was sold to Pescanova S.A., Vigo and converted into the fish-factory ship *Galicia*. After spending most of her time off the coast of Southern Africa, her long career was brought to a close when she was sold to Vigo ship breakers in 1978.

Red Star Line's largest passenger ship

Because of increased competition from Holland America Line, the 27,132gt *Belgenland* was ordered before the First World War from Harland and Wolff as Red Star Line's largest passenger ship. She was a triple-screw, 17-knot, three-class liner designed for the Antwerp to New York route. Launched at Belfast on the last day of 1914, work was suspended until 1917 when she was completed as White Star Line's cargo-only ship *Belgic*. At the time both White Star and Red Star were part of the International Mercantile Marine Company (IMM). One of the last Atlantic ships to have combination machinery, she had two funnels, a cruiser stern, three masts and virtually no superstructure. In 1918 she was fitted with accommodation for 3,000 troops for a new role as a troopship. In 1922 she returned to Belfast for completion as a passenger liner using her original design. She was transformed beyond recognition with the addition of three more decks, a third dummy funnel and the removal of her mainmast. Renamed *Belgenland*, she entered service in April 1923 on Red Star Line's Antwerp to New York route. She initially carried 500 first, 500 second and 1,500 third class passengers but with a decline in emigrant traffic and an increase in Americans wishing to visit Europe, in 1929 second and third were combined into a new class known as tourist. She was used regularly as a cruise ship based at New York and Tilbury and was for a time, the largest liner operating in the Thames. She also undertook several world cruises. However, because of financial problems during the Great Depression Red Star Line ceased operations in 1934. *Belgenland* was briefly transferred to IMM's Panama Pacific Line as *Columbia* but was sold for scrap in Scotland in 1936.

The largest freighters in the world

Another of the IMM companies which ceased trading in the early 1930s was the American-owned, British-flagged Atlantic Transport Line which ran passenger-cargo services between London and New York. In 1919 it placed an order with Harland and Wolff for four giant, twin-screw, 16-knot, turbine-driven passenger-cargo liners to replace war losses. Because of shortages of raw materials, the first in the series, the 21,716gt *Minnewaska*, left, was only completed in 1923 whilst her sister *Minnetonka* was delivered the following year. The second pair was never built. At the time they were not only the largest freighters in the world but also the biggest ships trading from London. The cargo capacity was over a million cubic feet whilst the ten holds were served by thirty-six electric winches and six pairs of king-posts. Three hundred and sixty-nine first class passengers were carried in spacious accommodation which included cabins on 'B' and 'C' deck, most of which were outboard. There was a wide-promenade deck with the main public rooms on 'A' deck decorated in period styles. The forward-facing lounge offered views on three sides whilst the dining saloon on 'D' deck was sufficiently large to accommodate all passengers in a single seating. The fortnightly service to New York included an eastbound call at Cherbourg. Whilst the two ships were initially successful, it soon became apparent that with falling rates and other cargo lines cutting into the trade it was becoming increasingly difficult to fill the immense cargo space. In November 1931 the London route closed and so did Atlantic Transport Line. After a brief spell on Red Star Line's Antwerp to New York service, the two ships were sold to Scottish breakers in 1934. They were barely ten years old.

British India's coolie ships of the 1920s

In 1904 British India (BI) Line, in competition with Blue Funnel Line, entered the lucrative Chinese coolie trade from Amoy (Xiamen) and Swatow. The British used these labourers to work in tin mines and rubber plantations in the Straits Settlements. Eight years later, BI acquired Apcar & Co., an Armenian-owned, Calcutta-based company which owned coal mines and ran ships to Amoy via Singapore and Hong Kong under the Apcar Line banner. British India's Chinese service became an important part of the company and it continued to use the Apcar name until the 1950s. In 1923, *Talma*, the first of a pair of two-funnelled ships for the Far East run was introduced. They were designed to impress the Chinese market and were the first in the fleet over 10,000gt. They were followed in 1924 by a trio of slightly smaller 8,000gt ships. These three-funnelled ships, on which the aft funnel was a dummy, were among the most distinctive-looking of all BI ships. *Tairea*, shown here, was the first to be delivered and was constructed on the Clyde by Barclay, Curle. She had accommodation space for 3,263 deck passengers in addition to 56 in first and 80 in second class. Her top speed was over 17 knots and she was the first BI ship with raised gravity davits which gave passengers an unobstructed view from the promenade deck. She was transferred to the Bombay-East Africa service in 1932 and was the only one of the trio to survive the war. In 1949 she returned to her original Far East run and was broken up in 1952.

Japanese motor ships

In 1924 Sulzer Brothers entered into a technical agreement with the Japanese shipbuilder Mitsubishi to build its engines. The first ocean-going Japanese passenger liner with diesel engines entered service in 1925. She was Osaka Shosen Kaisha (OSK)'s 7,267gt *Santos Maru*, the first of three 15.7-knot, twin-screw liners designed to carry Japanese immigrants to Brazil. Brazil has the largest Japanese community outside Japan and the USA and for almost a quarter of a century OSK operated a unique round-the-world service from Japan to South America around the Cape of Good Hope, returning to Japan via Panama and Los Angeles. Outbound, the ships carried emigrants to Brazil, and on the return journey, various cargoes were picked up en route including raw cotton, Japan being at that time the world's major textile producer. *Santos Maru*, built at Mitsubishi's Nagasaki yard and driven by Sulzer engines manufactured in Switzerland, reduced the time from Kobe to Santos from sixty-three days to forty-six days. She carried 40 first class and 102 third class cabin passengers with 681 immigrants housed in large dormitories. She also had substantial cargo capacity including 17,000ft^3 for silk. Requisitioned by the Japanese Navy in 1941 she became the submarine support ship *Manzyu Maru*. Three years later she was sunk by a US submarine with the loss of 724 lives.

Brazilian coastal motor ships

Brazil has the longest coastline in South America and in the days before air travel the easiest means of transport was by sea. In the 1920s the two main coastal companies were Cia. Nacional de Navegacao Costeira and Lloyd Nacional. The latter, which was founded in 1917, had a very old fleet which included five ships built in the nineteenth century. Both companies decided to modernise their passenger fleets with each ordering four motor ships of just under 5,000gt. Whilst Costeira had three built in Britain and one in France, Lloyd Nacional placed its order with Cantiere Navale Triestino, Monfalcone. The 4,872gt *Ararangua*, *Araraquara*, *Aracatuba* and *Aratimbo* (shown here) were delivered at regular intervals between August 1927 and April 1928. The four ships were virtually identical with two masts, a relatively small raked funnel and two Fiat engines driving twin screws which produced a service speed of 14.5 knots. The cargo space was considerable and was worked mainly by ten hydraulic cranes. Interestingly, each ship had its name featured amidships. They also carried 100 passengers accommodated in two and four berth cabins whilst the public rooms consisted of a music room forward on the boat deck and a smoking room and veranda at the aft end of the deck. The dining saloon could seat all passengers in a single sitting. Despite defaulting on payments to the yard, which were eventually settled in the early 1930s, the ships were a success. *Ararangua* and *Aratimbo* were only broken up in 1969 and 1966 respectively. *Aracatuba* was wrecked in 1933, whilst *Araraquara* was torpedoed and sunk by a German submarine in August 1942 with the loss of 131 passengers and crew. At the time Brazil was a neutral country and this sinking contributed to Brazil's decision to declare war on Germany later that year.

Singapore, the Malay States and Borneo

The great port of Singapore lies at the crossroads between India and the Far East. Until the Japanese invasion in 1942, it had been the capital of the Straits Settlements, a federation of Malay states which came under British control following the Anglo-Dutch Treaty of 1824 which divided the Malay Archipelago between Britain and Holland. Under British rule in the twentieth century the area became one of the largest producers of tin and rubber. To meet the needs of the trades between Singapore and Penang, Sumatra, south Siam and the west coast of the Malay Peninsula, the Straits Steamship Company Ltd. was founded in 1890. It was acquired by Blue Funnel (Alfred Holt & Co) in 1914, hence the blue middle band of the funnel colours. Although the large fleet of small ships with white hulls were used as a feeder service for Blue Funnel's main line cargo ships, they also played an important role in the transportation of passengers in the region. The finest of all the Straits ships was the 2,499gt *Kedah* of 1927. Built at Barrow-in-Furness by Vickers Ltd., this twin-screw, turbine-driven ship had a service speed of 18 knots and was used on the weekly express Singapore–Penang–Belawan cargo-passenger service. All cabins for the seventy-four first class passengers had portholes or windows whilst the dining saloon could accommodate everyone in a single sitting. The large walnut-panelled lounge forward on the boat deck was one the coolest parts of the ship, an important factor in the high humidity of the tropics. *Kedah* also carried 800 deck passengers and was very popular with first class travellers. In fact, the United States shipowner Robert Dollar was so impressed with the ship that he ordered a slightly larger version for his subsidiary the Philippine Inter-Island Steamship Company. *Mayon* (1930/3,371gt) ran between Manila and Zamboanga and was sunk by the Japanese in 1942. After an eventful war career as the Royal Navy auxiliary HMS *Kedah*, she returned to the UK in January 1946 and was sold to Harris & Dixon. Her passenger capacity was increased to 121 first class and 142 tourist and renamed *Kedmah* she became the newly-formed Zim Lines' first passenger ship. Claimed to be the fastest merchant ship in the Mediterranean, she started a new fortnightly service between Haifa and Marseilles in 1947. In 1952 she reverted to Harris & Dixon ownership and was renamed *Golden Isles*. She was broken up in 1956.

French Africa liners

The great French company Chargeurs Réunis Compagnie Française de Navigation à Vapeur was founded in 1872 and in 1875 was given exclusive rights by the French government to carry emigrants from Le Havre to Brazil and Argentina. Two years later it started a regular postal and passenger service to the new French colonies in West Africa. This was the start of its long association with Africa which included the airline UTA. Numerous liners were built for the route from Bordeaux to Dakar and various ports along the coast terminating at Pointe-Noire in the French Congo. In the 1930s the two main Chargeurs Réunis West Africa liners were *Brazza* (1924/10,387gt) and *Foucald* (1923/11,028gt). The *Brazza* was a very interesting ship. She started life as an 8,898gt, twin-screw, 12-knot cargo ship *Camranh* – the first French-built motor ship. In 1927 she was converted into *Brazza*, a three-class, 273-capacity passenger liner with two funnels, the forward one being a dummy. By the mid-1930s she was considered too slow for the route and was sent to Ateliers et Chantiers de France, Dunkirk for a major rebuild, which would see her service speed increased by 5 knots to 17 knots. Not only did she have new Sulzer diesels, she was lengthened by 19ft and given a new bow designed by the famous naval architect Vladimir Yourkevitch who designed the hull of *Normandie*. This image shows her at Southampton in 1936 shortly after the rebuild. In May 1940 *Brazza* was torpedoed and sunk by a U-boat off the Portuguese coast and sank in four minutes with the loss of 383 lives.

Italy's first liners over 30,000gt

Delivered by Ansaldo in 1926 and 1927 respectively Navigazione Generale Italiana (NGI)'s quadruple-screw *Roma* (32,583gt) and *Augustus* (32,650gt) were the first Italian liners over 30,000 tons, Although both had similar profiles, *Roma* was powered by geared steam turbines whilst *Augustus* had MAN diesels and was the world's largest passenger motor ship. They originally had four classes with the first and second class interiors designed by Ducrot in a similar classical style to NGI's earlier *Giulio Cesare* and *Duilio*. Because she had smaller engine exhaust uptakes the layout of the public rooms on *Augustus* was different from her running mate. However, one of the greatest innovations on this pair was provision of cabins for third class passengers instead of dormitories. *Augustus* was also the first liner to have an open-air lido-style area aft which included a swimming pool. Despite differences in speed, the 19-knot *Augustus* was three knots slower than *Roma*, they were very successful ships. In 1939 the company decided to re-engine the pair with the most powerful marine diesels ever built producing a maximum speed of 26 knots. Each plant, consisting of four engines and three auxiliaries, would have produced a staggering 83,750bhp. The ships would also have been rebuilt with a single funnel, cruiser stern and streamlined bow. This work never happened because of the war. They were converted into aircraft carriers and later destroyed. However, the four engines which were manufactured for *Augustus* were installed in the post-war *Giulio Cesare* and *Augustus*.

The grand *Saturnia*

Not to be outdone by NGI and Lloyd Sabaudo, the Trieste company Cosulich Società Triestina di Navigazione ordered two powerful, twin-screw, 19-knot motor ships from Cantiere Navale Triestino, Monfalcone for delivery in 1927 and 1928. They were designed for the South American run but with changing economic conditions were placed on the New York service. The first to enter service was the 23,940gt *Saturnia*. Driven by two Burmeister and Wain-type engines, she was at the time the world's largest motor ship. Because these engines produced less exhaust fumes than other ships, she had a short, squat funnel which gave her a unique and rather racy profile. However, this modern, motor ship look did not extend to her interiors which included an over-the-top, fifteenth-century style first class social hall and ballroom and Pompeian indoor pool designed by the Coppedè brothers. Despite this, she was the first liner to have a complete deck of staterooms with private balconies overlooking the sea. There were forty of these on 'A' deck including two large suites. All first class staterooms also had baths running hot and cold fresh and sea water. Her sister *Vulcania* (seen here) carried 279 first, 257 second, 310 third and 1350 fourth class passengers. Because they were required as secondary liners for the express service to New York, in 1935 and 1936 both ships had their engines replaced with lighter and more powerful engines which increased their service speed to over 20 knots. The refurbishment of their interiors also included the Coppedè-ballrooms being replaced by a more appropriate modern, airy style which used various types of wood. Unlike so many of their running mates, the pair survived the war and remained in the Italia fleet until the mid-1960s.

Dutch East Indies

The Netherlands was another small country in Europe which controlled vast territories in the East. For over 300 years the Dutch ruled the Dutch East Indies, now modern-day Indonesia, one of the most densely-populated regions in the world. Following the opening of the Suez Canal in 1869, two famous Dutch lines were established, each operating mail services between the Indies and Holland's major sea ports, Amsterdam and Rotterdam – Stoomvaart Maatschappij 'Nederland' (SMN) in 1870 and Rotterdamsche Lloyd (RL) in 1883. The Koninklijke Paketvaart-Maatschappij (KPM) was founded in 1888 to run mail, passenger and cargo services throughout the myriad of islands that made up this vast territory. Because its mail contract did not allow it to operate beyond the East Indies, with Dutch government assistance it formed the Java-China-Japan-Lijn (JCJL) in 1902 with SMN and RL to provide services between Java, China and Japan. In 1907 routes to Australia commenced with the Java-Australië Lijn. It was for this route that KPM ordered its first liners over 10,000gt from two Dutch shipyards in the mid-1920s, the twin-funnelled *Nieuw Zeeland* (1928/10,906gt) and *Nieuw Holland* (1928/10,903gt). Although KPM was an early champion of motor ships, probably because of their size, this twin-screwed, 15-knot pair was powered by geared steam turbines. They were also among the first fast passenger ships to use oil fired water tube boilers. Marketed as the 'Great White Yachts' these attractive-looking liners with a counter stern carried 155 first class passengers between Singapore and Sydney in great comfort and included two suites with private facilities. They also had wide, open decks for games and sports and a large open-air swimming pool. They were held in high esteem by the Australian Government and in 1933 *Nieuw Holland* was chosen as an Australian trade exhibition ship to the East Indies and Malaya. After the German invasion of the Netherlands in 1940 both ships were chartered as British troopships. Unfortunately *Nieuw Zeeland* (seen here being towed under the semi-completed Sydney Harbour Bridge in 1930) was sunk during the North Africa landings in 1942. After an extensive refit in 1948 at Hong Kong, *Nieuw Holland* returned to service. However, a year after the government seized all Dutch assets in Indonesia in 1958, she sailed on her final voyage from Australia and was sold to Hong Kong breakers.

NIEUW ZEELAND

Bibby Line's four-masters

Since 1889 Henderson Line's main rival on the Burma run was the Liverpool-based Bibby Line. This long-established company had been in the shipping business since the early nineteenth century. Its *Venetian* (1859/1,508gt) was the first ship built by Harland and Wolff whilst *Cheshire* (1891/5,907gt) was the first twin-screw ship to operate east of Suez. Although it ran an agreed parallel service to Burma (from Liverpool and London) with Henderson (from Glasgow and Liverpool), Bibby's ships were always superior. They also had a very distinctive profile with four masts and a tall funnel equidistant between the mainmast, just abaft the bridge, and the mizzenmast. In 1903 *Warwickshire* introduced a unique form of cabin layout which was soon copied by other companies operating in tropical regions. The Bibby tandem cabin units were designed to maximise available space whilst providing portholes for all cabins. In the mid-1920s Bibby broke with tradition when it placed an order with Fairfield Shipbuilding and Engineering Co Ltd instead of Harland and Wolff, which had built all its ships to that date. The 10,550gt *Shropshire* of 1926 introduced the diesel engine into the Bibby passenger fleet and was the first of a series of five similar, first class-only, passenger-cargo liners. The last to be delivered in 1935 was the 11,650gt *Derbyshire*, shown here. Like her Fairfield-built running mates, she was fitted with single-acting, two-stroke Sulzer-type engines and had a service speed of around 15 knots. She carried just under 300 passengers in superior accommodation and was the first Bibby liner to have a built-in swimming pool. She was also the last of the four-masters to be built. After the war Bibby returned to a radically-transformed Burma. Within a few years Burma gained independence from Britain and soon turned its back on its former colonial masters. These changing conditions meant fewer first class passengers and the four surviving pre-war liners were rebuilt with reduced accommodation. *Derbyshire* reappeared with two masts and a lower elliptical funnel. With dwindling passenger numbers the passenger services ceased in 1965, a year after *Derbyshire* was sold for scrap.

The first British turbo-electric powered liner

During the 1920s, to replace war losses, P&O ordered a series of two-funnelled liners for the Australian and Bombay mail services. These included two 20,800gt 'M'-name ships and three 15,100gt ships with 'C' names for the Australia routes and four 16,000gt ships with 'Ra' names for the London–Bombay run. The final ship of the decade was the 19,648gt *Viceroy of India*. With a similar profile to the earlier ships, she was a one-off for P&O. and was designed for the Bombay service. Unlike other P&O liners built in the 1920s which had quadruple-expansion engines, she was the first ocean-going, British passenger ship to have turbo-electric power, i.e. steam turbines driving electric motors connected to twin screws. Not only did these engines require fewer engine room staff, they also created less vibration which was why *Viceroy of India* was a popular cruise ship in the 1930s. The passenger accommodation for 415 first and 258 second class was also superior to any previous P&O liner. The first class public rooms based on period designs were opulent and she had the first built-in swimming pool in the P&O fleet. Built on the Clyde by Alexander Stephen and Sons Ltd., she was delivered in March 1929. At 19 knots, she was fast and in 1932 reduced the London to Bombay record to seventeen days, one hour and forty-two minutes. In 1940 she was requisitioned for service as a troopship and in November 1942, off Oran, she was torpedoed and sunk by a German submarine with the loss of four lives.

New Zealand Shipping Company's first motor ships

In the early 1920s the New Zealand Shipping Company planned replacement ships for its ageing passenger fleet. Following the success of *Aorangi* on the transpacific run the company decided that its next passenger liners would be diesel-powered. In 1925 plans were prepared for three ships of around 20,000gt but when the order was placed with John Brown in 1927 the size of ship was reduced to just under 17,000gt. The first to be completed in January 1929 was the 16,697gt, twin-screw *Rangitiki* (below). She and her sisters were not only New Zealand Shipping's first motor ships but also the first with two funnels. Unfortunately, during her trials, *Rangitiki* was found to be relatively unstable in ballast conditions. After her first voyage from Southampton to New Zealand, via the Panama Canal, a number of changes were made to alleviate the problem. These included the installation of permanent ballast and the shortening of her funnels. This photo shows her before the changes which were also introduced to her sisters *Rangitata* and *Rangitane*. These two ships were delivered in October and November 1929 respectively. All three were given John Brown Sulzer diesels which produced a service speed of 15 knots. Although they carried 100 first, 86 second and 413 third class passengers, they were mainly cargo liners with passenger accommodation fitting around the engine trunking and seven cargo hatches. The cargo capacity was large with 425,000ft^3 of insulated and 150,000ft^3 of uninsulated cargo space. The public rooms in first class were decorated to a high standard although the décor was rather old-fashioned and based on period designs. At the opposite end of the spectrum, third class conditions were cramped, especially in the dining saloon, which had tables for eight or ten diners. In 1940 the trio was requisitioned for war duty by the British Government. Although *Rangitiki* and *Rangitata* survived the war *Rangitane* was sunk by German raiders in November 1940 with the loss of thirteen passengers and crew. The post-war refit for *Rangitiki* and *Rangitata* included a change in their passenger accommodation to 121 first and 284 tourist class and new Doxford diesels which increased their service speed to 16 knots. Both liners were sold for demolition in 1962.

Union-Castle Line motor ships

Although the mailship *Carnarvon Castle* (1926/20,063gt) was Union-Castle Line's first motor ship she was originally designed as a steamship. The first motor ship ordered by Union-Castle Line was in fact the 11,951gt, twin-screw intermediate liner *Llangibby Castle*. She was intended to be the first of two sisters designed for the round-Africa passenger-cargo service from London. Her 1924 order with Harland and Wolff was delayed for two years because of poor financial results. When she was delivered in 1929 she was at the time not only the largest intermediate liner but also the first with two funnels. These intermediate ships called at a wider range of ports and tended to be slower than the mailships. The Great Depression and the failure of the Kylsant group of companies, which included Union-Castle, put paid to plans for a sister for *Llangibby Castle* although the 10,002gt *Dunbar Castle*, a smaller version ordered for the west coast intermediate run, was completed in 1930. The two funnels on *Llangibby Castle* which gave her a distinctive profile looked rather odd on such a small liner. She carried 256 first and 198 third class passengers in spacious but rather simple accommodation. The décor in first class was, like most British colonial liners of that time, based on period styles. This included a Louis XVI lounge in soft greys and whites and a dining saloon designed in the Empire style. Only 12 of the 212 first class cabins had en-suite baths and toilets although these were shared with the adjoining cabin. The ship also had no swimming pool. Her Burmeister and Wain engines produced a service speed of 16 knots whilst her refrigerated cargo space was 123,970ft^3. In 1940 she was requisitioned as a troop transport. During the war she was a very lucky ship having survived an air raid, having had her stern blown away by a torpedo, being hit by a shell and being damaged in a collision. She returned to the round-Africa route in 1947 where she remained for another seven years until her demolition at Newport, Monmouthshire in 1954.

French motor ships

After the loss of many ships during the First World War, Messageries Maritimes (MM) set about a rebuilding programme which would not only re-establish its pre-eminence but also introduce a series of arguably the most unattractive passenger liners ever built. MM's first diesel-driven liner was *Théophile Gautier* (1927/8,194gt) and with two tiny twin funnels her look was more that of a steamship than a modern motor ship. However, the next liner delivered in 1929, the 9,928gt *Eridan*, caused a sensation with her straight stem, counter stern, and two low, square-shaped funnels with overhanging tops. She was the first of six ships built in this style, the slightly larger, 11,000gt *Jean Laborde* and *Maréchal Joffre* and an even bigger trio designed specifically for the Far East service, and headed by the 16-knot, twin-screw *Félix Roussel* (1930/16,753gt). To reinforce their unique Frenchness, MM suggested that these ship be called not motor ships but '*nautonaphtes*' i.e. petrol ships. *Félix Roussel* (seen here) and her near-sisters *Georges Philippar* and *Aramis* had stunning first class interiors, with a different theme for each ship, the last two being French and Minoan respectively, whilst *Félix Roussel* featured the Khmer art of Cambodia. They were also the first French ships to have a permanent swimming pool (indoor) and among the first liners to have cabins (ten either side) with individual balconies. Three-class ships, the forward funnel was a dummy and included the dome above the first class lounge, which on *Félix Roussel* was illuminated to show various Cambodian sculptures set in niches. As

with most French ships, the main staircase led directly into the dining room, and the balustrades culminated on either side in a magnificent multi-headed snake god from Angkor Wat. *Georges Philippar* was lost in tragic circumstances during her homeward-bound maiden voyage and in 1935 the remaining pair were given a new raked bow and more powerful engines which increased their maximum speed to 18.5 knots. They were also were painted white with green boot-topping, which greatly enhanced their appearance. With *Aramis* seized by the Japanese during the Second World War and later sunk, *Félix Roussel* became an Allied troopship and was the last of her class at the end of the war. In 1950, after a two-year overhaul in Dunkirk, the ugly duckling emerged as a swan, her two square funnels replaced with a single oval-shaped stack. With most of her original interior intact, she became a two-class ship. These were, however, troubled times for the French Indo-China colonies and the *Félix Roussel* spent more time carrying troops than regular passengers. Surplus to requirements in 1955 she was sold to Arosa Line and was converted into the emigrant ship *Arosa Sun*. After Arosa's bankruptcy in 1959 she became an accommodation vessel for workers at the Dutch steel works in Ijmuiden and was scrapped in 1974.

NYK transpacific liners

For its new route, known as the Orient-California service, Nippon Yusen Kaisha (NYK) ordered three of the finest passenger ships ever built in Japan. Known affectionately as the *Queen of the Sea*, the 16,947gt, quadruple-screw *Asama Maru*, shown here, was the first to be completed in 1929. Despite being motor ships, she and her sister *Tatsuta Maru* had raked twin funnels and masts which produced an elegant profile. They were also fast and, powered by four Sulzer engines, had a top speed of 21 knots. The accommodation in first class was outstanding, with an English-style design and facilities such as a 'talkie' cinema, swimming pool and, for the first time on a ship, a tatami room for those who wished to experience the Japanese style of living. She also carried a French chef. Although classed as a sister to *Asama Maru* and *Tatsuta Maru*, *Chichibu Maru* (1930/17,498gt) had twin screws and a low single funnel. She was often seen as the flagship of the Japanese merchant marine. In 1939, the keels for the 27,700gt *Kashiwara Maru* and *Izumo Maru* were laid. The largest passenger ships to be built in Japan, these 24-knot turbine-driven ships would have reduced the journey time from Yokohama to San Francisco by two days but unfortunately, like the earlier San Francisco ships, they were lost during the war.

Russian motor ships

In 1925, determined to be no longer dependent on foreign shipbuilders, especially the British, the new Soviet Government set about modernising its former naval yards so that they could build ocean-going merchant ships. Russia had been one of the first countries to adopt oil-engines for ships and by the early 1930s became the foremost motor shipbuilding nation. Among the first large motor ships to be built were six 3,870gt cargo-passenger ships designed for the all-important Leningrad (St. Petersburg)–London route. These ships from the Severnaya yard, Leningrad, had small funnels and were fitted with accommodation for 28 first, 24 second and 240 in third class. They also had considerable refrigerated space. The first in the series *Aleksey Rykov* was delivered in 1928 whilst *Sibir*, seen here off Gravesend in 1938, was the last to arrive in 1930. She was lost in 1941 during a German aerial attack in the Baltic. Only two of this class survived the war, including *Kooperatsiya* which was only scrapped in the 1980s.

The glorious *Ile de France*

In 1927 Compagnie Générale Transatlantique (French Line) took delivery of a new enlarged running mate for *Paris* (1921/34,569gt). The three-funnelled, quadruple-screw, 24-knot, 44,153gt *Ile de France* had a very similar profile to the earlier liner apart from gravity davits on the upper decks. These davits were among the first to be used on the North Atlantic and provided passengers with uninterrupted deck space. However, the greatest difference between the two ships was the interior décor. Whilst *Paris* looked back to pre-war French designs, *Ile de France* was all about the future. The decorative scheme of the first class interiors was entirely in the modern art or art deco-style. Her designs were heavily influenced by the L'Exposition Internationale des Arts Décoratifs et Industriels which was held in Paris during 1925. The term art deco is a shortened version of Arts Décoratifs. France's leading designers were commissioned to work on the *Ile de France*'s impressive public rooms. Carefully chosen wooden veneers were much in evidence as were specially-designed furniture, tapestries, tablewares and lights. The three-deck-high dining saloon designed by Pierre Patou was vast and could seat all first class passengers in a single sitting. It was also the largest ever built on a liner to that date and made great use of indirect lighting, the *Ile de France* being one of the first transatlantic liners to use it in many of its public rooms. Constructed at St-Nazaire by Chantiers de l'Atlantique, she was the sixth largest ship in the world. Not only were her turbine engines more powerful than *Paris* but because of the 1924 emigration restrictions to the United States, she also carried fewer third class (646) and more second class (603) passengers than her running mate. In 1928 she was fitted with a seaplane-launching catapult on her after deck, a first for a liner, so that the transatlantic mails could be delivered a day earlier than scheduled. Similar catapults were installed on NDL's *Europa* and *Bremen* although the one on *Ile de France* was only used until 1930. Despite increased competition in the 1930s she was a very popular ship, especially among first class passengers. Laid up in New York at the start of the war, in 1940 she was detained by the British Government at Singapore after the fall of France and became a troopship managed by P&O. In 1942 her interiors were stripped out at Port Elizabeth, South Africa when she was converted into a 9,706-capacity troopship. The only thing left of her old interior was the Gothic-style chapel. Managed by Cunard Line from 1944, she was returned to her owners in 1946. Between 1947 and 1949 she was rebuilt at St-Nazaire and emerged transformed. Her three funnels were replaced by two streamlined stacks with smoke deflectors whilst the removal of the after funnel meant that the enclosed upper decks and open promenade decks could be completely redesigned. Partial air-conditioning was installed for some of the public rooms including a new 350-seater theatre. Her passenger capacity was reduced from 1,548 to 1,345 whilst leading French artists and designers again joined forces to create the new interiors. Although she never regained her pre-war mystique, *Ile de France* played an important role in the post-war revival of French Line. At the end of 1958 she was sold to Japanese breakers. Soon after her arrival at Osaka she suffered the indignity of being partially sunk and refloated for the movie *The Last Voyage*.

Holland America Line's long-awaited flagship

Red Star Line's major competitor on the North Atlantic was Holland America Line. However, the Dutch company was beset by financial problems throughout the 1920s, especially after the reduction in emigrant quotas introduced by the United States government in 1924. The shortage of cash meant that the building of the new 29,511gt flagship *Statendam* was delayed numerous times. She was eventually delivered in 1929, eight years after her keel was laid. She had been ordered from Harland and Wolff, Belfast in 1919 as a replacement for the 32,234gt *Statendam* which had been completed during the First World War but was requisitioned by the British Government and subsequently sunk by a German submarine in 1918. The new *Statendam* had the same three-funnelled profile as the earlier ship but with a cruiser stern instead of a counter stern. She was eventually launched in 1924 but was laid up because of a dispute over her fitting out costs. In 1927 she was towed to Schiedam for her final fitting out by Wilton-Fijenoord. Her maiden voyage from Rotterdam to New York in April 1929 coincided with the 300th anniversary of *Halve Maen*, the first Dutch ship to arrive at what is now New York. Despite being the largest ship in the Dutch merchant navy *Statendam* was distinctively old-fashioned

looking compared with other large transatlantic liners of her day. Her interiors were also a throwback to the past, with ornate wood-panelled interiors in first class based on classical designs, many of which had been prepared for the earlier *Statendam*. One of the finest rooms was the Palm Court with its domed ceiling and uninterrupted views of the sea through large, square windows. These windows were a feature of the ship and it was claimed that she had more windows than any other ship afloat. There were sixty-four windows in the main dining saloon alone. Her machinery was also radically different from the previous ship. She was fitted with two three-stage geared turbines driving twin-screws. Her service speed was 19 knots and she carried 510 first, 344 second, 374 tourist and 426 third class passengers. She also became well known as a cruise ship operating during the winter months. Laid up at the Holland America terminal in Rotterdam she caught fire during the German occupation of Holland in May 1940 and was completely destroyed.

The Canadian 'Lady' Boats

From the formation of the Dominion of Canada in 1867 to the outbreak of the First World War, Canadian politicians felt threatened, both commercially and politically, by their giant neighbour to the south. After a number of serious disputes over fishing rights and geographical boundaries, Canada sought new ways of freeing itself from the overwhelming power of the United States, one of these being increased trade with the British West Indies which also wished for greater autonomy from the United States. For many years Royal Mail Line ran a regular subsidised service between Canada and the West Indies. However, in 1927, after its tender for a new contract was rejected, the contract was awarded to Canadian National Steamships, part of the recently nationalised Canadian National Railways. The new trade agreement between Canada and the West Indies required a triangular service to Canada via Bermuda. One route would cover the Western Caribbean and would mainly convey bananas whilst the Eastern Caribbean service would be a general cargo operation. Five virtually-identical ships were ordered from Cammell Laird. Named after the wives of famous British admirals associated with the West Indies, the Lady ships were divided into two distinct groups. The 8,194gt *Lady Rodney*, below, and *Lady Somers*, designed for the Western Caribbean run carried only first class passengers and were essentially 'banana boats', whilst the slightly smaller 7,813gt *Lady Nelson*, *Lady Hawkins* and *Lady Drake* island-hopped along the Eastern Caribbean, picking up cargo and passengers en route. The 16-knot *Lady Nelson*, the first in the new fleet, sailed from Halifax on her maiden voyage in December 1928 bound for Bermuda and the Eastern Caribbean. Her passenger capacity was 103 first class, 32 second class and 100 deck passengers. She had twin-screws and was turbine-driven. By the end of April 1929 all five were in service and during their first year carried over 25,000 passengers. Considering their size, they were extremely handsome ships, painted white with red white and blue topped funnels. They were also perfect for the inter-island trades with shallow drafts, long-reach derricks and facilities for deck passengers. Passenger accommodation in first class was superb, with cabins all situated on the bridge deck, each with beds and portholes. At the forward end of this deck were two deluxe suites with private verandas. On the promenade deck, the drawing room and garden lounge, with their comfortable cane furnishings, epitomised the unpretentious style of these ships. All passengers could be seated at a single sitting in the one-and-a-half deck-high dining room which like the smoking room, was designed in the half-timbered 'ye olde Tudor' style popular in British colonial liners of the 1920s. For Canadians, the Lady ships played a major role in the development of cruising in the Caribbean. With tailor-made rail connections they allowed an easy escape from the harshness of the Canadian winter. With the entry of Canada into the war, the ships were painted grey, fitted with a 4in gun and initially continued to keep the link between Canada and the West Indies open despite the constant threat from submarines which later claimed *Lady Drake*, *Lady Hawkins* and *Lady Somers*. In 1947, the two survivors, *Lady Rodney* and *Lady Nelson*, returned to their original route. However, faced with a spiralling increase in costs and a government less willing to take on the large losses the service had incurred, both ships were withdrawn in 1952. They were sold to the Khedivial Mail Line of Egypt the following year and renamed *Mecca* and *Gumhuryat Misr* respectively. Both ships were used primarily as pilgrim ships. In 1967 *Mecca* was scuttled in the Suez Canal by the Egyptians during the Arab-Israeli War. A year later her sister was sold for demolition.

Chapter 4
The Reshaping of the United States Merchant Fleet

At the start of the First World War the number of US-flagged merchant ships was tiny in comparison with other world powers. As the war progressed, it became apparent that something had to be done to redress this imbalance.

US Shipping Board standard type combi-liners

The US Shipping Board, created in 1916, ordered a series of twin-screw, geared-turbine standard-type ships from US shipyards for delivery between 1920 and 1922. These vessels became the backbone of the US merchant marine in the post-war years. Of the passenger-cargo ships, there were two types of rather functional-looking vessels, the 10,496gt 502s and the 14,124gt 535s, so-called after their length in feet. They were initially given 'State' names but were renamed after US presidents in 1922. The seven 502s originally had accommodation for 84 first class passengers and 494,605ft^3 of cargo space with a speed of 14 knots. The sixteen 535s had accommodations for 260 first class passengers and 300 steerage passengers with 143,636ft^3 of cargo space and a speed of 17 knots. A number initially operated across the Atlantic for the government-owned United States Lines including *President Roosevelt* (seen here). With none of the sophistication of the large transatlantic liners she offered a more economical, intimate and friendly style for passengers on the New York, Southampton, Cherbourg and Bremen run. She became a US Navy transport during the war and was scrapped in 1948.

Enter the Dollars

The seven 502s were acquired by the Dollar Steamship Company for its round-the-world service in 1923. Formed by Robert Dollar in 1892, Dollar Line had the largest US-owned passenger liner fleet in the 1920s after it acquired ten 535s 'Presidents' from the US Shipping Board. In the late 1920s Dollar took advantage of the Merchant Marine Act of 1928, also known as the Jones-White Act, which was designed to further stimulate the US merchant navy by offering generous mail subsidies and support for new ships. For the San Francisco–Far East route it ordered from the Newport News Shipbuilding and Drydock Company two 21-knot, 22,000gt, steam turbo-electric liners, *President Hoover*, seen here, and *President Coolidge*, which were delivered two months apart in 1931. The largest ships built to that date in the United States, they were the only liners to be named by wives of US Presidents. They had twin funnels, a counter stern and, uncommon for that time, a bulbous bow. Carrying almost a thousand passengers in four classes, they also had two open-air pools and outstanding first class accommodation which included baths in most cabins, a gymnasium and a private dining saloon. Unusually for an American liner, the first class dining saloon was approached via a descending staircase and they were the first liners to have a bar with a soda fountain and ice cream dispenser. They were also the first US liners with a contemporary décor. There was so much ornamental glass work that an art glass shop was established in the shipyard. Unfortunately *President Hoover* was lost after she ran aground off the coast of Taiwan in 1937. This was a mortal blow for Dollar Line which had been struggling to repay its government loans. In 1938 it was taken over by the US Maritime Commission and was reconstituted as American President Lines. Four years later *President Coolidge* struck a mine at Espiritu Santo in New Caledonia and sank close to the shore where she remains as the world's largest diving site.

PRESIDENT HOOVER

The *Morro Castle* disaster

The first ships to be financed under the 1928 Merchant Marine Act were a pair of 21-knot, 11,520gt liners designed for Ward Line's prestigious New York to Havana passenger and subsidised mail service. The twin-screw, 20-knot *Morro Castle*, shown here, and *Oriente* were completed in 1930 by the Newport News Shipbuilding and Drydock Company. Powered by turbo-electric machinery, they significantly reduced the sailing time on the route and, fitted with bulbous bows, were at the time the world's fastest turbo-electric liners. Not only were they were among the first liners to be constructed under the rules of the 1929 SOLAS agreement but they also had outstanding accommodation for 430 first and 100 tourist class passengers. In first class there were sixteen suites and large, stylish public rooms. Hailed as among the safest ships afloat, they were immensely popular. Therefore, it came as a great shock when the four-year-old *Morro Castle* caught fire close to the shore of New Jersey in September 1934 and 133 lives were lost in the blaze. Following an extensive enquiry, new regulations were put in place which ensured that US-operated passenger ships had some of the world's strictest fire-safety regulations. *Oriente* became the troopship *Thomas H. Barry* in 1941. Later owned by the US Department of Commerce, she was broken up in 1957.

United States Lines

Another pair of liners built with Merchant Marine Act of 1928 loans were the 24,289gt *Manhattan* and *Washington*, delivered in 1932 and 1933 respectively. They were ordered from the New York Shipbuilding Corporation in 1930 by P W Chapman and Company which had bought United States Lines from the US Shipping Board a year earlier. A condition of the sale was that four new liners should be introduced onto the transatlantic run. Two would be 45,000gt ships for the express service whilst the second pair were intended as intermediate liners for the New York–Southampton–Hamburg route. Because of the economic uncertainty following the 1929 Wall Street Crash, the large ships were not ordered and Chapman defaulted on its payments to the US Shipping Board. Although the line came under new owners in 1931, work continued on the new ships which had counter sterns and raked bows. Powered by geared steam turbines, these 22-knot, twin-screw ships were the USA's first purpose-built large transatlantic liners. Art deco was starting to make its mark in New York, especially after the magnificent Chrysler Building was completed in 1929 and it is surprising that the décor on these important ships was so old-fashioned. For example the style of the first class smoking room, themed around the American West, not only had a large painting of American Indians but it also had a large wood-burning fireplace and animal heads including buffalo and moose. Despite this, the more than 1,000 passengers in three classes enjoyed considerable comfort and the pair often had load factors higher than other transatlantic liners. *Manhattan* was the first to be completed and her small motor ship-type funnels (seen here) were soon replaced by larger ones. During the war they played an important role as troopships and although *Washington* returned to service briefly from 1946 to 1951 as an austerity liner the pair were laid up in the reserve fleet until their demolition in 1965.

The Panama Canal

After ten year of work, and eleven days after the outbreak of war in Europe, the Panama Canal was officially opened on 15 August 1914 by Panama Steamship Line's *Ancon* (1902/9,606gt). Like the Suez Canal forty-five years earlier, this great engineering feat saved thousands of miles of sea travel. The International Mercantile Marine Company (IMM) formed the Panama Pacific Line in 1915 to operate passenger-cargo services between New York, Havana, Los Angeles and San Francisco via Panama using liners from its subsidiary Red Star Line. In 1925 the company placed an order with Newport News Shipbuilding and Drydock Company for a trio of 18-knot turbo-electric liners of just over 20,000gt. Assisted by US Government loans and mail subsidies *California*, *Pennsylvania*, shown here, and *Virginia* were completed in 1928 and 1929 and were not only the largest liners built in the US to that date, but also the first in the world to be powered by turbo-electric power. With less vibration these ships provided greater comfort for the 384 first and 363 tourist class passengers. They were outstanding ships with large public rooms in both classes, all outboard cabins, single-seating dining, suites with verandas and the first American ships to have open-air swimming pools and only the second group after the Italian liners *Roma* and *Augustus* of 1926 and 1927 to have this facility. Passengers could also bring their cars as there was garage space for 140 vehicles which were driven aboard on side ramps. After the removal of the government mail subsidy the trio were withdrawn in 1938 and subsequently bought by the US Maritime Commission for American Republics Line's 'The Good Neighbor Fleet' which was operated by Moore-McCormack Line and ran between New York, Rio de Janeiro, Santos, Montevideo, and Buenos Aires. Renamed *Uruguay*, *Brazil* and *Argentina* their appearance was marred by the removal of the aft dummy funnel. They were broken up in 1964.

American motor ships

American shipowners were slow to take up diesel power and generally preferred steam-driven ships. The first purpose-built, ocean-going passenger motor ships built for a United States owner were constructed at Gothenburg, Sweden by Götaverken. The *City of San Francisco* and *City of Panama* (right) were delivered in August and October 1924 respectively for the San Francisco-based Pacific Mail Steamship Company. These small, twin-screw, 2,434gt passenger-cargo liners were designed for the coastal trade between San Francisco and Panama. They carried fifty-nine passengers in first class and a similar number in steerage. Their six-cylinder B&W-style engines produced a leisurely service speed of only 12 knots. A year after their arrival, Pacific Mail's coastal routes were sold to Grace Line's subsidiary, the Panama Mail Steamship Company. In 1932 they were given Grace Line *Santa* names and in 1937 were sold to the United Baltic Corporation.

Grace Line motor ships

Grace Line was sufficiently impressed with the performance of the Götaverken pair that it specified diesel engines for its new two pairs of passenger ships. The first two, delivered in 1928, were unusual in the fact that they were not only built in England by the Furness Shipbuilding Company Limited, Haverton Hill-on-Tees but also because they had two funnels, the forward one being a dummy. The 7,858gt *Santa Barbara* (right) and *Santa Maria* were at the time the largest and fastest ships in the Grace Line fleet. They only carried 157 first class passengers in extremely fine accommodation with all cabins outboard. All passengers were seated in a single seating whilst children had their own dining room. Sulzer engines drove twin screws which produced a service speed of 16.5 knots. The flexibility of diesel machinery was ideal for the New York to Chile via Panama express service which often involved at least fifteen ports of call. This handsome pair had five cargo holds and were very successful in capturing a sizeable share of the west coast of South America cargo and fruit business. By 1940 they were outdated and were sold to the US Navy as troop transports. Renamed USS *Crawley* (ex-*Santa Barbara*) and USS *Barnett* (ex-*Santa Maria*), the former became a war loss whilst the latter was sold to Achille Lauro in 1948. After a major refit at Genoa she emerged as the 10,699gt emigrant ship *Surriento*, still two-funnelled and with her original engines but with her capacity increased to 187 in first and 868 in tourist class. She was broken up in 1966.

Matson Line and Hawaiian tourism

In the inter-war years Matson Line sought new ways to diversify and one of these was the tourism market. In 1924 it decided to build not only one of the finest hotels in the world, the Royal Hawaiian Hotel, Waikiki Beach, but also a passenger liner which would complement it. Built at Philadelphia by William Cramp & Sons, and designed by the renowned naval architect William Francis Gibbs, the 17,232gt, twin-screw, 22-knot, geared steam turbines *Malolo* was completed in 1927. An elegant-looking ship, with raked funnels and masts, her lifeboats were halfway up the superstructure, a common feature on the cruise ships of today. The largest, fastest and most luxurious liner yet built in America, she was very spacious with seven passenger decks for the 650 first class passengers. All cabins had beds and telephones, many with baths or showers, and the ventilation system ensured that the air was changed every three minutes. The public rooms were decorated in classical American eighteenth-century style whilst the large library contained over 2,000 specially-bound volumes. She also had a grand Pompeiian-Etruscan-style indoor swimming pool and a single-sitting dining saloon with a musicians' gallery. With the journey time to Hawaii reduced from a week to four and a half days, *Malolo* was a great success and two new larger liners based on the *Malolo* design were subsequently ordered for the Matson subsidiary The Oceanic Steamship Co. which had the mail contract between San Francisco and Sydney. Named after California counties, the 18,000gt *Mariposa* and *Monterey* were completed in 1931 and 1932 respectively. This pair revolutionised sea travel in the Pacific not only in terms of speed but also passenger comfort. They carried almost 700 passengers in two classes, each of which had its own open-air swimming pool. In first class there were eight cabins with private balconies and they were the first American liners to have air-conditioning, albeit only in the dining saloon. With a top speed of 22 knots, these heavily-subsided liners ran from San Francisco and Los Angeles to Hawaii, Samoa, Fiji, New Zealand and Australia and by 1935 carried around 60 per cent of passengers on the route. Meanwhile, a third sister, *Lurline*, had been completed in 1933 as a running mate for *Malolo*, subsequently renamed *Matsonia*, on the Hawaiian run. Used as transports during the Second World War, all four ships had successful second careers as cruise ships. *Homeric* (ex-*Mariposa*) was the first to broken up 1974. *Queen Frederica* (ex-*Matsonia*) followed in 1977 and *Ellinis* (ex-*Lurline*) in 1987. *Britanis* (ex-*Monterey*) sank in 2000 whilst under tow to the breakers.

The four Graces

By the 1920s, Grace Line had developed an extensive network between New York and the west coast of North and South America, as well as to the Orient, following their purchase of the Pacific Mail Steamship Company in 1915. At the end of the decade, it was decided to take advantage of the generous subsidies provided by the Merchant Marine Act of 1928, and ordered four virtually identical liners from the Federal Shipbuilding and Dry Dock Company of Kearney, New Jersey. Designed by William Francis Gibbs, *Santa Rosa* (seen here), *Santa Paula*, *Santa Lucia* and *Santa Elena* of 1932 and 1933 were exceptional vessels. With two funnels, the handsome 19-knot quartet had a 'big liner look' about them, even though their gross tonnage was only 9,135. They had twin-screws and were turbine-driven. The forward funnel also featured a pair of fins for smoke deflection, which was later used to great effect on Gibbs' most famous ships, *America* and *United States*. The layout of the passenger accommodation was also highly innovative, with all the public rooms on the promenade deck, including the two-deck-high dining room, which featured a roll-back roof between the funnels for al-fresco dining. They were the first American ships to have all outboard cabins with baths or showers and only 225 first class passengers were carried. Another unusual feature was the use of waitresses in the dining room, and Chinese-Americans as cabin stewards. The ships also had an exceptionally large, 20ft by 35ft, open-air swimming pool. Placed initially on the New York to San Francisco coastal run, the new Grace liners also had a large cargo capacity which was essential if the service was to be profitable. In 1938, following changes to the government contracts and the purchase of two companies which operated in the Caribbean, three of the four Grace sisters were moved to the New York-Caribbean route, whilst the fourth, *Santa Lucia*, ran to Chile and was later joined by *Santa Elena* as a running mate. After war duty, during which two of the original quartet were lost, *Santa Rosa* and *Santa Paula* returned to the New York–Caribbean service in 1947. In 1961 they were sold to the Greek firm Typaldos Brothers. After the collapse of that company in 1967 both ships were laid up and eventually scrapped.

Chapter 5
Increased Competition on the Routes to South America

After the First World War the routes between Europe and South America were very important not only because of the immigrant trade but also the wealthy and sophisticated passengers who demanded great quality of service.

New liners from Italy

By 1910, the Genoa-based Navigazione Generale Italiana Società Riunite Florio & Rubattino (NGI), founded in 1881, had become Italy's largest shipping company. Despite its size the company was unable to compete effectively with foreign competition on its main transatlantic routes. At stake was the almost endless flow of Italian emigrants to both North and South America. With relatively small ships, Italy was only able to capture less than half the market. Although the routes to the United States remained important for NGI, South America offered the greatest opportunities with large numbers of Italian emigrants bound for Argentina and Southern Brazil and first class clientele who demanded the highest standards of luxury. In 1914 the company ordered two ships which in terms of speed, service and size would become the leading ships on the route. The 21,658gt *Giulio Cesare* (Julius Caesar) was built on the Tyne by Swan, Hunter & Wigham Richardson, whilst her slightly larger, 24,281gt sister *Duilio* (named after the Roman admiral Gaius Duilius who defeated the Carthaginians) was constructed at the Ansaldo shipyard Sestri Ponente, Genoa. The First World War interrupted construction and *Giulio Cesare* was only completed in 1922 whilst *Duilio* entered service the following year. Designed by the Italian naval architect Nabor Soliani, *Giulio Cesare* was not only the first Italian vessel over 20,000gt, but she was also the largest on the Europe to South America run up to that date. A handsome quadruple-screw ship, she had a straight stem, neatly curved cruiser stern, and a well-proportioned pair of black funnels, each with a broad white band. Her geared turbines produced a top speed of over 20 knots. With limited cargo space, she carried 243 first class, 306 second class and 1,824 steerage passengers. Most of the interiors were designed and furnished by the Ducrot Company of Palermo who also decorated the Italian Royal Yacht *Savoia*. The main first class public rooms were based on an eighteenth-century palazzo, with two similar-sized large chambers, a hall and a ballroom. The two-level dining room, situated high up on the ship, was overlooked by a large domed skylight. Comfortable accommodation was provided for second class in the poop, whilst emigrant accommodation was situated between second and first. The Great Depression created financial problems for the major Italian shipping lines and in 1932 the Italian Government ordered the merger of the three leading transatlantic companies into the Italia Flotte Riunite Cosulich-Lloyd Sabaudo-NGI Commonly known as Italia, its funnels bore the *tricolore* colours of Italy: red, green and white. The following year the South African and Italian Governments announced that the newly-formed Italia would provide a five-year subsidised passenger service between the Union of South Africa and Italy. *Giulio Cesare*, seen here at Cape Town, and *Duilio* were placed on the run in 1934. The arrival of these two crack Italian liners had a profound impact on the South Africa to Europe route as they showed up the inadequacies of the Union-Castle Line passenger-mail service, not only in terms of speed but also comfort. As a result, the next new mail contract in 1938 stipulated that the mail service be reduced by a full three days to fourteen. This brought about a complete overhaul of the Union-Castle fleet. In the meantime, Italian shipping was again reorganised in 1937 into the Finmare Group which exists today. Both ships were transferred to Lloyd Triestino and although they were popular with South Africans, the service was not profitable and, at the end of the five-year contract in 1939, both ships were withdrawn and *Giulio Cesare* was transferred to the Genoa–Hong Kong route. Both ships were laid up at Trieste in 1944 where they were sunk during an Allied air raid.

Lloyd Sabaudo's 'Contes'

Until the formation of Italia in 1932, NGI's main rival at Genoa was Lloyd Sabaudo which had been founded at Turin in 1906 with support from the Italian Royal House of Savoy. In 1914 Lloyd Sabaudo ordered a 15,000gt liner from the Glasgow shipbuilder William Beardmore. With two tall, thin funnels, she was based on the design of Allan Line's Beardmore-built *Alsatian* (1914/18,485gt). However, because of the outbreak of the First World War, the first ship *Conte Rosso* (named after Amadeus VII, the fourteenth-century 'Red Count' of Savoy), was completed as HMS *Argus*, the Royal Navy's first flush-decked aircraft carrier. In 1919 a new contract was signed with Beardmore for two similar but larger, 18,000gt, twin-screw, 20-knot ships. *Conte Rosso* and *Conte Verde* were delivered in 1922 and 1923 respectively. *Conte Rosso* was not only the first large Italian liner to be completed after the war, but also the first merchant ship to be fitted with geared steam turbines. The exotic interiors of this rather old-fashioned looking liner caused a sensation when she entered service. While the creative world looked forward to a new era of modernity, the Coppedè brothers' designs for *Conte Rosso* were an eclectic mix of Italian-historic styles from ancient Roman to the Baroque. with painted ceilings and elaborate chandeliers. She also had unusual dining arrangements for first class passengers. In addition to a formal two-deck, oak-panelled main dining saloon situated high up on 'B' and 'C' decks, there was also a *ristorante all'aperto*, an open-air restaurant with wicker chairs forward on the promenade deck. In 1925 Beardmore completed the 24,416gt *Conte Biancamano*. She was the last Italian ship built abroad. Under pressure from Benito Mussolini's government which came to power in 1922, Lloyd Sabaudo was forced to order its final Coppedè-designed ship from the Stabilimento Tecnico shipyard, Trieste. Delivered in 1928, the 25,661gt *Conte Grande* was the finest ship in this quartet of unusual liners. *Conte Rosso*, shown here in Lloyd Triestino colours, carried 208 first class, 268 second and 1,890 third class passengers. After operating on Lloyd Sabaudo's New York and South American services in 1932 following the absorption of Lloyd Sabaudo into the Italia group, she was transferred to Lloyd Triestino's Trieste–Shanghai route. As a troopship she was sunk in May 1941 off the coast of Sicily by a British submarine with the loss of 1,276 lives.

Royal Mail Line's response

Faced with increased foreign competition on its major South American routes, Royal Mail Line ordered a pair of 22,000-ton, twin-screw motor ships from Harland and Wolff in 1924. The first, *Asturias*, was completed in 1926 and was described as the largest, most luxurious and highest-powered motor ship of her time. She and her sister *Alcantara* (right), completed in 1927, also introduced a new type of profile with a pair of squat, horizontally-topped funnels and the first Royal Mail liners with cruiser sterns. These features appeared on other Harland and Wolff liners constructed for Union-Castle Line and White Star Line, which were also part of the Royal Mail group of companies. Despite the modern motor ship look, the interiors of the new 'A' ships were a throwback to pre-First World War liners. *Asturias*'s first class aft-facing veranda lounge was designed in a Moorish style whilst the two-deck-high dining room, which could seat all 408 first class passengers in a single sitting, was inspired by the French Empire period. Every first class cabin had hot and cold running water whilst many had a private bath and toilet. She also carried 200 second and 674 third class passengers. The latter were mainly accommodated forward. Unfortunately for Royal Mail, the eight-cylinder, four-stroke engines were a disappointment. Both ships suffered from excessive vibrations when travelling at their 16-knot designed speed, which after a few years was well below that of the competition. During 1934 and 1935, the diesel engines were replaced with steam turbines. At the same time, their funnels were heightened whilst their hulls were extended forward by 10ft. These changes increased their speed to 19 knots. During the war they were refitted for war service and had their forward dummy funnel removed. After suffering serious damage in 1943 *Asturias* was bought by the Ministry of Transport and ran as a troopship until 1957 when she was scrapped. *Alcantara*, which returned to Royal Mail service in 1948, went to the breakers in 1958.

Pacific Steam's Queen of the Pacific

Meanwhile, on the west coast of South America, another Royal Mail Line associate, the Pacific Steam Navigation Company (PSNC) had a series of old-fashioned, steam-driven liners with 'O' names operating in the 1920s on its main routes from Liverpool to Valparaiso, via Spain and the Panama Canal. Grace Line, one of its major competitors, had also introduced a pair of handsome passenger-cargo motor ships, *Santa Barbara* and *Santa Maria*, on the Valparaiso to New York run in 1928. In the same year PSNC ordered the 17,707gt *Reina del Pacifico*, Queen of the Pacific, from Harland and Wolff. Delivered in 1931, she was not only the highest-powered British motor vessel but also one of the most powerful quadruple-screw motor ships in the world. She reached 21 knots on her trials. To re-emphasise a break with the past this attractive two-funnelled liner was not given an 'O' name and was painted white with green boot-topping. She carried 888 passengers, 280 in first class, 162 in second and 446 in third. As the majority of her passengers were Spanish-speaking, her interiors were based on Moorish and Colonial Spanish styles. The designer Ashby Tabb, after an extensive tour of Spain, co-ordinated all the designs. The Winter Garden at the aft end of 'E' deck showed the early Arab influence with fretted arches and two Moors holding silver shells with up lights whilst the single-sitting first class dining saloon featured wrought ironwork and dining chairs based on those in the Escorial Palace near Madrid. Although the swimming pool was indoors, there was a 76ft by 63ft Games Deck which included two tennis courts. Large diesel engines had advanced considerably since *Asturias* and *Alcantara*. In her first three-and-a-half years of operation *Reina del Pacifico* made 792 port calls and logged almost 330,000 miles without a single incident. During the Second World War she played an active role not only as a troopship but also as an assault ship and took part in the North African and Sicilian landings. In 1946 she returned to Belfast for her post-war refit. In September 1947 during her trials an engine-room explosion killed twenty-eight men, many of whom worked for Harland and Wolff. She was joined by a new consort, *Reina del Mar*, in 1956 but after a series of mishaps, including grounding at Bermuda, she was withdrawn from service in 1958 and sold to Welsh breakers at Newport.

REINA DEL PACIFICO

Blue Star's 'A' class

In the 1920s one of the most important South American routes was the transportation of frozen meat to Britain between London and the River Plate. The two main shipping lines were Vestey Brothers' Blue Star Line and Nelson Line, which had been acquired by Royal Mail in 1913. In 1925 Blue Star placed an order with various British shipyards for nine refrigerated ships, five of which were designed for a new fortnightly passenger-cargo service. With luxurious accommodation for 164 passengers, the new 12,850gt, twin-screw, 16-knot liners would be the only ones on the South American trades to carry just first class passengers. The amount of space per passenger was larger than any of the established lines on the route and with passenger ships at Buenos Aires given priority treatment at the improved docking facilities, the turnaround time in port was also greatly reduced. Two ships came from the John Brown yard on the Clyde, whilst the remaining three were built by Cammell Laird at Birkenhead. The amount of refrigerated space was considerable, with three holds forward and three aft, each subdivided into insulated 'tween-deck compartments, forty-nine in total. The lack of large holds also meant that the vessels had relatively little sheer and this, combined with a straight stem, resulted in a rather stiff-looking appearance. The two, closely-spaced, raked admiralty-cowled funnels with the distinctive Blue Star colours, however, gave the ships a unique identity. The aft funnel was a dummy and provided ventilation for the engine room – the admiralty cowls were removed within a year of completion. The two sets of geared-turbine engines were also powerful enough to enable the ships to do the entire voyage from London to Buenos Aires with stops at intermediate ports in 18–19 days. The passenger accommodation was situated amidships on four decks and the public rooms were as good as, if not better than, any of the Conference carriers on the route. The overall style of these rooms was that of an

eighteenth-century English country house, with fluted columns, parquet floors, richly-designed carpets and silk-covered furnishings. The large dining room was situated forward on the main deck and could accommodate all passengers in a single sitting. The main public rooms were on the promenade deck with the usual layout of smoking room and veranda aft and lounge forward. All staterooms were outboard with beds, whilst a number also had bathrooms attached. With Spanish A-names, the five ships were initially difficult to tell apart and the first to be completed was *Almeda* which inaugurated the new service in February 1927. She was followed later that year by *Avila*, *Andalucia* (shown here), *Avelona* and *Arandora*. The success of the ships was immediate and before the end of the year, Blue Star Line had joined the South American Freight Conference and its services were dovetailed into the Conference line schedules. With fewer ships needed to operate the route, it was decided to convert *Arandora* into a full-time cruise ship. Also in 1929, because of confusion with Royal Mail's 'A-class' liners, all the Blue Star 'A' ships were given the *Star* affix. In 1934 *Avelona Star* was rebuilt as a cargo ship with a single funnel whilst *Almeda Star, Avila Star and Andalucia Star* were each lengthened in 1935 and given a maier-form bows. All five ships were lost during the war.

The 'Compass Princes'

Prince Line had a long association with New York which went back to the late nineteenth century. Taken over by Furness, Withy in 1919, it operated a regular service from New York to South America. To consolidate its position on the fortnightly, 5,800-mile service between New York and Buenos Aires, it ordered four, virtually identical, twin-screw passenger-cargo motor ships from two Clyde shipyards, Napier & Miller and Lithgows. Known as the 'Compass Princes', each was named after one of the principal points of the compass. The 10,917gt *Northern Prince* was the first to be delivered in April 1929. Like her sisters, she was a handsome ship with a straight stem, cruiser stern, and a rather squat funnel. She had six holds, twenty-two derricks, and considerable cargo space, much of which was insulated. She also carried only 101 first class passengers in luxurious accommodation. The amount of space for passengers was exceptional for a ship of her size. Not only did she have a single-sitting dining saloon but most of the cabins also had a bath and beds with satin bedspreads. There was extensive use of wood panelling and one of the first open-air swimming pools to be installed on a British ship. The Burmeister-type engines produced a service speed of 16.5 knots. The remaining sisters, *Eastern Prince*, *Southern Prince* and *Western Prince*, shown here, were delivered throughout 1929. Despite their arrival around the time of the Wall Street Crash and the introduction of US Government-subsidised ships on the run, they were very successful ships. Only *Eastern Prince* and *Southern Prince* survived the war. The former became the troopship *Empire Medway* and was scrapped in 1953 whilst the latter was sold to the Italian firm, Costa. Renamed *Anna C.* she lasted until 1971 when she too was scrapped.

Enter the 'Highlands'

Meanwhile Nelson Line, which had not built a new passenger liner since 1911, responded to the Blue Star threat by ordering from Harland and Wolff five 15-knot, twin-screw, 14,100gt motor ships for the London route. With over half a million cubic feet of refrigerated space they were also designed to carry 135 first and 66 intermediate class passengers with additional open-berth space for 600 mainly Spanish and Portuguese emigrants. They were functional-looking ships with squat, closely-spaced funnels, a long forecastle, and short deep well between the bridge and superstructure. The first class interiors were decorated in an Old English style with oak beams and panelling with wooden decks and minimal carpeting. This plain style was more like second class on some lines but appealed to those who did not like the stuffiness on more formal ships. *Highland Monarch* was the first to be completed in 1928 for the fortnightly service to Brazil and River Plate via Spain and Portugal. She was followed a year later by *Highland Chieftain* and *Highland Brigade*, seen here, whilst *Highland Hope* and *Highland Princess* were delivered in 1930. Unfortunately *Highland Hope* was wrecked when she was less than a year old so a new sister, *Highland Patriot*, was ordered for delivery in 1932. By a strange twist of fate, this replacement ship was the only one of the quintet to be lost in the war. In peacetime, the survivors returned to the South American run and were eventually replaced by more modern vessels. *Highland Monarch*, the last to go in 1960, was also the first of these unique ships to be built.

Chapter 6
The Race for the Transatlantic Speed Record, 1929 to 1936

The race for the fastest transatlantic ships became an obsession in the 1930s, especially as these liners were increasingly seen as symbols of national pride.

Bremen 1929 and *Europa* 1930

In the early 1920s Germany underwent a period of great social unrest and hyperinflation. However, in 1924 the Reichsmark was introduced and with a stable currency the country started to prosper not only industrially but also creatively. Progressive German thinking was exemplified by the Bauhaus movement, with its simple designs which were a complete contrast to the grandeur of Imperial Germany before the war. By the mid-1920s the two leading German shipping lines, Hamburg America Line and its Bremen-based rival Norddeutscher Lloyd, had re-established themselves on the world's major shipping routes. It was also now time for Germany to recapture the prestigious transatlantic speed record it had lost in 1907 after the arrival of *Lusitania* and *Mauretania*. On 13 December 1926 Norddeutscher Lloyd simultaneously placed orders with two German shipyards for a pair of 50,000gt, 27-knot liners to be named *Bremen* and *Europa*. They were designed to operate on a weekly service in each direction between Bremen and New York with the crossing from the English Channel to New York only taking five days. Both ships featured great advances in engineering technology and hull design. Each had four propellers driven by powerful geared steam turbines. The bow had a bulbous forefoot which is common these days but was extremely unusual in the 1920s. This not only created more stability but also improved the overall speed of the ship. Despite being built at different yards, *Europa* at Blohm & Voss, Hamburg and *Bremen* at AG 'Weser', Bremen, both ships were ready for launch on consecutive days in August 1928 and were due to enter service together a year later in a simultaneous bid to regain the Atlantic speed record. However, *Europa*'s completion was delayed by eight months following a fire whilst fitting out. *Bremen*'s maiden voyage to New York took place in July 1929 when she broke *Mauretania*'s twenty-year record in both directions at an average speed of almost 28 knots. She was joined on the route by *Europa*, also a record-breaker, in March 1930. Both ships had an impressive appearance with a streamlined superstructure, tall masts and two low, pear-shaped funnels. Because of problems with soot on deck, the funnels of both ships were raised in 1930 which rather spoiled their racy look. The interiors of the ships were designed to be like a hotel with standardised first class cabins with built-in closets instead of wardrobes. However, the large public rooms were rather bland and traditional compared with the opulence of the pre-war German liners and there was certainly no nod given to the modern designs of the Bauhaus. Like the *Ile de France* in 1928, an aircraft catapult was installed but between the twin funnels, not on the after deck. Despite losing the Atlantic speed record to the Italian liner *Rex* in 1933, the two liners had a successful career with NDL in the 1930s. In 1939 they returned to Bremerhaven where they became naval accommodation ships. Unfortunately *Bremen* sank following a fire in 1941. After the fall of Germany in 1945 *Europa* was seized by the US Navy and used as a troop transport before being handed over to France as reparations in 1946. Despite a sinking, a fire, and major delays at the shipyard in St-Nazaire, she re-emerged as French Line's 51,839gt *Liberté* in 1950 and was placed on the Le Havre to New York route. In 1961 she was sold to Italian breakers.

Rex 1932

Although Italy had been unified since 1861, from that time up to the outbreak of the First World War tremendous social change had taken place as the new nation struggled with the diversity of regional interests and the problems of industrialisation. Each year thousands of poor Italians left their homeland in search of a better life abroad. Numerous Italian shipping lines sprung up to carry this lucrative human cargo, and the most famous of these were the two great rivals which operated out of the north Italian port of Genoa: Navigazione Generale Italiana (NGI) and Lloyd Sabaudo. By the early 1920s the number of immigrants allowed into the USA was dramatically curtailed, so Italian ships on the North Atlantic needed to attract not only wealthy travellers, but also the new, burgeoning tourist market. Although the arrival of Norddeutscher Lloyd's record-breakers *Bremen* and *Europa* coincided with the Wall Street Crash and the start of the Great Depression, for Italy's Prime Minister Benito Mussolini, the Depression was a great opportunity to unite Italians to move forward to a common goal. NGI and Lloyd Sabaudo ordered a pair of large liners, which would establish Italian supremacy on the Atlantic. These two, quadruple-screw, 29-knot, turbine-driven ships, the 51,062gt *Rex* (NGI) and the 48,502gt *Conte di Savoia* (Lloyd Sabaudo), were built at Genoa and Trieste respectively. Often seen in the same light, the new liners had radically different designs, both inside and out. Although *Conte di Savoia* (below) was undoubtedly a more modern ship overall, *Rex* had far more character. Her profile was almost yacht-like, with tall raked funnels and masts, counter stern and flared bow. Like Italy itself, the design of the passenger facilities on *Rex* was a curious mix, which somehow seems to have worked. Not only was she a four-class ship but also her décor had one foot in the past and the other in the present, with none of the excess of the latter, and little of the starkness of the modern era. Her first class public rooms also did not have the cavernous grandeur found on other large North Atlantic liners. On *Rex*, the rooms were like those in a top Italian hotel ashore. Many of the first class cabins were suites, with silk-covered chairs and fixtures and fittings of the highest quality. Some even had private verandas. However, *Rex*'s best-known feature was the Lido, which had been designed to attract Americans to travel the 'Sunny Southern Route' to Europe. Situated at the after end of the promenade deck, the Lido and pool area was the largest seen on any ship to that date. *Rex* was also among the first liners to have air-conditioning in all first class public and dining rooms. Completed in September 1932 she sailed from Genoa on her maiden voyage to New York. A few months later, she was joined by her new consort *Conte di Savoia*.

Earlier that year, Mussolini tightened his grip on Italian shipping lines by forcing the major players on the Atlantic to merge into a single company, commonly known as Italia. In August 1933 *Rex* reduced *Bremen*'s record to four days, thirteen hours and fifty-eight minutes. However, the record was relatively short-lived. In May 1935 French Line's *Normandie* broke the record on her maiden crossing. Despite this loss, *Rex* and *Conte di Savoia* remained popular ships on the express route across the Atlantic. Unfortunately neither liner survived the war as they were destroyed in air raids in 1944 and 1943 respectively.

Normandie 1935

The arrival of *Bremen* and *Europa* also had a profound effect on Britain and its old adversary France. Whilst Britain wished to regain its lost record, France, which had never won the Blue Riband, as the Atlantic record became known, was also determined to get in on the act. Thus, the two nations started a race to see who could produce not only the fastest but also the most magnificent liner ever built. France had also embraced the new art deco style which had been inspired by the 1925 Paris exhibition of modern art and industrial design. Despite the onset of the Great Depression, work started weeks apart in December 1930 and January 1931 on Cunard line's unnamed new liner, known only by its yard number 534, and French line's *Normandie*. By the end of 1931, however, with the British Government unwilling to help financially, construction of Cunard's great ship at John Brown's shipyard on the Clyde ceased. Her massive hulk remained on the stocks for over two years before work recommenced. Meanwhile across the Channel, the French pressed ahead with the building of the 79,280gt *Normandie* at St-Nazaire and in October 1932 she was launched by the wife of the President of France. Despite the national importance of the new ship her completion took two years longer than planned because of labour disputes. The cost of her building was also immense and was estimated to be around £8 million. She was not only the first ship to exceed 1,000ft in length but also, up to that time, the largest ship ever built. She was a revolutionary ship both inside and out. Her hull with its sweeping lines and clipper-bow was designed by a Russian émigré naval architect, Vladimir Yourkevitch. Her unique streamlined profile was enhanced by three large black and red funnels, which reduced progressively in height, and a superstructure, which was stepped back in terraces towards the curved stern. Her turbo-electric engines were also unusual for a ship of this size and provided enough power to cross the Atlantic in four days at an average speed of 29 knots.

A floating showcase for French art and style, *Normandie* had cohesion to her design which has never been surpassed. Everything from the Christofle tableware to the Lalique glass and elegant furniture aboard the ship has become synonymous with French chic. The most impressive chamber in the ship, and the largest afloat, was undoubtedly the main dining room. Air-conditioned, with seating for 700 passengers, it was longer than the Hall of Mirrors at Versailles, extending over 300ft and three decks high. She also boasted the first purpose-built theatre aboard a liner and two six-room suites de grande luxe, each with its own private terrace. In May 1935 she sailed on her maiden voyage and arrived at New York proudly flying the Blue Riband pennant, which she had won on her first attempt, averaging just under 30 knots. She broke the record again on her return journey with an average of 30.31 knots. Although she never paid her way, *Normandie* was immensely popular with the rich and famous but after only four years in service, her career came to a sudden end with the outbreak of war in Europe. Laid up in New York, she was seized by the United States for conversion into a troopship after the fall of France. In February 1942 she caught fire. With none of the French crew on hand to work the fire-control system, one of the best in the world, she was soon ablaze from stem to stern. The chaotic response from the New York fire crews flooded the ship and the following day, the pride of France capsized.

Queen Mary 1936

In March 1934, work recommenced on Cunard's idle giant. In exchange for agreeing to merge with the ailing White Star Line, the British Government gave Cunard a £9.5 million loan to complete not only 534 but also to build a running mate, the future *Queen Elizabeth*. 534 was launched as *Queen Mary* in September 1935 and completed in March 1936. As Cunard wanted to signal a complete break with the past, she was the first Cunard express liner not to be given a name ending in '-ia'. Although she was completely different from *Normandie* in exterior appearance, type of engines and interior design, her dimensions were virtually the same. At 80,774gt she was also briefly the world's largest ship but was surpassed by *Normandie* after the French liner's 1936 refit which increased her size to 82,799gt. Her exterior had very little streamlining and she was rather backward looking with three large raked funnels and massive bulk. Compared with *Normandie* she looked more like a great-aunt of the seas instead of a child of the modern age. Her quadruple screws were driven by powerful geared turbines. *Queen Mary* was Cunard's first liner to dispense with period decoration. Again, unlike *Normandie*, she did not totally embrace modern contemporary design. Her interiors were an eclectic mixture of British conservatism and American art deco. There was also an extensive use of wood panelling. Over fifty varieties of wood from all over Britain and the Commonwealth were use throughout the ship. The first class public rooms had high ceilings, with contemporary but rather conservative artwork and comfortable chairs and sofas. It is this sense of informality which made *Queen Mary* a very popular ship particularly with Americans who were probably overwhelmed by the sense of *Normandie*'s extreme modernity. Despite her outdated appearance, certainly in comparison with the streamlined *Normandie*, *Queen Mary*'s maiden voyage in May 1936 received an extraordinary amount of publicity around the world. She also claimed the Blue Riband record from her French rival, with her 1938 record crossings in both directions of just under four days at an average speed of around 31 knots unbroken for fourteen years. In 1939 she was laid up in New York following the outbreak of war. After a successful period as a troopship she was returned to Cunard in 1946. For twenty years from 1947 to 1967 she operated on the transatlantic route with her consort *Queen Elizabeth*. In 1967 she was sold to the city of Long Beach, California, for use as a museum, hotel and convention centre.

Chapter 7
The Glorious 1930s

Having suffered one of the world's worst financial crises, the shipping industry soon recovered from the Great Depression and entered a new golden age of passenger liners.

The largest motor passenger fleet in the world

During the early 1930s Union-Castle Line had a virtual monopoly of the passenger-mail service between the United Kingdom and the Union of South Africa. In 1928 it had signed a lucrative new freight contract and ordered two new, 16-knot, twin-screw liners, *Winchester Castle* (1930/20,109gt), below, and *Warwick Castle* (1931/20,445gt). With their low, modern motor ship funnels, they were improved versions of *Carnarvon Castle* and heralded the start of a new era for the company which now had the largest motor passenger fleet in the world. *Winchester Castle*'s passenger capacity was 259 first, 243 second and 254 third class. As usual on Union-Castle liners few cabins had private facilities and those which did incurred an extra charge of £10. The interior décor was once again based on period styles. The two deck-high first class lounge with its tall, mullioned windows and heavy oak beams across the ceiling was based on an old colonial house. It also had a large fireplace and a lounge gallery on the deck above. The smoking room featured a Dutch-style fireplace and a reproduction of King Arthur's Round Table, the original of which hangs in Winchester Castle, whilst the raised open veranda aft was constructed in half-timber and furnished with reproduction old Windsor chairs. The only concession to modernity on the ship was an American cocktail bar in the corner of the smoking room which was subsequently removed in her 1938 refit. Her double-acting four-stroke Burmeister and Wain engines produced a top speed on trials of 17.3 knots whilst her refrigerated cargo space was 216,267ft^3. In 1937, the South African Government awarded a ten-year mail contract to Union-Castle on condition that the weekly mail service between Southampton and Cape Town be reduced by a full three days to fourteen days. To meet this obligation it would be necessary to overhaul the mailship fleet completely, and between 1937 and 1938 five of the mailships constructed between 1921 and 1931 were sent back to their builders for major work to bring them up to the required speed. *Winchester Castle* was the last to be completed and emerged in January 1939 with a single streamlined funnel and new double-acting two-stroke engines which increased her service speed to 20 knots. The following year she was requisitioned as a troopship and at the end of her war service in 1947 was used as an 877-capacity emigrant ship to South Africa. Unfortunately in November 1942 her sister *Warwick Castle* had been torpedoed and sunk by a German submarine with the loss of sixty-three lives. After a refit at Harland and Wolff *Winchester Castle* returned to the mail service in 1949 with her passenger capacity changed to 189 first and 389 tourist. In 1960 following the introduction of the 28,582gt *Windsor Castle* she was surplus to requirements and was sold to Japanese breakers.

Largest British motor ships

In 1926 White Star Line became part of the giant Royal Mail Group. Two years later it announced that it had signed a contract with Harland and Wolff for *Oceanic*, a 60,000gt liner which would be not only the largest in the world but also the first with an overall length of over 1,000ft. Unfortunately this diesel-electric liner never got past the keel-laying stage. Because of the precarious state of the White Star and Royal Mail Group's finances the project was cancelled in 1929. Despite this setback, work continued on White Star's first diesel-powered liner, the 26,943gt *Britannic* (right), which was completed in 1930. The largest British motor ship and the second largest in the world after *Augustus* (1927/32,650gt), she introduced a new funnel style to the North Atlantic with a pair of squat funnels. The forward one was a dummy. She was one of the last motor ships of the 1920s to have an angular forward superstructure whilst her period-style interior décor was also rather conservative, especially for a modern motor ship. The cabin class dining room was designed in the style of Louis XIV, the main lounge in Adam style with the ubiquitous Tudor smoking room featuring a ceiling with wooden beams. Designed for the Liverpool to New York route she carried 504 cabin, 551 tourist and 498 third class passengers. Twin-screwed, her Burmeister and Wain-type diesels produced a cruising speed of 17.5 knots. In 1932, she was joined by a slightly larger sister, the 27,759gt *Georgic*, which was also the last liner built for White Star Line. She was a more modern version of *Britannic*, with a rounded bridge front and stylish contemporary interiors. These included furnishings with brightly-coloured upholstery, a long gallery with geometric-patterned carpets and an indoor pool with distinctive art deco shaped tiles. Following the 1934 merger with Cunard Line, both ships were transferred in 1935 to the London–Southampton-New York service. During the war they were requisitioned as troopships. In 1941 *Georgic* was attacked by German aircraft in Egypt. Although she suffered serious damage she was rebuilt as a single-funnelled, 3,000-capacity troopship. By then she had been sold to the British Government. Used after the war as an immigrant ship and for charters to Cunard Line, she was sold for scrap in 1956. *Britannic* meanwhile returned to peacetime duties in 1948 on the Liverpool to New York run. She remained in White Star livery until her sale to the breakers in 1960.

Elder Dempster's only two-funnelled liner

In the late 1920s Elder Dempster, the Liverpool-based line which had a near-monopoly of British trade on the West Coast of Africa, introduced its largest passenger liners to that date, *Accra* (1926/9,337grt) and *Apapa* (1927/9,333grt). Although their size was restricted by the primitive port conditions in West Africa, the two liners carried over 243 first class passengers in English country house splendour. They were also motor-driven – Elder Dempster being one of the earliest champions of the oil engine for cargo-passenger ships. The success of these two led the company to place an order with Harland & Wolff for another slightly larger version, the twin-screw, 15-knot, 9,576gt motor ship *Achimota*. With a layout similar to the earlier pair the major difference was the number of funnels. Instead of a single stack *Achimota* had a pair of squat Harland and Wolff motor ship funnels, the forward one being a dummy, with horizontal tops of the type seen on the latest Union-Castle and Royal Mail liners. Designed to carry 236 first class and 64 second class passengers, *Achimota* was a hot-weather ship with two open promenade decks and public rooms with high ceilings to allow added ventilation and comfort from the extreme heat of West Africa. All cabins had natural light and the quality of the first class public rooms was of an exceptionally high standard, with much use of veneered wood. The 260-capacity first class dining saloon with its vaulted dome was designed in a Spanish style and was situated on the main deck. The main public rooms were on the promenade deck and consisted of a lounge and library forward and not one but two smoking rooms aft and no swimming pool. As the Elder Dempster ships carried mainly colonial administrators and traders, they were designed to provide a male-dominated club atmosphere, hence the provision of a smoking room and a so-called smoking lounge. The new ship was awaiting her main engines when the Kylsant empire, which included Elder Dempster, collapsed. Without capital the company was unable to take delivery of their new flagship which was eventually completed in July 1931. *Achimota* was taken over by Harland & Wolff and laid up until a new buyer could be found. As luck would have it, the Australian company Huddart Parker was looking for a new ship to place on their trans-Tasman service between Sydney, Wellington and Auckland which they operated in conjunction with the Union Steam Ship Company of New Zealand. *Achimota* was bought in 1932 and renamed *Wanganella*. For most of the 1930s she operated the trans-Tasman route in summer and cruised in the Pacific during the winter months. After an eventful war career she returned to her regular route in 1947 where she remained until 1962. For a number of years she was used as a floating hostel for construction workers before being sold to Taiwanese breakers in 1970.

The short-lived *L'Atlantique*

Because of her relatively short career, the 42,512gt, 1,238-capacity *L'Atlantique* is often overlooked but is one of the most significant liners of the 1930s. At the time of her completion, she was the second largest French liner after the *Ile de France* and the largest passenger liner ever designed for service to South America. She had quadruple screws and geared turbines which produced a maximum speed of almost 24 knots. Built four years before *Normandie*, the design of her interiors was arguably more stylish and introduced some unique features which are common place on modern cruise ships. For example, the large entrance hall with its shops and purser's office on 'D' deck formed a two-deck-high atrium, with a balcony, from which ran a wide, fore and aft, central corridor with first class outboard suites on either side. Two decks above were magnificent first class public rooms which included a circular forward lounge and a large salon which led to a wide staircase descending into an enormous two-deck-high dining room. These large, free-flowing spaces were achieved by dividing the engine room uptakes for the fore and middle funnels and by designing the hull with the minimum of sheer. The lack of sheer gave *L'Atlantique* a rather box-like exterior. As she operated in hot-weather waters, she also had a wide-open, wraparound promenade, full-size tennis court and swimming pool with a domed roof. She entered service in September 1931 and the following year her funnels were heightened. Unfortunately in January 1933, whilst on a positioning voyage without passengers, she caught fire off Guernsey. Because of the large open spaces of her accommodation, the fire spread rapidly and she was destroyed.

The world's first air-conditioned liner

In 1931 one of the most attractive liners of the twentieth century entered service on Lloyd Triestino's weekly express service between Trieste and Alexandria. The quadruple-screw, 13,062gt *Victoria* was the company's answer to Società Italiana di Servizi Marittimi's (Sitmar Line) *Ausonia* (1927/12,955gt) which operated on the rival service from Genoa. Built at Trieste, *Victoria* attained over 23 knots on her trials, making her the world's fastest motor ship at that time. Designed to replace two slower ships, *Helouan* (1912/7,367gt) and *Vienna* (1911/7,367gt), her two inner propelling engines were installed in one engine room whilst the two outer engines were in another. She had two tall masts and a pair of squat elliptical funnels. Her passenger capacity was 239 first, 245 second, 100 third and 82 fourth class. All first class cabins had baths whilst the first class public rooms were designed by the famous Italian marine architect Gustavo Pulitzer Finali. *Victoria* was his first complete-ship commission and his moderne style with its great use of natural materials was a complete contrast to the over-the-top, classically-influenced designs of the Coppedè brothers. The most impressive room on the ship was the two-deck-high, air-conditioned first class dining saloon which was situated at the after end of the promenade deck. With its tall windows and sea views it was probably influenced by Hamburg Sud's *Cap Ancona* (1927/27,560gt) which had a similar dining arrangement. It was also the first time that air-conditioning had been installed in a passenger ship. Six months after *Victoria* entered service the major Italian shipping lines were rearranged with Lloyd Triestino taking over Sitmar Line's ships and routes. *Victoria* was transferred to the Genoa-Bombay route in 1932 and was a serious competitor to P&O's new 'Strath' liners, which were also painted white. In 1940 she became a troopship and was sunk in January 1942 by torpedoes from British aircraft in the Gulf of Sidra, Libya.

Dutch rivalry to the Dutch East Indies

Despite strong competition from the family-run Rotterdam Lloyd on the mail service between the Netherlands and the East Indies, Stoomvaart Maatschappij 'Nederland' (SMN) was the leading line to the Dutch East Indies in the inter-war years. After a successful experiment in 1924 with diesels in the cargo ship *Bintang* (1916/6,480gt), it was decided that all its new ships would be diesel powered. The first passenger motor ship *Pieter Corneliszoon Hooft* (1926/14,642gt) had a tall steamship-style funnel whilst *Christiaan Huygens* (1927/16,286gt) was given a small single funnel which did not look right. The addition of a second dummy funnel for the next pair of even larger 16.5-knot liners gave the ships a more modern look. Built at the height of the Depression, *Johan van Oldenbarnevelt* (19,428gt) (shown here) and *Marnix van Sint Aldegonde* (19,355gt) were both delivered in 1930 and, like the earlier liners, were named after famous sixteenth- and seventeenth-century Dutchmen. Despite their strange profiles, it is the layout and interiors of these ships which set them apart from other liners of the period. In true Dutch style, they were 'democratic' ships with second class passengers enjoying almost as much space as those in first. Great care was taken to provide relief from the tropical heat and humidity. Every cabin had a porthole whilst the windows of the public room were almost at deck level and when opened allowed a free flow of air. With many families travelling to the East Indies, children were especially well catered for with separate decks in both first and second class. The exotic public rooms also made great use of raw materials from the East Indies whilst another unusual feature in first class was the situation of the enclosed swimming pool in front of the forward dummy funnel. Although great rivals, Stoomvaart Maatschappij 'Nederland' and Rotterdam Lloyd shared the route, and offered passengers weekly sailings to the East Indies. During the war both ships were used as troopships although *Marnix* was lost during an air raid off Algeria in 1943. During the post-war years *Johan van Oldenbarnevelt* initially carried troops to the Indies and returning settlers fleeing the conflict. In 1952 she was converted into a single class 1,144-capacity emigrant ship and seven years later she reverted to her role as a passenger liner. She was given a new look which included heightened, dome-topped funnels and the removal of her mainmast. In 1963 she was sold to Greek Line for use as a cruise ship. Renamed *Lakonia* she caught fire later that year on a Canary Islands cruise from Southampton with the loss of 128 lives.

Rotterdam Lloyd's response to SMN's new ships was the slightly smaller but faster 17,000gt, 18.5-knot motor ships *Baloeren* and *Dempo*, seen here at Sourabaya, which were delivered in 1930 and 1931 respectively. They were named after volcanoes in Java, a mailship tradition which started in 1888. They were distinctive-looking vessels with silver-grey hulls, cruiser stern, large unbroken superstructure and two tall masts, the foremast just abaft the bridge. They also had a recessed hull below the promenade deck so that passenger cabins were less exposed to direct sunlight. The forward part of the superstructure had large windows on both the promenade and boat decks which could be opened to allow a free flow of air in tropical waters whilst the tiled first class swimming pool was unusually situated on the forecastle. The magnificent first class dining saloon had a three-deck-high well and was approached from the deck above by a sweeping staircase and both ships were promoted in classic art deco-style posters. This popular pair were lost during the war. *Baloeren* had been seized by the Germans and hit a mine in 1943 whilst *Dempo* was torpedoed and sunk in 1944.

The great Canadian Empress

In 1931 Canadian Pacific took delivery of its finest liner, the 42,348gt, quadruple-screw *Empress of Britain*. This extraordinary ship was designed as a dual-purpose transatlantic and 400-capacity worldwide cruise ship. During the summer period, when the St Lawrence was ice-free, she sailed from Southampton via Cherbourg to Quebec where passengers would disembark on special trains to Montreal and US cities. The company hoped that she would entice passengers from direct services with the promise of only three days at sea and '39 per cent less ocean' by using the St Lawrence Seaway route. The ship was also, at 24.5 knots, the fastest liner to operate across the Atlantic to Canada. In the winter months she made four-month cruises from New York. She was constructed on the Clyde by John Brown which also built the engine machinery. Each of her four propellers was driven by a set of single reduction turbines. During world cruises, when less power was needed, her two outer propellers were removed. Her dimension also meant that she was able to use both the Suez and the Panama Canals. Externally, she had a very distinctive but rather top-heavy appearance with three large buff funnels atop a gleaming white superstructure. She carried 465 first, 260 tourist and 470 third class passengers. Her first class accommodation was among the finest seen on the Atlantic run, with large public rooms each of which was designed by a well-known British artist and unusually given different names. For example, the smoking room with its oriental designs by the illustrative artist Edmund Dulac was called the Cathay Lounge whilst the single-sitting Salles Jacques Cartier dining saloon had large frescoes by Frank Brangwyn. The large enclosed sports deck also had a full-sized tennis court. However, it was the cabins in first class which received the greatest praise. All were wood-panelled with comfortable beds and outboard windows or portholes. Three-quarters of the cabins also had private facilities. During the 1930s she made around eleven round-trip transatlantic crossings per annum although she never attracted as many passengers as originally envisaged by Canadian Pacific. However, she was a very prestigious ship for the company especially as she was then the world's largest cruise ship. Unfortunately, in October 1940 she became Britain's largest war loss when she was attacked and sunk by German bombers near Ireland with the loss of forty-five lives.

The only East Asiatic Company passenger-cargo motor ships with funnels

Pioneer of the diesel engine, the Danish East Asiatic Company took delivery of its first passenger-cargo motor ship with funnels in 1930. The 10,218gt *Amerika* was the first of three handsome twin-funnelled liners designed for the company's Copenhagen to the West Indies and North Pacific coast route. This single-screw motor ship had a service speed of 15 knots and carried fifty-six first class passengers in superior accommodation. She was followed a year later by a slightly improved sister, *Europa*, shown here. Both ships had a straight stem and counter stern whereas *Canada*, the final ship in the trio, had a raked stem and cruiser stern. She entered service in 1935 and was a great improvement on the earlier pair. Not only was she a more powerful ship but also the spacious facilities for her fifty-five passenger were much better. Most of the cabins had private facilities whilst there was also now a permanent open-air swimming pool. She had ten refrigerated compartments for fruit and a separate one for meat and fish. Unfortunately, all three were lost during the war. *Canada* struck a mine in 1939, *Europa* was destroyed in a Liverpool air raid in 1941 whilst *Amerika* was torpedoed and sunk by a German submarine in 1943 with the loss of eighty-six lives.

The millionaire's run to Bermuda

One of the greatest legacies of the shipping giant Furness, Withy, has been the development of tourism between the United States and Bermuda. In 1919 Furness, Withy bought the Quebec Steamship Company and started a three-ship service between New York and Bermuda. In the same year Prohibition was introduced in the USA, and this offered Bermuda and Furness, Withy a golden opportunity. Now, affluent Americans could not only enjoy Bermuda for its delightful climate and attractive scenery, but also because alcohol was freely available at sea and ashore. In the first year, 22,000 passengers were carried, and the company soon started developing hotels and golf courses on the colony. By the mid-1920s, it was apparent that increasing demand could only be met by the building of a large and luxurious liner. The 19,086gt, two-funnelled motor ship *Bermuda* completed in 1927 was the prototype for the next generation of New York-Bermuda liners. Despite the voyage to Bermuda being less than two days, *Bermuda* was essentially a miniature transatlantic liner but with first class accommodation taking up almost the entire ship. Designed for long-distance cruising, she was used all year round on the run between New York and Bermuda. In 1931, she was to be joined by a larger consort, the three-funnelled, 20-knot, 22,424gt *Monarch of Bermuda*. Unfortunately, *Bermuda* was lost in a fire at Hamilton but a replacement was immediately ordered. Two years later *Monarch of Bermuda*'s new sister, the 22,575gt *Queen of Bermuda* (below), entered service. With each ship operating a weekly round trip to Bermuda, it was essential that they were reliable so turbo-electric engines were installed. This type of power also limited the amount of noise and vibration from the engines, an important factor for such a short sea crossing. The amount of space for passengers was impressive, as was the décor, which was an interesting mixture of New York art deco and Bond Street conservatism. The ships were very stylish and it is little wonder that they were an immediate success with wealthy patrons. Unlike the spectacular and cavernous chambers of the transatlantic flagships, the main public rooms were unpretentious, comfortable and relaxing and offered the perfect escape from the frenetic pace of New York City. All first class cabins had private facilities whilst at the after end of 'A' deck was a substantial gymnasium and an oval indoor mosaic swimming pool with decorations of wrought metal and teak. At the forward end of this deck was a large old-fashioned British country-house style library, with separate writing rooms for ladies and gentlemen. The weekly sailings from New York continued year round virtually uninterrupted until the outbreak of war when both liners were requisitioned for war service as troopships. Although they survived the conflict, *Monarch of Bermuda* was destroyed by fire in 1947. *Queen of Bermuda* returned to the Bermuda run in 1949 and two years later a new ship, *Ocean Monarch* (1951/13,654gt), was delivered. By now, Bermuda was no longer the preserve of the well-to-do and catered for a broader spectrum of traveller. Fifteen years later in 1966 the Furness Bermuda Line ceased operations and *Queen of Bermuda* was sold for scrap.

P&O's 'Straths'

Turbo-electric machinery, which had been installed in *Viceroy of India*, was also used in the next pair of P&O liners, *Strathnaver* and *Strathaird*, the largest and fastest ordered for the company to that date. These 22,540gt, 21-knot ships entered service in 1931 and 1932 respectively and were designed not only for comfort but also with sufficient speed to operate via Bombay without compromising the requirements of the Australian mail contract. They broke the traditional P&O mould on a number of fronts. Firstly, they had three low raked funnels painted buff instead of the usual P&O black. The fore and aft funnels were dummies. Their hulls were white with red boot-topping in place of the sombre P&O black hull with stone-coloured upper works. The white hull reduced the hull temperature by about 4° F, a welcome relief in the stifling heat of the Red Sea. They also carried more second class passengers (670) than first class (498) and had considerable cargo space in six holds, two of which were insulated for fruit and meat. The ship names were unusual as they were not named after places, mainly in India, but after the ancestral homes of P&O's chairman Lord Inchcape's MacKay (*Strathnaver*) and William Mackinnon, co-founder of BI, Mackinnon (*Strathaird*) clans. In 1932 they made the first of many cruises from the UK to the Mediterranean, a pattern which would continue throughout the 1930s. In the same year *Strathaird* (shown here) made the first cruise for P&O in Australian waters. They survived the Second World War, returned to service with a single funnel and were later used as one-class ships, subsequently being broken up in Hong Kong in the early 1960s.

Maierform bows

One of the most distinctive bow shapes in the 1930s was the curved Maierform bow which had been designed by the Austrian naval architect Fritz Maier. A year after his death his sons established the Bremen-based Maier-Schiffsform-Verwertungsgesellschaft m. b. H. The main advantage of this design was the improvement in water resistance compared with a conventional bow especially in rough weather. Because the slamming motion in a head-on sea was reduced significantly, engines could be used without a reduction in power. It was very popular with German and Dutch shipowners and the first large passenger ship to be fitted with this bow was the 16-knot, twin-screw motor ship *Colombia* (1930/10,782gt) which was constructed at Rotterdam by P Smit Jr for Koninklijke Nederlandse Stoomboot-Maatschappij (KNSM). She had a rounded bow with an icebreaker-like rise to her stem. Established in 1856 KNSM was the principal carrier of freight and passengers between the Netherlands and the Dutch colonies in the Caribbean and *Colombia* was the largest liner owned by the firm. A one-off, she carried 310 passengers in three classes and her passenger facilities, which included an indoor swimming pool, were a great improvement on earlier ships. In February 1942 whilst en route to Simonstown she was torpedoed by a German submarine off the coast of South Africa with the loss of eight lives. During the war the company lost forty-eight of its eighty-six ships.

In 1934, N.V. Vereenigde Nederlandsche Scheepvaart Maatschappij (The United Netherlands Company), took delivery of two 10,000gt passenger-cargo motor ships with Maierform bows. The twin-screw ships *Bloemfontein*, shown here, and *Jagersfontein* were designed for the company's new express service to South and East Africa, via Southampton, which operated under the Holland-Afrika Lijn banner. Each carried ninety-three first class passengers in superb accommodation with all cabins featuring windows or portholes. The main public rooms on the promenade deck were very light and airy and included at the forward end was a palm court overlooking the bow for relaxation and dancing. The single-sitting dining room was situated on the deck below and was also forward facing. Externally this pair were very distinctive but rather stiff looking with no rake to the funnel or masts. Their service speed of over 16 knots was faster than any of the Deutsche-Ost-Afrika-Linie liners and most of the large Union-Castle Line mailships. *Bloemfontein* was also the first ship launched by long-distance wireless when General Hertzog, Prime Minister of South Africa pressed a button at the Netherlands Legation in Pretoria at noon on 16 June 1934. Although *Jagersfontein* was lost during the war, *Bloemfontein* remained in service until 1959.

Japan to Europe

The Japan–Europe run was the most prestigious of all NYK's services because of the growing importance of Japan as a major manufacturing nation, especially as it had become the world's largest textile producer. These routes also faced the greatest competition from the major European lines and to keep ahead on these services the company ordered a pair of modern, 12,000gt passenger-cargo motor ships from Japanese yards. *Terukuni Maru* (right) and *Yasakuni Maru*, completed in 1930, set new standards of luxury for travel between London and the Far East. Not only were they faster than previous NYK liners – their twin Mitsubishi-Sulzers produced over 18 knots on trials – but also they carried a much higher proportion of first class passengers – 118 out of 249. With a low profile, raked stem and counter stern, their spacious public rooms were also elegantly fitted out in a variety of European and Japanese styles. In those pre air-conditioned days, the fitting of a Punkah Louvre system of ventilation throughout the ship was also a most welcome improvement. Although these ships were very successful, by the mid-1930s they were eclipsed by a trio of fast German liners from Norddeutscher Lloyd.

French North Africa

Conquered in 1830, Algeria was France's oldest colony and the route between Marseilles and Algiers was vitally important to the French state. The oldest French shipping line operating to North Africa, Compagnie de Navigation Mixte was founded in 1850. Its main competitors were Compagnie Générale Transatlantique (CGT) which had been awarded the mail contract in 1880 and Société Générale des Transports Maritimes à Vapeur (SGTM). Speed and comfort on the 467-mile crossing to Algiers was always key and CGT usually had the edge over Mixte. In 1909 it introduced the 18-knot, 4,451gt *Charles Roux* on the route. She was France's first turbine-driven passenger ship. In 1932 Mixte upped the stakes with the arrival of the 5,079gt *El Kantara*, below, the first of three fast steam turbine ships. Constructed on the Tyne by Swan, Hunter and Wigham Richardson she was followed by a slightly larger, faster (22 knots) and more streamlined pair of French-built ships, *El Mansour* (1933/5,818gt and *El Djezair* (1934/5,790gt). This trio were flush-decked and had a cruiser stern, two low, raked funnels and carried over 350 passengers in three classes. Given the size of the ships, their stylish, wood-panelled first class public rooms were spacious and full of light. At the start of the Second World War, they became armed merchant cruisers but after the fall of France in June 1940 returned to Marseilles. In 1943 the Germans gave the trio to Italy and whilst *El Mansour* was scuttled at Marseilles, the other two were sunk by the RAF. *El Mansour* was raised after the war, rebuilt and returned to service. She was later used by the French Navy and was scrapped in 1974.

Largest and fastest to North Africa

CGT's response to the Mixte trio were the twin-screw, 10,172gt *Ville d'Alger* (right) and *Ville d'Oran* which were completed in 1935 and 1936 respectively. Turbine driven, not only were they the fastest on the route (over 23 knots), but also the first to exceed 10,000gt. With a raked bow, cruiser stern and two large funnels (the aft one was a dummy) they were impressive-looking ships. Their passenger capacity was just under 1,000 in four classes. The spacious art moderne-style first class public rooms and dining saloon were situated on the promenade deck whilst the main lounge had a sweeping staircase which led to cabins on the deck above. In 1939 they became armed merchant cruisers. The aft funnel was also removed which greatly improved their appearance. Whilst *Ville d'Oran* survived the war as an Allied troopship, *Ville d'Alger* was set on fire and sunk by the Germans in 1944, blocking the channel at Porte de Bouc in the south of France. Despite the extensive damage, she was raised after the war and rebuilt. By 1949 both ships were back in service and remained on the Marseilles-North Africa route until the mid-1960s when they were sold to the Greek shipowner Typaldos Brothers. Renamed *Poseidon* (*Ville d'Alger*) and *Mount Olympus* (*Ville d'Oran*) they were sold for demolition in 1969.

Bank Line's African trio

Shipping links between South Africa and India started in the mid-nineteenth century with the introduction of sugar cane into the newly formed Natal Colony. Unable to persuade many of the local Zulu population to perform this back-breaking work, the government turned to India as a source of labour. These workers were soon followed by a merchant class of Indians known as 'passengers', mainly from the Gujarat province of North Western India, who set up shops and businesses. In 1906, Bank Line (Andrew Weir and Company) entered the trade with the formation of the Indian African Line. Using chartered tonnage, the new company offered monthly sailings from Cape Town to Calcutta and Rangoon. After the First World War, Andrew Weir, now Lord Inverforth, set about a major rebuilding programme which would ensure Bank Line's prominence as one of Britain's leading cargo lines. Not only was the order for twenty-one ships, the largest given to a single shipyard (Harland & Wolff), they were also all motor ships. In 1932, the company placed an order with Workman, Clark, Belfast for three 7,000gt, twin-screw, 16-knot passenger-cargo motor ships for the Indian African Line. Given African names, *Isipingo*, *Inchanga* (below) and *Incomati*, the trio was a complete contrast to the rest of Bank Line's rather austere-looking fleet. Painted white, with a buff hull band, green boot-topping and a neat, low buff and black-topped motor ship funnel, their colour scheme and tall raked masts gave the trio a yacht-like quality. The first class interiors were equally stylish and with considerable space for the fifty passengers. This feeling of being in a floating English country house ensured that the ships were usually fully booked. The lounge was situated on the promenade deck with large windows looking forward, the comfortable soft furnishings and light green and pastel colour scheme offering a relaxing escape from the tropical heat outside. It was also flanked by enclosed tea terraces with screens which could be easily opened. Unusually for a British ship of this period, there was a large open-air swimming pool, whilst all first class cabins had windows and adjoining private shower and lavatory. The dining room on the upper deck accommodated all first class passengers in a single sitting, with a large number of small tables. The twenty second class passengers were situated aft, with room for up to 500 'natives' in the 'tween decks. They each had a dead-weight capacity of 8,000 tons and five holds, one of which was a deep tank for carrying palm oil, whilst No 4 hold had 17,000ft^3 of insulated space. Completed in 1934, the 'White Fleet' ran like clockwork, with regular departures from Calcutta for the four week voyage to Cape Town. There were calls at Rangoon, Madras, Colombo, Mombasa, Beira, Lourenço Marques (now Maputo in Mozambique) and all the main coastal ports of South Africa. The service continued until the latter part of 1941, when each ship was called up for liner service to West Africa, based in Liverpool. Whilst *Incomati* was torpedoed by a German submarine in 1943, her sisters returned to Calcutta in 1946, and restarted the service. They proved to be useful cargo carriers and with declining passenger numbers the passenger capacity was reduced to twelve. Both ships were sold for demolition in 1964.

The innovative *Orion*

Until the arrival of the 23,371gt *Orion* in 1935, Orient Line's large passenger liners had two funnels. Not only did *Orion* have only one funnel, which was very unusual for a British liner in excess of 20,000gt, she was also the first to feature a single mast. Her superstructure had minimal streamlining because on the long voyage to Australia, speed was not critical, and it was felt that curves would only restrict the amount of available passenger space. With the 'B' promenade deck extended aft, her basic hull shape also became the template for future generations of Orient and P&O liners. The hull, which traditionally would have been painted black, was a warm corn colour with green boot-topping. As well as being an attractive feature, this colour was less likely to fade and reduced the hull temperature by a few degrees. However, it was her interiors which set her apart from other British liners of the time. Out went period decoration and in came stylish contemporary interiors with large uninterrupted spaces, simple furniture and beautifully woven carpets. This understated British elegance influenced other liners, including *Queen Elizabeth*. In 1937 *Orion*'s sister *Orcades* was delivered with a taller funnel because of soot problems and also thicker and more widely-spaced stanchions which gave the ship cleaner lines. The latter became a feature of all P&O and Orient liners up to *Oriana* and *Canberra* including the next pair of P&O 'Straths', *Stratheden* and *Strathallan* in 1937 and 1938. Unusually for the British of that time, *Orcades* had air-conditioning not only in the first class dining saloon but also in the library and some of the best cabins. Unfortunately she did not survive the war and was torpedoed and sunk by a German submarine in the South Atlantic in October 1942.

Paquet's new flagship

Some of the finest passenger liners operating to France's African colonies were those owned by Compagnie de Navigation Paquet which was founded by Nicolas Paquet in 1860. Its main route was between Marseilles, Morocco, the Canary Islands and Dakar and its ships carried not only passengers but also mail, fruit and other cargoes. In 1935, one of its finest liners entered service. The 8,920gt, twin-screw *Chella* was ordered as a replacement for the company's flagship *Nicolas Paquet* (1929/8,517gt) which had been wrecked in 1933. She was a fine-looking ship, with a slightly raked bow, cruiser stern and a two short motor ship-type funnels, the forward one being used for the boiler uptakes. Driven by steam turbines she was the first Paquet ship to be fitted with high-pressure water-tube boilers. She was also the fastest ship on the route to that date and achieved almost 23 knots on trials. She carried 178 first, 192 second and 102 tourist class passengers and had tween-deck space for 700 in steerage. The first class accommodation was divided into four categories, standard, preference, deluxe and grand luxe which included a private sitting room. The first class

dining room, situated forward on the promenade deck, had ocean views on three sides and was decorated by Marc Simon who designed the Grill Room aboard *Normandie*. *Chella*'s career was short as she was destroyed by fire during a Luftwaffe air raid on Marseilles in June 1940. Some of her machinery was salved and used in other French ships whilst her remains were demolished in the mid-1950s.

NDL's Far East Express Service

After it came to power in 1933 the Nazi Party took a keen interest in the major German shipping lines. This state intervention resulted in the building of a number of 'ships of state' which would represent the face of the new Germany abroad. Among these was a trio of fast twin-screw, 23-knot, 18,000gt passenger-cargo liners for Norddeutscher Lloyd's Far East Express Service. *Scharnhorst* was the first to be delivered in 1935 and she was not only the first German sea-going ship to be fitted with turbo-electric machinery, she also had the world's largest Maierform bow at that time. The main advantages of this curved stem was the minimising of speed in rough weather. A significant part of her hull was also welded and this saved a considerable amount in weight. She carried 152 first class and 144 second class passengers in outstanding, spacious and stylish accommodation. There was a swimming pool for first class passengers and nearly all their cabins had private facilities. Her sister *Gneisenau*, delivered in 1936, had geared turbines whereas the slightly smaller *Potsdam*, which had been ordered by Hamburg America Line, also had turbo-electric engines. These liners were way ahead of their time and operated on a four-weekly service from Bremen to Yokohama. Many of their passengers were British and the ships stopped briefly at Southampton where the company had its own locally-based passenger tender *Greetings* (1915/781gt). *Potsdam* was the only survivor of the war and she subsequently became a British troopship and Haj pilgrim ship before being sold to breakers in 1976.

NYK trio

NYK's reaction to the German liners was a trio of streamlined, 17,100gt, 22-knot liners. Had it not been for the war the 285-passenger vessels *Nitta Maru*, *Yawata Maru* (below) and *Kasuga Maru* (the first initial of each spelt the NYK name) would undoubtedly have been a tremendous success. They were the first Japanese liners with air-conditioning and in first class every cabin had an attached bathroom whilst the public rooms were beautifully designed in a modern Japanese style. They were also driven by two sets of geared steam turbines. *Nitta Maru* and *Yawata Maru* were completed in 1940 and used briefly on the San Francisco run before being converted into aircraft carriers, the same fate which befell their semi-completed sister *Kasuga Maru*. They were all torpedoed and sunk by US submarines.

Ellerman beauty

For much of the first half of the twentieth century, Ellerman Lines owned one of the largest fleets of cargo ships in the world. It also operated a number of cargo-passenger liners on its services to India to South Africa. These ships usually carried more first class passengers than second. However, by the mid-1930s the company faced increased competition on its Indian trades and decided to upgrade its fleet. The first of a series of new passenger-cargo ships was the extraordinary 11,081gt, turbine-driven, 15-knot *City of Benares* which was completed by Barclay, Curle and Company in 1936. She was ordered for City Line's Glasgow and Liverpool to Bombay, Colombo, Madras and Calcutta service. Ellerman's only two-funnelled liner, she had a distinctive profile with two raked funnels (the forward one was a dummy), a raked stem and a cruiser stern. She was also designed to enter the Manchester Ship Canal and carried 219 first class passengers in arguably the finest accommodation on the Indian routes. The style of her décor was elegant moderne with much use of polished veneered wood panels. Although none of her public rooms were air-conditioned they were well ventilated through the use of large windows. There was also a large sheltered promenade and a permanent swimming pool with underwater lighting for evening bathing. The dining saloon could also seat all passengers. It is surprising to note that not only was she was one of the largest single-screw passenger liners to that date but also that she was a coal burner. Her furnaces could burn oil if needed whist the galley ovens were fired by coal. *City of Benares* was a one-off. Because of increased shipbuilding costs, Ellerman decided to postpone further passenger liner construction, opting instead to renovate the accommodation of its existing passenger fleet. Unfortunately, she was lost during a tragic sinking when she was less than four years old. In September 1940 she was torpedoed by a German U-boat in the Atlantic whilst bound for Canada, and 258 lives were lost including 77 evacuee children.

'The Queen of the Tasman'

Matson Line's *Mariposa* and *Monterey* both made record crossings of the Tasman Sea between Auckland and Sydney. However, in 1937 their record was smashed by Union Steam Ship of New Zealand's stunning *Awatea*, affectionately known as 'The Queen of the Tasman'. Her record crossing of two days, seven hours and twenty-eight minutes at an average speed of 23.1 knots stood for twenty-four years. This twin-screw, turbine-driven, 13,482gt liner was completed in 1936 at Barrow by Vickers-Armstrongs Ltd. Designed to carry 377 first, 151 tourist and 38 third class passengers, she looked like a mini-*Queen Elizabeth*, especially after her funnels were raised in 1937. Her wood-panelled moderne-style first class interiors were a match for any of the prestige transatlantic liners. The two-deck-high lounge was described as 'one of the finest rooms afloat'. It was panelled in grained ash and featured a floor-to-ceiling decorated screen which folded away to reveal a movie screen. There was also an observation lounge forward whilst many of the first class cabins had private facilities. In 1940, after the loss of *Niagara*, she was transferred to the strategically-important Sydney–Vancouver route. The following year she was requisitioned for war service. Designated a Landing Ship Infantry she took part in the November 1942 Allied landings in North Africa where she caught fire and sank during an enemy air attack.

Revitalised Deutsche Ost-Afrika-Linie

In 1935, the revitalised Deutsche Ost-Afrika-Linie placed an order with Blohm & Voss for two fast, 18-knot, twin-screw, 16,662gt liners. *Pretoria* (1936), below, and *Windhuk* (1937) were designed to generate much-needed foreign currency for Germany by competing directly with Union-Castle Line's London west coast intermediate and Southampton mail services. The southbound voyages from Hamburg included calls at Rotterdam, Southampton, Las Palmas, Walvis Bay, Cape Town, Port Elizabeth, East London, Durban and Lourenço Marques. Driven by geared steam turbines with experimental high-pressure boilers, they were only 1.5 knots slower than Union-Castle's fastest motor ships, which is why their clever fifteen-day sailing schedule included a departure from Southampton the day before the mailship, with both ships arriving in Cape Town the same day. Flush-decked, with a relatively high superstructure, surmounted by two imposing raked funnels, the aft one being a dummy, *Pretoria* and *Windhuk*'s passenger facilities for 152 first and 338 tourist class passengers were superior to those on the conservative Union-Castle Line ships. The main passenger accommodation and facilities were on four decks and the amount of space allocated to tourist class was relatively large, certainly in comparison with the new, slightly smaller, intermediate Union-Castle Line liners where tourist passengers were confined mainly to the stern area of the ship. The main tourist class public rooms on 'A' deck extended just aft of amidships whilst these passengers also had use of a swimming pool, which was fitted in the opening of cargo hatch No 5. In 1942 *Windhuk* was taken over at Rio de Janeiro by the United States Government and transformed into a 4,666-capacity troopship, USS *Lejeune*. She was demolished in 1966. Her sister meanwhile was only sent to the breakers in 1987 having been a German hospital ship, a British troopship, a pilgrim ship and, latterly, an Indonesian Navy accommodation vessel.

Changes to the South African mail contracts

Because of increased competition from the Italian and German liners *Giulio Cesare* and *Duilio* and *Pretoria* and *Windhuk*, in 1937 the South African Government awarded a ten-year mail contract to Union-Castle, in which it stipulated that, from 1938, the weekly mail service between Southampton and Cape Town had to be reduced by a full three days to fourteen days. To meet this obligation it would be necessary to overhaul the mailship fleet completely, and between 1937 and 1938 five of the mailships constructed between 1921 and 1931 were sent back to their builders for major work to bring them up to the required speed. The new 25,000gt motor ships *Stirling Castle* and *Athlone Castle* entered service in 1936 and were followed by a larger, 27,000gt version, *Capetown Castle* (right), in 1938. In terms of overall impact, this handsome trio were arguably the finest mailships ever placed on the Cape mail run. Not only were they the most powerful British motor ships of their day, the public rooms in first class also broke away from the period style of the earlier Union-Castle Line mailships. They were the first British liners to use indirect lighting throughout the public rooms which were designed in a modern and uncluttered style. They also introduced the concept of a long gallery which linked the main first class lounge to the smoking room and aft veranda whilst cabin class passengers had the use of an open-air swimming pool. In September 1936, *Stirling Castle* shattered *Scot*'s 43-year-old southbound record and she and her sister were the last mailships whose length was restricted by the dimensions of the Victoria Basin in Cape Town. With the construction of the new dock, later called the Duncan Dock, well underway, *Capetown Castle* was the first mailship over 700 feet between perpendiculars. She also had one first class open promenade and was the first Union-Castle liner named after a South African location although Union Line owned two mailships with South African place names, *Durban* (1877/2,875gt) and *Pretoria* (1878/3,198gt). The three large motor ships played an active role during the Second World War as troopships and in 1947 returned to the South Africa mail run. Too slow for the accelerated mail service, they were phased

BI's express Calcutta–Rangoon mail service

In the 1930s the express Calcutta–Rangoon mail service was considered to be the British India Line's most important route in the east. It was also the first service in 1857 for the newly-formed Calcutta and Burmah Steam Navigation Co Ltd, which later became the British India Steam Navigation Company. In 1937 Burma was granted a new constitution and was separated from British India where it had been a province since 1886. Three 8,300gt liners with 'A' names were ordered for the run from Swan, Hunter and Wigham Richardson as replacements for an earlier trio of 'A'-class ships which were half the size of the new vessels. The first to be delivered at the end of 1938 was *Amra*. She was an impressive-looking ship with a wide, cowl-top funnel. With twin screws and turbine-driven, she was also fast and managed 18.5 knots on trials but was one of the last coal-fired liners to be built. Her original passenger capacity was 45 first, 50 second and 2,327 on deck. With the outbreak of war she and her sisters, completed in 1940 and 1941, were requisitioned as troopships. With the independence of Burma in 1948 and its withdrawal from the Commonwealth, *Amra* never returned to her designated route and spent the remainder of her career on the Bombay to East and South Africa service. She was converted to oil-firing in 1951 and was sold to Taiwanese breakers in 1965.

New look Union-Castle intermediates

In 1936 two new-look single-funnelled, round-Africa motor ship liners were completed, the 15,000gt *Dunnottar Castle* and *Dunvegan Castle*. These were followed in 1938 and 1939 respectively by a larger and faster pair for the west coast run. The 17,400gt, twin-screw, 18-knot *Durban Castle* and *Pretoria Castle* were the first intermediate ships named after South African cities. The size, speed and names of the last two ships must have been influenced by the arrival of Deutsche Ost-Afrika-Linie's crack liners *Pretoria* and *Windhuk* in 1936 and 1937 on the Hamburg–Southampton–Las Palmas–Walvis Bay–Cape Town–Durban–Lourenço Marques route. These four motor ships introduced a new style to the intermediate fleet and, like the mailships, had indirect lighting in the public rooms and a long gallery which linked the main first class lounge to the smoking room and after veranda. They also had an open-air swimming pool for first and tourist class passengers. *Durban Castle*, left, was launched three months after *Capetown Castle* and had a very similar profile to the larger mailship with a single first class promenade deck, pear-shaped funnel, raked stem, cruiser stern and a rounded bridge front. She carried 220 first and 335 tourist class passengers. Her interiors were relatively plain with limited art work and decoration. All the floors were rubberised with a few rugs scattered here and there. Only four first class cabins had an en suite bathroom which incurred a £15 surcharge. This was probably because of Union-Castle Line's rather austere and traditional-minded chairman Sir Vernon Thompson, who was also a strict teetotaller and did not allow open bars to be a feature on Union-Castle ships. However, the two dining rooms could seat all passengers in a single sitting. She also had considerable reefer space, 178,850ft^3. After war service, she and her renamed sister *Warwick Castle* were placed on the mail service until the mail service was back to full strength in 1950. *Pretoria Castle*'s name was given to the new mailship *Pretoria Castle* which was completed in 1948. After a dozen years on the round-Africa run, they were both sold to breakers in 1962.

Burma

For much of the nineteenth century Burma had been a troubled region for Britain. In 1852 lower Burma and the delta of the mighty Irrawaddy River were seized by the British. In 1886 all of Burma came under British rule and became a province of British India. Under colonial administration the country prospered and became one of the wealthiest in South East Asia. At one time, it was not only the world's largest exporter of rice, it also produced most of the teak and precious stones such as rubies. One of the first shipping lines to recognise the opportunities offered by Burma was the Scottish firm P Henderson and Company, often known as 'Paddy Henderson'. Its subsidiary Albion Line, which was later acquired by Shaw, Savill, first started calling at Rangoon in the 1850s. Hendersons also formed the Irrawaddy Flotilla Company which had a vast fleet of river boats and in the 1920s carried some nine million passengers a year. Many of the river steamers and ocean-going ships were built by Denny at Dumbarton which also had a stake in the company. Operating under the banner of the British and Burmese Steam Navigation Company, services ran between Glasgow, Liverpool and Rangoon. The 7,050gt *Prome*, right, and *Salween*, delivered in 1937 and 1938 respectively, were the last of the Henderson passenger-cargo liners. Given that Dennys first built turbine-driven ships at the turn of the century, it is surprising that this 15-knot pair were the first Henderson ships to have turbine machinery. Designed to carry mainly civil servants and businessmen, the comfortable accommodation for the seventy-six first class passengers was in single- and two-berth cabins, each with square windows instead of portholes. Much care was taken to ensure that the dining saloon and main public rooms had ample ventilation whilst the amount of promenade space per passenger was said to be greater than the *Queen Mary*. *Prome*, seen here at Liverpool, and *Salween* both survived the war and were scrapped in 1962.

Polish transatlantic liners

In 1930 the Polish Government took over the assets of the Danish East Asiatic-controlled passenger and cargo services of the Baltic American Line and formed a new company, the Gydnia-Amerika Line. In 1934 it ordered two 14,300gt, twin-screw, 18-knot motor ship liners from the Italian yard, Cantieri Riuniti dell' Adriatico. This was a barter agreement which included payment in Polish coal. Delivered in 1935 and 1936 respectively, *Pilsudski*, shown here, and *Batory* were designed as 'tourist class' liners for the Gydnia to New York route. They carried 377 tourist and 400 third class passengers. The main tourist class public rooms were situated on the promenade deck which, unusually for a transatlantic liner, had an open promenade. There was a large main lounge, an enclosed veranda overlooking the bow and a few cabins with private facilities. The overall décor was modern but not ostentatious. Because they offered good value for money, the two liners were very popular and the company considered building a third in the class. Unfortunately, war intervened and both ships were refitted as troopships under the British flag. *Pilsudski* struck a mine off the mouth of the Humber in November 1939 and sank with the loss of ten lives. *Batory* returned to service in 1947 but in 1951, because of anti-Soviet Bloc sentiment in the United States, was no longer allowed to operate in New York. She was then placed on a new route from Gydnia to India via Southampton where she remained until 1957. The final phase in her career took place between 1957 and 1968 when she sailed between Gydnia and Montreal as a 76 first and 740 tourist class liner. She was a great success and carried 122,620 passengers during this period. Replaced by *Stefan Batory* (ex-*Maasdam*, 1952/15,024gt) she became a hotel ship in Danzig before being sold to Hong Kong breakers in 1971.

The largest purpose-built liner on the Sydney–Fremantle run

Diesel-powered passenger ships had been operating on the Australian coastal service since 1925. In the mid-1930s each of the main interstate shipping lines, Adelaide Steamship Company, Melbourne Steamship Company and McIlwraith McEacharn Limited, took delivery of a new ship which was over 10,000gt. The 10,985gt, 17-knot, twin-screw *Kanimbla* was not only the largest purpose-built liner on the Sydney–Fremantle run, she was also the finest. Completed in 1936 by Harland and Wolff for McIlwraith McEacharn, she was a beautifully-proportioned ship with a streamlined superstructure and an exterior profile which was well advanced for the time. She carried 203 first and 198 second class passengers and had five holds and a cattle deck forward. She was also the first interstate vessel to have an automatic sprinkler system fitted throughout the accommodation and public rooms in case of fire. In addition to wood-panelled public rooms in first class, there was also a permanent swimming pool and glass-enclosed dance floor amidships. Unusually, *Kanimbla* was the first and probably the only passenger ship equipped with a permanent radio broadcasting studio. The station, call sign 9M1, made regular broadcasts until the ship was requisitioned for war service in 1939 as the armed merchant cruiser, HMS *Kanimbla*. She was paid off in 1949 having covered some 470,000 miles during her war service. She returned to the coastal trade in 1950 and usually undertook voyages from Sydney to Fremantle in the summer months and Sydney to Cairns in the winter months. Faced with falling passenger number because of air travel, she was sold in 1961 to a Liberian firm and renamed *Oriental Queen*. After a period as a pilgrim ship and a Japanese cruise ship she was sold to Yokohama breakers in 1973.

KPM, the largest Dutch shipping company

By 1930 the Koninklijke Paketvaart-Maatschappij (KPM) had grown to an enormous size, with a fleet of some 129 ships, carrying 1.2 million passengers per annum. The equivalent of British India Line, it was also the largest Dutch shipping company, not only in terms of tonnage but also numbers of ships owned. However, hard-hit by the Depression and with few external routes, the company sought new opportunities to improve its profitability. In 1931, it started an experimental passenger and freight service between the Far East and South Africa via Batavia (Jakarta) and in 1935 ordered three purpose-built, 17-knot, 14,100gt passenger-cargo liners, each capable of making the round trip in three months. The variety of ports of call and lengthy sectors also required that the three new liners, named after the founders of KPM, needed to be extremely flexible not only in terms of engine power but also for cargo handling – hence the numerous fixed jib cranes and triple-screw diesels. They were also the world's first triple-screw passenger motor ships. The first to be completed, in 1937, was *Boissevain*. Unlike her sisters, *Tegelberg* and *Ruys*, which came from Dutch yards, she was built in Germany under a unique barter arrangement. With Germany short of foreign currency, and the tobacco planters in Java and Sumatra unable to sell their produce to the Reich, it was agreed that the ship would be paid for in tobacco. Externally she looked magnificent with her white hull, gently curved cruiser stern, tall masts and low buff funnel. Most of the eighty-two first class passengers were accommodated in outboard cabins on the bridge deck, whilst those in intermediate (for 'superior Chinese') were housed aft of amidships. 'Tween deck space was also available either for cargo or 500 steerage passengers. Public rooms in first class were light, airy and comfortable and most suitable for tropical travel. The décor was modern but unostentatious and, if anything, slightly formal. They had a built-in swimming pool and were the first ships on the route to have suites with private balconies whilst nearly every cabin in first class was provided with a bath. After the Japanese invasion of Java, they were chartered by the British Government as troopships and all three survived the war unscathed. However, the 1945 declaration of independence in Indonesia left KPM in a vulnerable position. In 1947 it merged the non-local Indonesian routes with those of the Java-China-Japan-Lijn to form the Hong Kong-based Koninklijke Java-China-Paketvaart Lijnen, more commonly known as Royal Interocean Lines. Their hulls and funnels were painted black as seen here on *Tegelberg* passing through the Malacca Straits. The Far East–South Africa route was extended to South America (although no longer via Indonesia) and offered a fascinating variety of ports during the two-month voyage from Kobe to Buenos Aires. By 1968 with the impending arrival of 20-knot freighters and diminishing passenger numbers, this handsome trio was sold to Taiwanese breakers.

The largest Dutch-built liner

Launched by Queen Wilhelmina in April 1937, for many, Holland America Line's 36,287gt *Nieuw Amsterdam* was one of the finest liners of the twentieth century both externally and internally. Despite not being one of the largest or fastest transatlantic liners, she had a beautifully-balanced profile with a shapely curved stem, lofty superstructure, two streamlined funnels, two tall masts and a cruiser stern. She was built by the Rotterdam Drydock Company at a time of great unemployment among Dutch shipyard workers. Assisted by the Netherlands Government, much of her building work was shared out among other leading Dutch shipbuilders. The trade unions also agreed to a temporary wage reduction during the ship's construction which took two years to complete. A three-class ship, the passenger capacity for *Nieuw Amsterdam* was 568 cabin (first), 455 tourist (second) and 209 third class. Unlike other transatlantic liners, the gap between the various classes was not that great, with each class enjoying excellent facilities. For example the third class dining room could not only seat all passengers in a single sitting but it was also air-conditioned. In fact, at that time the air-conditioning on *Nieuw Amsterdam* was the most complete of any ship afloat. She also had the largest proportion of cabins with private baths or showers on the transatlantic run. All cabin class cabins had en-suite facilities as did a relatively high number in tourist class. Many leading Dutch artists, designers and decorators were employed for her modern interior décor which was neither bland nor studied. The overall effect in all classes was typically Dutch and is best described as one of comfortable elegance without the need for overwhelming cultural statements. The main cabin class public rooms were situated on the two promenade decks, upper and main. The rooms on the centre line were unhindered by boiler and engine casings which were divided throughout most of the ship. The Grand Hall was 73ft long and 52ft wide and extended the height of two decks. It had twenty tall, engraved windows and a natural-coloured aluminium ceiling depicting various stages of life in half-reliefs. At the forward end of the main promenade deck was a 350-capacity theatre. One of only two permanent theatres afloat (the other was on *Normandie*), it was also the first theatre at sea to be air-conditioned. However, one of the most impressive rooms on the ship was the 180ft long, 427-seater cabin class dining saloon with its arched dome ceiling covered with padded gold material. It was connected to the tourist class dining saloon by glass doors enabling the two rooms to be used as one large, 765-capacity dining saloon during cruises. Unusually all the dining saloons were connected to the galleys by four escalators. *Nieuw Amsterdam* also had almost a quarter of a million cubic feet of cargo space and could carry up to sixty cars. She was one of the largest twin-screw liners whilst her engine machinery consisted of two sets of quadruple expansion turbines which produced a service speed of 20.5 knots. Delivered in April 1938 she was only in service for just over a year before war broke out in Europe. Plans for a running mate were put on hold following the invasion of Holland in May 1940. She was subsequently chartered to the British Ministry of Shipping and converted into a 6,700-capacity troopship. Although managed by Cunard White Star Line, she continued to operate with a Dutch crew under the Dutch flag. By the time she returned to her owners in April 1946 she had completed 530,452 nautical miles and carried 378,361 troops during the war. After her post-war refit she returned to service in October 1947. In 1957 her hull was painted grey, seen here. Five years later she became a two-class ship during a major overhaul. By 1971 she was only used for cruises and in 1974 was sold to Taiwanese breakers.

A selection of smart Danish-built motor ships of the late 1930s

Although most Soviet ships between the wars were built in Russia, a few specialised vessels were constructed elsewhere including the 4,125gt *Svanetiya*, below right, the USSR's first streamlined passenger ship. She was built at the Danish yard Helsingor Vaerft and with a raked bow, cruiser stern and funnel was typical of the smart, fast Scandinavian-designed ships of the late 1930s. Her twin Burmeister and Wain engines produced a service speed of 16.5 knots. Completed in 1937 for the Odessa–Alexandria express service she carried 244 passengers in three classes. For a country which boasted a 'classless' society, there was some irony in the fact that *Svanetiya*

had two deluxe suites, each with a sitting room, double bedroom and bathroom. Sadly, her career was short-lived and whilst in the Black Sea she succumbed to German aerial bombardment in April 1942.

The Romanian Government also ordered two small, twin-screw passenger-cargo ships for the Constantza–Alexandria service operated by Serviciul Maritim Român. Constructed in 1938 at Burmeister and Wain's Copenhagen yard the 6,672gt *Transilvania*, bottom, and *Basarabia* were then the world's fastest passenger motor ships with trial speeds of 24.5 knots and 25.3 knots respectively. They carried 80 first, 100 second and around 230 third class passengers. The first class accommodation was light and airy with polished woods and stylish furniture. All passengers could be seated in the spacious, air-conditioned dining saloon which was situated on the main deck, the same deck as the second class dining saloon. Despite being designed as auxiliary cruisers in time of war, Romania refused to allow them for use by its ally Germany and they spent most of the war laid up at Istanbul. In 1945 they were surrendered to the Soviet Union and although *Basarabia* was retained as war reparations, *Transilvania* was later returned to her owners. She remained in service until 1979 when she capsized off Galati in the Danube. Her sister, renamed *Ukraina*, was only broken up in 1987.

Meanwhile, in Chile the long-established Compania Sud-Americana de Vapores (CSAV) took delivery in 1937 and 1938 of three 7,729gt, single-screw, passenger-cargo motor ships for its Valparaiso–New York service via the Panama Canal. Operating under the banner of the Chilean Line, *Aconcagua*, *Copiapo* and *Imperial* were built at Nakskov, Denmark by Nakskov SV. *Aconcagua*, seen here, was named after the highest mountain outside of Asia. She and her sisters were handsome ships with cruiser sterns and engines by Burmeister and Wain. They each carried 34 first and 126 third class passengers with considerable space for cargo. Cattle were also transported in 'tween deck space. Unfortunately, the South American careers of these fine ships was cut short after the entry of the United States into the global conflict. In 1943 they were sold to the US War Shipping Administration for $2 million each and converted into 1,600-capacity troopships. They retained their CSAV names and were sold between 1948 and 1949 to Turkish Maritime Lines and renamed *Giresun* (*Aconcagua*), *Ordu* (*Copiapo*) and *Trabzon* (*Imperial*). For a while they were the largest Turkish passenger liners and carried 528 passengers, including 352 third class in dormitories. The first two were scrapped in 1970 whilst *Trabzon* was used as a cruise ship until her sale to breakers in 1983.

First diesel-electric liner

Hamburg America Line operated a passenger and cargo service from Hamburg to the west coast of South America via the Panama Canal. The schedule included over a dozen ports which were often short calls and involved complicated manoeuvres. To meet this need for flexibility in power, a common requirement for the cruise ships of today, the company ordered three diesel-electric passenger-cargo ships for delivery in 1938 and 1939. Two were 6,951gt, 58-capacity ships whilst the third was the 16,595gt liner *Patria*, below, the world's first large passenger ship to be powered by diesel-electric. A remarkable ship, she is often overlooked because of her short career of less than a year with HAPAG. Her handsome profile was similar to the 12,000gt *Caribia* and *Cordillera* which were delivered in 1933 for the Caribbean and middle America service. Twin-screwed with a service speed of 17 knots she carried 185 first and 164 second class passengers. Despite her size, the first class public rooms were grand and included a wide central staircase and two-deck-high balconied dining saloon which was situated on the upper decks. During the war she was used mainly as an accommodation ship and briefly in 1945 as the seat of the German Government. From 1946 until her demolition in 1985 she was the Russian liner *Rossiya*.

The mighty *Dominion Monarch*

In 1939 Union-Castle Line's *Capetown Castle* was eclipsed on the South African run by Shaw Savill Line's new quadruple-screw, 45,000bhp, 27,154gt motor ship *Dominion Monarch*, right, which was not only slightly larger but also considerably more powerful. She was built by Swan, Hunter and Wigham Richardson for a new fast passenger and cargo service to New Zealand via the Cape and Australia. At the time of her completion she was the highest-powered motor ship afloat and the largest and fastest vessel trading between Great Britain and New Zealand and Australia. She was also the largest ship built on the Tyne since *Mauretania* in 1907 and her distinctive twin-funnelled profile belied the fact that she was a motor ship. In fact, she had none of the streamlining usually associated with motor ships of the late 1930s although she was extensively welded. Her interiors were also rather old-fashioned and include a Tudor-style smoking room. However, she was a first class only ship and her 517 passengers enjoyed a vast amount of space including a 250ft-long games deck. At the time she was the only British ship to carry a fully-qualified golf professional. Air-conditioning was another feature which was limited to the dining saloon, hair dressing saloon and entrance foyer. Arguably, her main role was that of a cargo ship. She had six holds with a total cargo capacity of 673,000ft^3, 511,000ft^3 of which was insulated including 72,240ft^3 for frozen and chilled meat. Her design speed was 19.5 knots but was capable of over 21.5 knots if required. *Dominion Monarch* was in New Zealand on her second voyage when war broke out. Designed for long-distance travel she was an ideal candidate for her new role as a troopship and transport and was only returned to her owners in 1947. After a major refit, she returned to peacetime work in 1948. However, during the 1950s her schedule was constantly disrupted by strikes at ports in New Zealand and Australia. As she relied heavily on cargo she became increasingly unprofitable and in 1962 she was withdrawn from service and sold to Japanese breakers.

Cunard's largest intermediate liner

In 1926 Cunard Line started a weekly London–Le Havre–Southampton–New York service. This route became of major importance to the company. After the formation of Cunard White Star Ltd. in 1934, White Star Line's large new motor ships *Britannic* and *Georgic* were transferred to the service in 1935. At the time, they were the largest ships to operate on the Thames. After the completion of *Queen Mary* in 1936, tenders were sought for the building of a pair of large intermediate liners for the London-Southampton-New York service, which would be similar to *Georgic* in terms of size, passenger layout and comfort. The new ships would also need to be able to use the entrance lock for London's King George V Dock. The contract for the first ship was awarded at the end of December 1936 to Cammell Laird and Company Ltd., Birkenhead. With a profile similar to *Queen Elizabeth*, the 35,739gt *Mauretania* was completed in May 1939. She was at that time the largest ship built by an English shipyard and the biggest ship to enter the Thames. Twin-screwed and turbine driven she had a service speed of 22 knots and was also designed as a replacement liner when either of the 'Queens' was taken out of service for the annual refit. She also had a substantial cargo capacity of 390,000ft^3 with space in her 'tween decks for seventy cars. With ten passenger decks, she carried 486 cabin, 368 tourist and 502 third class passengers. The style of her British modern décor was similar to *Queen Elizabeth* with simple lines and much use of rare decorative woods. The facilities for all classes were a great improvement on earlier ships and included air-conditioning in many of the main public spaces. Interestingly, tourist and third class each had its own cinema. Unfortunately, the intervention of war once again put paid to Cunard's ambitions and after only three voyages, *Mauretania* was sent to New York for layup and subsequent transformation into a troopship. Plans for a second ship were put on hold. On her return from war duty in 1947, she was placed on the Southampton–Cherbourg–New York route. In 1949, she was joined by a new running mate, the 34,183gt *Caronia*, which had originally been conceived as her sister. However, because post-war conditions were radically different from the 1930s, the new ship was designed as a dual-purpose transatlantic liner and cruise ship. *Mauretania* was also used as a cruise ship in the early 1960s and in March 1963, she inaugurated a new passenger-cargo service between New York and Cannes, Genoa and Naples. Because of poor passenger numbers this service only lasted seven months. In 1965, she was withdrawn and sold to breakers.

Streamlined Japanese liners

In 1939 Osaka Shosen Kaisha (OSK) took delivery of a magnificent pair of fast 12,755gt liners designed for its round-the-world service from Japan to South America around the Cape of Good Hope, returning to Japan via Panama and Los Angeles. Designed by Dr Haruki Watsuji, one of the leading marine architects in Japan and Chief Designer at OSK, *Argentina Maru*, below, and her sister *Brazil Maru* with their streamlined appearance were the epitome of modern style and engineering. They were essentially state subsidised emigrant ships with dormitory accommodation for most of the 800 third class passengers. However, the 101 first class passengers had the use of fine facilities on the three upper decks, including a swimming pool, nursery, gymnasium and well-lit lounges decorated in a modern Japanese style. The dining room was high up in the ship and had large windows opening on to the promenade deck. The cargo space included four silk rooms and seven refrigerated chambers. They were also powerful ships with twin diesels producing a maximum total output of 16,500bhp. With a mean speed of 21.5 knots, *Argentina Maru* set a record voyage by covering the distance between Japan and Cape Town in twenty-five days. She made only four voyages before the attack on Pearl Harbor and soon after the outbreak of war was switched to the Japan–Darien service, before being taken out of service for trooping duties. From 1942 to 1943 she was converted by her original builders into the aircraft carrier *Kaiyo*. As such, in March 1945, she was attacked by US aircraft in Northern Kyushu and beached. Her sister became a troop transport and was torpedoed and sunk by a US submarine in August 1942.

The Congo boats

The origins of Compagnie Belge Maritime (CMB) go back to 1895 when the first regular Belgian-owned passenger-cargo service was established between Antwerp and the port of Boma at the mouth of the Congo River. The so-called Congo Free State was a huge area which had been annexed in 1891 as the personal fiefdom of King Leopold II of Belgium. In 1908 it became a Belgian colony, the Belgian Congo, and was served by 'Congo boats' with 'Ville' names until 1967. Without doubt the finest liner built for CMB was the 13,544gt, twin-screw, 17-knot motor ship *Baudouinville* which was delivered by the John Cockerill shipyard in June 1939. Designed for the restrictions of Matadi which is 80 miles up the Congo River, she had a distinctive, well-balanced appearance with a raked bow and cruiser stern. A three-class ship, she carried 395 passengers and had a cargo capacity of over 300,000ft^3. As to be expected for a liner sailing in the tropics, there was a considerable amount of open promenade space although only the first class dining saloon was air-conditioned. She also had two swimming pools, a permanent one aft of the funnel on the boat deck and a fitted pool in the trunk of No 4 hatch for those in second class. The main public room in first class was the large forward-facing lounge which was designed, like the rest of the accommodation, in a constrained modern style. For senior civil servants and businessmen there were two large suites, each with three separate rooms. *Baudouinville* only made three round-voyages to the Congo before Belgium was overrun by the Germans who later seized the ship at Bordeaux and destroyed her in 1944.

Pasteur, the replacement for *L'Atlantique*

L'Atlantique's replacement was the 29,253gt *Pasteur*, completed at the start of the Second World War. Although significantly smaller than her predecessor, she was a more powerful ship. Turbine-driven, she had quadruple-screws and a top speed of almost 26 knots. At the time she was the fastest liner designed for the South American run. She also had a relatively shallow draft which allowed her to enter Buenos Aires and for Bordeaux passengers to be handled at the port of Le Verdon at the mouth of the River Gironde. Her passenger capacity was 287 first, 126 second and 338 third class. Although her accommodation was not as luxurious as *L'Atlantique*, her interiors were very stylish. Lessons had also been learnt from *L'Atlantique*'s fire and her less-spacious public rooms were subdivided by fireproof bulkheads. The first class lounge, smoking room and dining saloon were all situated on the same deck above which was a sports deck with swimming pool, sunbathing areas, full-size tennis court and a very unusual space below the bridge called Le Club. This airy, teak-deck area was designed in a nautical theme with large columns wrapped with thick ropes and included a bar, deck games and cane furniture. Advances in boiler design also meant that less space was taken up by boilers and instead of having two funnels, *Pasteur* was given an enormous, tall funnel which would take the fumes for all ten boilers. Because of the war *Pasteur* never operated to South America and remained a troopship until 1957 when she was sold to Norddeutchscher Lloyd and was converted into the liner *Bremen*. Bought by Chandris in 1972, she sank under tow to the breakers in 1980.

The USA's first truly modern liners

After the formation of the US-controlled Panama Canal Zone in 1904, the US Government also took over the Panama Railroad Steamship Line. In 1937 the Panama Line, as it was then known, ordered from the Bethlehem Steel Company three 10,000gt passenger-cargo ships for the strategically-important New York–Haiti–Panama route. Promoted as being 'years ahead of any ship afloat', *Panama*, *Ancon* and *Cristobal*, completed in 1939, were arguably the USA's first truly modern liners. They were also designed by two of the twentieth century's most innovative designers, the naval architect George G Sharp and the French-born industrial designer Raymond Loewy. Twin-screw, turbine driven with a service speed of 16.5 knots, they were the first significant ships to incorporate the new US fire-safety regulations and among the first liners to have kingposts in place of tall masts. With no sheer, they had a low, sleek profile with a cruiser stern and large streamlined funnel. The 202 first class passengers enjoyed Loewy's stylish modern interiors which made great use of plastics, stainless steel, aluminium and glass. Like Orient Line's *Orion* of 1935, there was no period decoration. The two-deck-high Great Hall with its tall windows and staircase leading to an upper lounge was impressive whilst the dining room was air-conditioned. Many of the cabins were grouped in fours around a small lounge with large sea-view windows. This Sharp-design feature was first used on American Export Line's 'Four Aces' in the early 1930s and was subsequently also incorporated into the post-war 'Four Aces'. The same 'court cabin' concept was later used in *Oriana* and *Canberra* in the 1960s. With no visas or passport required, an open-air swimming pool and wide promenade decks, these ships were ideal for those who wanted a carefree cruise. They also had considerable cargo and reefer space and provided a vital link between the Canal Zone and the USA. All three became war transports and returned to service between 1946 and 1947. In 1961 the company suspended commercial passenger and cargo services. *Ancon* became the training ship *State of Maine* whilst *Cristobal* operated a single-ship government-only service from New Orleans until 1981 when she was sent to the breakers. The former *Ancon* was sold for scrap in 1973 and *Panama* ended her career as Chandris Cruise's *Regina Prima* before being scrapped in 1985.

Royal Mail Line's new flagship

The outbreak of war also put paid to the Royal Mail Line centennial maiden voyage on 26 September 1939 of the company's new flagship, the 25,689gt *Andes*. Although she had similar dimensions to *Pasteur*, she was slightly smaller and slower. Also driven by geared turbines, she had two screws instead of four and a service speed of 21.5 knots. However, she was a two class ship and carried a higher number of first (403) and second class (204) passengers. As Royal Mail had a very successful cruise operation *Andes* was also designed for cruising when necessary as a one-class ship. All cabins either had a window or porthole whilst in first class all had private facilities, a high proportion of which also had a bath. In some cabins the bed folded into a recess so that the cabin could be a sitting room during the day. After the grandeur of the earlier Royal Mail liners, the décor of *Andes* was not ostentatious but more in the conservative moderne-style of Cunard's *Queen Elizabeth*. The first class dining saloon, which could seat all passengers in first, was air-conditioned and on the upper decks were four tennis courts and a large swimming pool. After her completion at Belfast by Harland and Wolff in September 1939 she was briefly laid up prior to her conversion into a troopship. During the war years she carried around 350,000 troops and sailed over half a million miles. She was returned to her owners in 1947 and the following year she made her maiden commercial voyage from Southampton to South America. In 1953 she was fitted with stabilisers and throughout the 1950s did regular cruises. Just prior to the arrival of Royal Mail's *Three Graces* in 1960 she ceased her liner voyages and was painted white and converted into a full time, single class, air conditioned cruise ship. Although she became one of the UK's top cruise ships in the 1960s she was expensive to operate and in 1971 she was sold to Belgian ship breakers.

Oranje, the fastest motor liner in the world in 1939

In 1939, shortly before the outbreak of war in Europe, Stoomvaart Maatschappij 'Nederland' took delivery of its new flagship, the 20,017gt, triple-screw *Oranje*. Intended to be the first of a trio of fast motor ships, she was designed to meet the future needs of the service between Holland and the East Indies. Attaining 26 knots on trials, *Oranje* was at that time not only the fastest motor liner in the world but also one of the most innovative ships of the 1930s. Although only slightly larger than the 1930-built, twin-screw SMN motor ships, she had more than twice their power. A four-class ship (fourth class was for troops), she had a flexible arrangement between classes so that she could also be used as a cruise ship. The dining saloons in first and second were sufficiently large to accommodate passengers in a single sitting. However, the most striking feature of *Oranje* was her unusual tumblehome hull, which meant that the breadth of the ship was at least 17ft narrower at the upper deck level than down below. This was partially due to stability reasons and the need to provide all passengers with outboard cabins but also the lower gross tonnage meant a considerable saving in Suez Canal dues which were based on gross tonnage. She had a single mast and no ventilators, the air being taken into the ship via two large unobtrusive structures on the top deck. Her stylish public rooms were large and airy with more opening windows than on previous Dutch East Indies ships. She also had large floor-to-ceiling windows overlooking the bow in the first class observation lounge. Unfortunately, the start of her career on the East Indies run was interrupted by the war and after her outward maiden voyage in September 1939 she was laid up at Batavia. Following the invasion of Holland, she was converted into a hospital ship and spent the next five years carrying over 32,000 patients round the globe. She returned to service in 1946 but after the problems in Indonesia came to a head in 1957, SMN decided to withdraw from the route and came to an agreement with Rotterdam Lloyd to operate *Oranje* alongside her rival *Willem Ruys* on a round-the-world service to Australia and New Zealand. This lasted only five years and both ships were sold to the Naples-based Lauro Lines in 1964 and completely transformed into the cruise ships *Angelina Lauro* and *Achille Lauro*. The former *Oranje* was destroyed in a fire whilst on a Caribbean cruise in 1979.

Rotterdam Lloyd's new flagship

In January 1939, at the Flushing yard of 'De Schelde', the keel was laid for Rotterdam Lloyd's (RL) answer to *Oranje*, a 21,300gt, 840-capacity liner known simply as 'Schelde 214'. As the Netherlands was a neutral country at the start of Second World War, work continued and only ceased after the Germans invaded in May 1940. Remarkably, the ship survived the war and was launched in July 1947 as *Willem Ruys*, in honour of RL's director who had been shot by the Nazis. This extraordinary liner had the largest geared diesel engines ever installed on a ship to that date and was able to do almost 25 knots. She had a similar tumblehome-hull shape to *Oranje* but was more streamlined with her lifeboats situated on the lower decks like a modern cruise ship. She also had two squat, streamlined funnels. There were no inboard cabins and four de-luxe cabins even had a private balcony. The forward first class lounge or social hall featured a second-level observation lounge with large plate glass windows. Another unusual aspect was that the adjoining first and second class dining saloons were identical and could be transformed for special occasions into one large room by the removal of a partition. When she entered service at the end of 1947, RL had been granted Royal status and became known as Koninklijke Rotterdam Lloyd. However, like *Oranje*, her career on the East Indies route was short-lived and after the passenger-mail service was brought to a close she was converted in 1959 into a fully air-conditioned, round-the-world-passenger liner with accommodation for 375 first and 753 tourist class passengers. Among the many changes to the ship, the most obvious was to her funnels which were raised and placed above a new deck house containing some of the air-conditioning plant. In 1964 she became *Achille Lauro* and is remembered not only for the hijacking which took place in 1985 but also the fire in 1994 which destroyed the ship, like her former running mate fifteen years earlier.

The world's largest ship

In 1936 Cunard awarded John Brown the contract for *Queen Elizabeth*, the running mate for *Queen Mary*. Although not as fast as *Queen Mary* the new quadruple-screw, turbine-driven, 28.5-knot ship would be the largest ship in the world, measuring 83,673gt. She was also longer and had a more streamlined and better-balanced profile than the rather old-fashioned-looking *Queen Mary*. Her two funnels, instead of the three, gave her passengers considerably more deck space. Designed to carry 822 first, 668 cabin and 798 tourist class passengers, *Queen Elizabeth* turned her back on the art deco excesses of *Queen Mary* and *Normandie*. Designed in an understated modern British style, her comfortable public rooms were elegant but not brash, with soft colour schemes and restrained hidden lighting. She was described at the time as being a 'vast show-palace of all the best in contemporary techniques of interior decoration. An extraordinary variety of materials has been used for her furnishings from traditional leathers and wood panellings to the newest wonders of metal alloys and plastics'. Despite catering mainly for American passengers, it is surprising that *Queen Elizabeth* only had air-conditioning in her first class public rooms and main restaurant. Full air-conditioning was eventually installed in the mid-1960s. Even though she was such a large ship, she rolled in the heavy North Atlantic swells and had no stabilisers until 1955. It was for this reason that her main restaurant was situated amidships, low down in the ship. This magnificent room could seat nearly all first class passengers in a single sitting. In the main restaurant, there were also three private dining rooms. However, for real exclusive dining, the 108-seater Veranda Grill situated aft on the Sun Deck was the place to be. High up on the ship and overlooking the stern area, this was the haunt of the rich and famous and despite a ten-shilling cover charge, was usually fully booked for the entire voyage. It had a separate kitchen and its own dance orchestra and was more like a supper club than a restaurant. *Queen Elizabeth* was launched in September 1938 and was due to be completed in 1940, Cunard's centenary year. Unfortunately, war intervened and, painted grey, she left the Clyde bound for New York. Later converted into a troopship she played a major role throughout the war transporting tens of thousands of personnel around the globe. Her first commercial voyage took place in October 1946 and a year later Cunard's planned express service between Europe and New York commenced when *Queen Mary* returned to service. This continued for twenty years until the sale of *Queen Mary* in 1967. Hard-hit by the arrival of cheaper air travel, the ships were no longer commercially viable and in 1968 *Queen Elizabeth* made her final voyage to New York. After an abortive attempt to use her as a visitor attraction at Port Everglades, Florida, she was sold to a C Y Tung company in Hong Kong in 1970. Renamed *Seawise University*, she was destroyed by fire in Hong Kong in 1972, whilst being converted into a floating university. Despite this unfortunate end *Queen Elizabeth*'s record size as a passenger ship remained unchallenged for fifty-six years. In November 1996, Carnival Cruise Line's 101,353gt *Carnival Destiny* entered service. Not only was she the first passenger ship over 100,000 tons but also she was the first to exceed the tonnage of *Queen Elizabeth*.

The largest and fastest liner built in the US

Encouraged by President Roosevelt, the Merchant Marine Act of 1936 was designed to produce a modern US-flagged merchant fleet through a more efficient use of government subsidies than the previous mail subsidy scheme. To pay for higher US shipbuilding and operating costs subsidies were paid to both shipyards and shipping lines. The US Shipping Board was replaced by the US Maritime Commission which was formed to design and then have built replacement ships for old tonnage. The first ship ordered by the Commission was the three-class, 1,202-capacity, 26,454gt *America* which was built for United States Line's transatlantic service. Completed by the Newport News Shipbuilding and Drydock Company in 1940 she was designed by the famous American naval architect William Francis Gibbs. The 24-knot *America* was easily identified by her pair of large funnels with swept-back winged tops, which were repeated twelve years later on her famous running mate *United States*. The décor on *America* was also relatively plain and under-stated whilst 90 per cent of the ship was constructed with non-flammable material, making her virtually fire-proof. At the time the US had the world's strictest fire safety regulations following the tragic 1933 fire aboard *Morro Castle*. With the outbreak of war in Europe *America* became a troopship and only made her first peacetime Atlantic crossing in November 1946, the same year designs were begun for a new larger and faster running mate. In 1963 *America* was withdrawn and the following year she was sold to the Greek Chandris Lines for service as an emigrant ship between Europe and Australia. Renamed *Australis*, she remained with the company for fourteen years and carried over a quarter of a million passengers. In 1994 she was wrecked on the island of Fuerteventura, Canary Islands, whilst under tow. The forward section can still be seen.

C-3P combi-liners

In the late 1930s the newly-formed US Maritime Commission decided to renew its fleet of cargo ships. Among the many standard types was the 7,700gt C-3 freighter, the hull of which was also used for two dozen outstanding passenger-cargo ships. The first in the series was the 7,997gt *Delbrasil*, one of six 16.5-knot, single screw, geared-turbine combi-liners ordered for the Mississippi Shipping Co., Inc. (Delta Line), the largest coffee carrier in the world, for its New Orleans to the East Coast of South America service. Completed in 1940 to the highest fire-prevention standards, *Delbrasil* had almost half a million cubic feet of cargo space, as well as extensive facilities for her sixty-seven passengers. All cabins had private facilities and windows instead of port-holes. The air-conditioned dining room could accommodate everyone at a single seating, whilst there was also a comfortable lounge, veranda cafe and swimming pool. The interior design was American art deco. Her profile was sleek, uncluttered, enhanced by a raked stem, low motor ship-type funnel (which was heightened on subsequent ships), and counter stern – a nice contrast with the modern interior. All six ships were requisitioned for war service and, at the culmination of hostilities, Delta Line decided that they were too small for their requirements and ordered a new trio of 119-passenger capacity ships. Meanwhile, following the US Navy's decision to retain its three advanced-looking *African Comet*-type C-3P ships, designed by George Sharp and the world's first all-welded passenger ships, Farrell Lines bought *Delbrasil* and *Deltargentino* in 1949 for its passenger-cargo service between New York and Cape Town, the longest non-stop ocean crossing in the world (6,795 miles). Renamed *African Endeavour* and the *African Enterprise* (above) respectively, they were seldom full, and incurred a great loss for Farrell Lines, and after only ten years of service, they were withdrawn and laid up in the James River until they were scrapped in 1969. The last survivor of the Delta Line C-3P group, the training ship *Golden Bear* (ex-*Delorleans*), was only broken up in 2012.

American President Lines also ordered seven C-3P ships for its east to west, round-the-world service. The first of this new class, the 9,255gt *President Jackson*, was delivered in October 1940. Her ninety-seven first class passengers enjoyed excellent accommodation designed by the renowned US naval architect George Sharp. The dining saloon was air-conditioned whilst all cabins were outboard with private facilities. The stylish lounge overlooking the swimming pool was two decks high with large windows, full-length curtains and a wood-burning fire. The ultra-modern décor added to the country club atmosphere. The 26,000-mile voyage usually took ninety-eight days and included calls at twenty-three ports in fourteen countries. Although the remaining ships were delivered between 1940 and 1941, just three entered commercial service before they all became US Navy transports later in 1941. All but one of the seven survived the war and in 1946 only *President Monroe* and *President Polk* were delivered to American President Lines for use as combi-liners. They were sold in 1965 and within five years both had been sent for scrap. Meanwhile, *President Jackson* remained in US Navy service until 1973 when she too went to the breakers.

Chapter 8
The Late 1940s and 1950s

Less than twenty years after the end of the First World War, the major shipping lines once again faced the task of renewing their fleets following huge losses during the Second. During the 1950s another threat appeared on the horizon. The rapid shift from sea to air travel in the latter part of the decade was a huge challenge, especially for the large liners on the transatlantic routes.

The first passenger-cargo liner completed after the Second World War

Designed by George Sharp, Delta Line's 9,537gt post-war trio were without doubt trend-setting ships. *Del Norte*, the first to be delivered in November 1946, was not only the first passenger-cargo liner to be completed after the Second World War but also the first with full air-conditioning for passengers and crew and among the first to be fitted with commercial radar. Although the all-welded hull with its raked stem, cruiser stern and no sheer was based on the C-3 design, the streamlined superstructure was topped with a large elliptical dummy funnel which housed the wheelhouse, chart room and living quarters. This structure and the lifeboats were made from aluminium which made considerable savings in the top weight of the ship. The engine-room smoke was emitted from a pair of tall kingpost-exhaust pipes abaft the dummy funnel similar to those seen on Moore-McCormack Lines' *Brasil* and *Argentina* twelve years later. The 18-knot *Del Norte*, *Del Sud*, shown here, and *Del Mar* only carried 119 first class passengers and, because the main passenger accommodation had a single fore and aft passageway situated amidships, the cabins with full-size beds were among the largest ever seen on a ship and ranged from single rooms to 334ft^2 apartments. The two-deck-high main lounge was a spacious living room with tall windows and venetian blinds to control the bright tropical light. There was also an elevator, wood-panelled library, large swimming pool and wraparound glass-enclosed promenade. These magnificent ships became cargo-only ships in 1967 and five years later they were sold for scrap.

US standard ship post-war conversions

A number of the C-3 and Victory US standard ships were converted after the war into large-capacity passenger ships. Among these was the 11,678gt *Fairsea* (right) which was transformed during 1949 into a 1,800-capacity emigrant carrier for Soc. Italiana Trasporti Marittimi (Sitmar). She was launched in 1941 as *Rio De La Plata*, one of four passenger-cargo ships ordered by the US Maritime Commission for Moore-McCormack Line's service between New York and South America. These 16.5-knot, single-screw ships had geared Doxford-type motor engines. Their interiors were designed by George Sharp and with 196 first class passengers they would have been the world's first fully air-conditioned ships. All cabins had baths, twenty had private verandas whilst the café had a sliding room for open-air dancing. Unfortunately, they were all converted into escort carriers soon after their launch and leased to the Royal Navy with *Rio De La Plata* becoming HMS *Charger*. As *Fairsea*, she was chartered initially by the International Refugee Organisation and later by the Australian Government to carry emigrants to Australia. Her career came to an end in 1969 when a fire caused serious damage to her engines and she was sold for scrap.

Alexandre Vlasov, the Russian émigré owner of Sitmar Line, also bought four steam turbine-driven Victory ships in 1947 for conversion into emigrant ships. In the end only two, *Castel Bianco* and *Castel Verde*, were used on the Italian and Spanish emigrant trades to Central and South America. They were initially fitted with austerity accommodation and were easily identifiable as former Victory ships but in 1953 they were completely transformed into two-class ships. The addition of extra decks made them look rather top-heavy and the 10,139gt *Castel Bianco*, which had one deck more than her sister, became well-known as a 'roller'. Although the 717 emigrants on *Castel Bianco* slept in dormitories, for the 477 in tourist class there was a lido and swimming pool, a ballroom and a number of cabins also had private facilities. In 1957 both ships were sold to Compañía Transatlántica Española and renamed *Begoña* (below) and *Montserrat*. The dormitory accommodation was stripped out and they carried around 830 in tourist. Used mainly on the Europe to Venezuela service they both suffered latterly from problems with their turbine engines and were withdrawn in the early 1970s.

Of the 531 Victory ships constructed between 1944 and 1945, 97 were converted into 1,587-capacity troopships. Three were bought in 1947 by the Dutch Government to transport troops between the Netherlands and the Dutch East Indies. These steam turbine ships were renamed after the constellations *Groote Beer* (Great Bear), *Waterman* (Aquarius) (right) and *Zuiderkruis* (Southern Cross). At the end of trooping duties, it was decided that the trio would be rebuilt as 9,177gt, 830-capacity emigrant ships. The bridge and charthouse were moved forward and additional decks added. They were very functional ships, designed to carry families and children in basic comfort to Australia, New Zealand and Canada. Whilst there was no swimming pool, there was a large open-air sports area and dedicated children's deck. There was also a laundry and ironing room to wash personal clothing and a separate children's bathroom. Passengers were accommodated in bunks in either dormitories or multiple-occupancy cabins, all with wash basins and coconut matting. Close to each cabin group were toilets and showers. The 250-seater dining saloon had long tables with closely-spaced chairs. The hospital also had an adjoining operating theatre. Across the Atlantic in the late 1950s and 1960s they were popular with students seeking a cheap crossing to Europe. In 1963 *Zuiderkruis* was transferred to the Dutch Navy as an accommodation ship whilst the remaining pair were sold to the Greek shipowner John S Latsis. By 1970 all three had been scrapped.

The first Victory ship to be delivered in February

1944 was *United Victory*. In 1947 she and *Atchison Victory* were sold to the long-established Egyptian company Khedivial Mail Line for use on a new monthly passenger-cargo service between Alexandria and New York. They were both extensively reconditioned at the company-owned yard in Alexandria into the ninety-eight first class-only, 8,190gt, 17-knot *Khedive Ismail* and *Mohamed Ali El Kebir*. Although the ships retained their distinctive Victory-ship profile their wood-panelled interiors were stylish and modern. Many cabins had private bathrooms whilst on the boat deck there was a swimming pool and veranda café. At some stage air-conditioning was also installed. After President Nasser became president of Egypt in 1956, *Khedive Ismail* (left) was renamed *Cleopatra* and five years later Khedivial Mail was nationalised. *Cleopatra* was sold to breakers in 1981 whilst her sister was badly damaged during a fire in 1965 and was scrapped in Spain.

Shaw Savill's 'Big ics'

In 1945 Shaw Savill and Albion ordered seven large cargo liners to replace war losses. Known as Shaw Savill's 'Big ics', *Corinthic*, *Athenic*, *Ceramic*, *Gothic*, *Persic*, *Runic* and *Suevic* were built between 1947 and 1950 for Shaw Savill's Australian and New Zealand routes. Although they all had over half a million cubic feet of reefer space, the first four ships also carried eighty-five first class passengers. The 15,200gt, twin-screw, steam turbine, 17-knot *Corinthic* and *Athenic*, the first in the series, entered service in 1947. The slightly larger and more powerful *Ceramic* and *Gothic* were delivered the following year. With little streamlining and rather boxlike exteriors they were solid, functional vessels with six holds worked by numerous winches and derricks. However, in the early 1950s *Ceramic* and *Gothic* were fitted with a streamlined Thorneycroft funnel top which greatly enhanced their overall appearance. The passenger cabins, situated on the top two decks, were all outboard with many also featuring en-suite facilities. There were two promenade decks with the top one including a smoking room and a covered veranda overlooking the stern. At the forward end of the lower promenade deck were the lounge and a relatively small dining room which required two sittings for meals. The décor of the public rooms featured wood panelling and was on the whole rather conservative but suited the needs of the mainly older passengers who wanted a leisurely voyage in the southern hemisphere. In 1953–4 *Gothic* was used as a royal yacht for the newly-crowned Queen Elizabeth's tour of the Commonwealth countries of the southern oceans, the first such visit by a reigning British monarch. In 1965 *Corinthic* and *Athenic* became cargo-only ships and were followed three years later by the remaining pair. By end of the decade three were sent to the breakers leaving *Ceramic* to soldier on until 1972 when she too was scrapped.

Argentinean ambitions

In 1947, two years after it came to power, President Perón's government placed an order with Vickers-Armstrongs for three fast, steam turbine, twin-screw passenger and cargo liners intended for an express service between Buenos Aires and London. They were designed to not only fly the Argentinean flag but also to compete directly with long-established British companies such as Royal Mail and Blue Star Line. The 12,459gt *Presidente Peron* was the first to be completed in 1949, having achieved 19 knots on her trials. Compared with other passenger-cargo liners of that time, she was an outstanding ship. Her superstructure was streamlined forward with gradually stepped-back decks towards the stern. This gave her a very sleek profile, She also had a pearl-grey hull, white upper works and a sky-blue funnel with a black top and narrow white band, the colours of the Argentinean flag. Unfortunately, not long after she entered service, her funnel was raised which rather spoiled her looks. This photo shows her as built. She carried only seventy-four first class passengers in great comfort. All cabins were outboard and had wide beds, fitted wardrobes, en-suite facilities and windows. At the forward end of 'B' deck were two large suites, each with a lounge overlooking the bow. There were two promenade decks with spacious air-conditioned public rooms on 'A' deck. These made great use of light-coloured veneered woods such a maple, walnut and elm. The main social lounge forward featured a large portrait of President Perón whilst the lounge further aft was used principally for music and dancing. The latter opened onto the veranda café and a large open-air swimming pool. The air-conditioned dining room, which could seat all passengers, also had a private dining area and a children's dining room. Her sisters *Eva Peron* and *17 de Octubre* entered service in 1950. Not only did they feature the raised funnel but they also did not have a lower promenade deck, the space being used for additional cabins, raising the passenger capacity to ninety-six. The cargo capacity for the trio was substantial with 315,000ft^3 of insulated space worked through four holds. They were initially managed by the state-owned Dodero Line. However, after the fall of Perón in 1955 they were all renamed. *Presidente Peron* became *Argentina*, whilst *Eva Peron* and *17 de Octubre* were renamed respectively *Uruguay* and *Libertad*. In 1964 *Libertad* was refitted as a single-class, 400-capacity tourist class whilst in 1966 and 1967 *Argentina* and *Uruguay* became cargo-only ships and in 1973 were sold to breakers. *Libertad* followed two years later.

Revival of the Portuguese merchant fleet

For much of the first half of the twentieth century, Portuguese liners tended to be very old. In August 1945 the nationalist government of António Salazar decided to set in motion a plan of the Ministry of Marine to modernise the Portuguese merchant fleet. Over the next ten years nineteen new liners were ordered by the leading Portuguese companies. Among these were four ships designed to serve the all-important routes between Portugal and its colonies in Southern Africa. These were jointly operated by Companhia Colonial de Navegação and Companhia Nacional de Navegação. Two steamships, *Império* (1948/13,186gt) and *Pátria* (1947/13,196gt), were built for Colonial on the Clyde by John Brown. These rather old-fashioned ships used existing plans prepared for Anchor Line whereas the two Nacional liners ordered from Swan, Hunter and Wigham Richardson were the streamlined, twin-screw motor ships *Angola* (1948/13,078gt) (below) and *Moçambique* (1949/12,976gt). With a service speed of 18 knots, they were able to do the round trip from Lisbon to Mozambique in forty-five days, which was a considerable saving on the previous schedule. With a large black funnel, raked stem, twin masts and cruiser stern they were more distinctive than *Império* and *Pátria*. Although they were designed mainly for the passenger trade, they also carried a considerable amount of cargo. However, the passenger accommodation was relatively cramped even in first class with its rather sombre décor. The first class swimming pool was also high up on the boat deck. They carried 78 first, 150 second and 98 third class, with 394 emigrants or troops in 'tween deck spaces. However, *Pátria* and *Império* had much better public rooms and passenger accommodation than their Nacional rivals. Not only did they have more spacious rooms but also they were fully air-conditioned in all passenger and crew quarters at a time when the best Union-Castle liners only had air-conditioning in major public rooms. The four liners were very successful as they formed the backbone of the Portugal to Africa run. They were withdrawn in the early 1970s not long before Angola and Mozambique declared independence from Portugal in 1975.

British India's post-war services to the Persian Gulf

The Bombay to the Persian Gulf passenger, mail and cargo services, started in 1862, were among the most demanding of all BI routes not only because of the intense heat but also the multitude of calls, often at ports with poor cargo-handling facilities. In the nineteenth century much of the coastline was uncharted and BI ships acted as unofficial surveyors until 1911 when the Indian Government took charge of lighting and buoying in the Gulf. Between 1946 and 1950 a quartet of 5,000gt motor ships with 'D' names was delivered for the service as replacements for the seven 'B' class ships built before the First World War. These mini-liners with a short well deck forward and short funnel abaft the bridge were constructed on the Clyde by Barclay, Curle. They also had Doxford diesels and top speed of between 15 and 16 knots. The last in the series was *Daressa* which was delivered in June 1950. She carried 26 first and 60 second class passengers in comfortable accommodation whilst her 659 deck passengers had sleeping platforms in the 'tween decks. She was also the first in the series to have air-conditioned public rooms. She was sold in 1964 to Chandris for conversion into the cruise ship *Favorita*. This did not happen and, after a period of layup, she was sold in 1968 to Guan Guan Shipping Ltd., Singapore. Renamed *Kim Hwa*, she was sold for scrap in 1974. The final 'D' ship on the Gulf service was *Dwarka*. She remained until 1982 and was also the last BI ship in the East to carry the line's famous funnel colours.

The Sarawak Steamship Company's *Rajah Brooke*

One of the subsidiary companies which came under Straits Steamship control in 1931 was the Sarawak Steamship Company which operated services between Kuching, the capital of Sarawak on the north-west coast of Borneo and Singapore. For a hundred years from 1841 to 1941, when the Japanese invaded Sarawak, the state had been ruled by the 'White Rajahs', the Brooke family. In 1946, it became a British colony and gained independence in 1963. The largest ship owned by the company was the 2,312gt *Rajah Brooke* of 1948. She was the first of six similar shallow-draught passenger-cargo ships built for the Sarawak and Straits companies between 1948 and 1954. Her unique design, with the navigation bridge close over the bows and main superstructure aft, allowed her to navigate the tight turns of the Borneo rivers with little obstruction to hinder the pilot's view. Constructed at Dundee by the Caledon Shipbuilding and Engineering Co Ltd, she was a twin-screw, diesel powered ship with a service speed of 11 knots. Her 249 unberthed passengers were housed in the 'tween decks whilst the 40 first class passengers were accommodated aft. Like a modern cruise ship, her wooden-floored dining saloon was situated aft, just below the boat deck and was fitted with large windows which could be opened to ensure maximum ventilation. In 1964 she was transferred into the Straits main fleet and was used on the routes between Singapore, Brunei and Sabah, North Borneo where she remained until her sale to Singapore breakers in 1980. Two years later, with the sale of her running mate *Kimanis* (1951/3,189gt), Straits' traditional point-to-point passenger services came to an end.

The rise of Scindia after Indian independence

Despite having to face enormous competition from the mighty British India Line and P&O, the only Indian-owned shipping company of any size was the Scindia Steam Navigation Company which had been founded in 1919. At the outbreak of the Second World War it had a fleet of twenty-two ships, including four passenger ships which were used primarily as pilgrim ships to Jeddah. Two of these ships, *El Hind* and *El Madina*, were brand new and were lost in the war. A pair of 8,500gt replacements with the same names were ordered for completion in 1948. However, by the time they were delivered not only had India gained independence from Britain but Pakistan had also broken away as a separate state. This put paid to Scindia's plan for its new pilgrim ships and, given traditional Scindia names, *Jal-Azad* and *Jaljawahar* were modified for service on the UK–India freight and passenger trade. Relatively slow ships (14 knots), they carried 56 first class passengers amidships, 44 in 'economic' class on the upper poop and up to 1,050 unberthed passengers in the 'tween deck spaces. When she arrived at Tilbury in August 1948 *Jal-Azad* became the first Indian-owned passenger ship to dock in Britain for almost thirty years. Unfortunately these rather old-fashioned ships were no match for the British and foreign competition to India and, in 1954, they were withdrawn and transferred to the Scindia-managed Eastern Shipping Corporation for use on routes in the Indian Ocean. *Jal-Azad* was renamed *State of Bombay* and ran on the Bombay to East Africa service, whilst *Jaljawahar* operated between Madras and Singapore as *State of Madras* (seen here). In 1961, they came under Indian state ownership with the formation of the Shipping Corporation of India. They were sold for scrap in 1972 and 1973 respectively.

In 1939 Scindia acquired the Bombay Steam Navigation Co., one of India's oldest shipping lines. Founded in 1845, it operated coastal services from Bombay along the west coast of India. With the waning influence of British India Line following Indian independence in 1947, a pair of striking two-funnelled passenger ships were ordered from Harland and Wolff for the Bombay Steam Navigation Co. Designed for the Bombay–Persian Gulf run, the 3,750gt *Sarasvati* (below) and *Sabarmati* were launched at Belfast on the same day in October 1948 and were completed two months apart the following year. They had two-berth cabins for 16 first class passengers, three berth ones for 24 in second class whilst the 1,200 deck passengers slept in the 'tween decks and there was space amidships on the upper deck for a dining saloon, fruit stalls and two galleys, one vegetarian and the other not. These unique single-screw, turbine-driven ships had a service speed of 17 knots and spent most of their careers on the Bombay-Karachi route. They were both broken up at Bombay in 1969.

New 'Presidents'

The first liners built for American President Lines after the war were also based on a US Navy P-2 standard type transport. Eleven 17,000gt P-2 ships with 'General' names were built on the US east coast whilst ten slightly larger ships with 'Admiral' names were ordered from the Bethlehem shipyard at Almeida, California. At the end of the war construction of the final two was suspended but was subsequently resumed and they were completed in 1948 as commercial passenger liners for the US Maritime Commission. Chartered to American President Lines, the 15,359gt *President Wilson* (left) and *President Cleveland* were the largest commercial ships built on the US west coast to that date. They had distinctive profiles with the promenade deck extending to the bow and two tapered funnels designed to reduce soot on the deck. Much non-combustible material was used in their construction as well as aluminium for the upper decks whilst the enclosed promenade featured rubber tiling in place of traditional teak decking. Engines were turbo-electric and with twin screws they managed a service speed of 19 knots. Each carried over 800 passengers in two classes. First class was air-conditioned whilst mechanical ventilation was used in tourist class which was mainly used by Chinese travellers. The air-conditioning plant was at the time the largest ever installed on a ship. The first class public rooms were designed by George G Sharp and were of a high standard and very spacious. Interestingly, in the children's playroom was a small electrically-operated merry-go-round. Many cabins had Pullman-type beds which could be transformed during the day into sofas at the touch of a button. Designed by Arnot and Company, these space-saving arrangements were first introduced in 1947 on the Alcoa-trio of combi-ships. *President Wilson* and *President Cleveland* sailed every three weeks from San Francisco and Los Angeles to Honolulu, Yokohama, Manila, Hong Kong and Kobe and were the backbone of the transpacific service until their sale in 1973 to the Hong Kong-based Tung group. By the mid-1970s this handsome pair had been scrapped.

The beautiful *Oslofjord*

In 1938 Norwegian America Line took delivery of the 18,673gt *Oslofjord*, its first motor-driven and final two-funnelled liner. This German-built ship was designed as a dual-purpose ship, which could operate in summer as a three-class, 860-capacity liner on the Oslo–New York route and as a single-class cruise ship during the winter months. Unfortunately her career was cut short in December 1940 when she struck a mine off the mouth of the River Tyne and was wrecked. In the autumn of 1942 the company started planning a replacement liner which would be built as soon as possible after the ending of hostilities. The 16,844gt, twin-screw, 635-capacity, two-class *Oslofjord* was completed in 1949 by the Amsterdam yard, N.V. Nederlandsche Dok en Scheepsbouw Maatschappij. The largest passenger ship in the Norwegian merchant fleet, she was also designed as a dual-purpose transatlantic liner and cruise ship and had a service speed of 20 knots. Her streamlined yacht-like exterior was ultra-modern for that time with very fine lines. She had stylish interiors and severe sheer lines forward with her forward section designed so that it would ship as little water as possible. The basic shape of her ice-strengthened hull was repeated for the next three NAL liners, culminating in *Vistafjord* of 1973. Her success as a cruise ship led to NAL becoming one of the leading luxury cruise lines. She made her last transatlantic crossing in 1967 and was chartered first to Greek Line and then to Costa when she was renamed *Fulvia*. Whilst on a Costa cruise to the Canaries in July 1970 she caught fire after an engine explosion and later sank.

France's first turbo-electric liner on the North African trade

In 1939 Compagnie de Navigation Mixte placed an order with Chantiers de la Méditerranée for an 8,800gt, twin-screw passenger and cargo ship. The remarkable *Kairouan* was the first turbo-electric liner on the North African trade and the first to be launched in France after the collapse of the country in 1940. Her powerplant was built by Alsthom who made *Normandie*'s turbo-electric engines. However, *Kairouan* had more advanced high-pressure boilers than *Normandie* which produced an increased reduction ratio between turbine and propeller. She had a very distinctive profile with a Maierform bow and machinery and funnel aft of amidships. She also had numerous side doors for cargo handling including two which were wide enough for cars. Semi-completed, she was scuttled by the Germans at Toulon in 1944. She ended up at a 50° angle with her bow on the bottom and her stern resting on the sunken Italian liner *Virgilio* (1928/11,718gt). In a complicated two-year salvage operation she was raised in 1947 and after rebuilding, entered service in 1950. Her sleek hull shape was enhanced by the addition of an F.C.M./Valenci-type funnel. Her original passenger capacity was 1,375 which included 595 deck passengers who were berthed in the 'tween decks. All first and second class public rooms were air-conditioned and, with a service speed of over 24 knots, she reduced the crossing time by two hours. In 1969 Mixte was absorbed by CGT and a new company, Compagnie Générale Transméditerranéenne was set up to run the North African services. *Kairouan* was sold to Spanish breakers in 1973.

The ill-fated *Magdalena*

Between 1949 and 1960 Royal Mail Line took delivery of four liners for the passenger and cargo service between London, Brazil and the River Plate. These would be the last Royal Mail liners ever built. The first of these ships was the ill-fated *Magdalena* which had been ordered from Harland and Wolff as a replacement for *Highland Patriot* which had been lost in the war. At 17,547gt she was a larger, faster and more streamlined version of the 'Highland' ships but with a single funnel instead of two. Driven by turbines and two propellers her service speed was 18 knots, three knots faster than her *Highland* running mates but with a similar amount of cargo space. She also only carried first (133) and third class (346) passengers. The first class accommodation was a vast improvement on the earlier ships. Not only was it more contemporary in design, it was also fully air-conditioned. In fact, *Magdalena* was the first British liner to have all her first class space air-conditioned. All first class cabins were outboard and had sliding windows and private facilities with either a bath or shower. There was also a single-seating dining saloon, an observation lounge on the top deck with sea views on three sides and a sheltered swimming pool aft. Third class passengers, mainly Spanish and Portuguese emigrants, were accommodated in a range of two- to ten-berth cabins. The medical facilities on the ship were impressive and included an operating theatre and a maternity ward. Unfortunately on the return sector of her maiden voyage in April 1949 she struck rocks near Rio de Janeiro and subsequently became a total loss, fortunately with no fatalities. The shame of this disaster was such that in a subsequent history of Royal Mail Line, *Magdalena* was not included in the fleet list.

East Africa in the 1950s

The granting of independence to India and Burma in the late 1940s had a profound effect on the fortunes of the British India Steam Navigation Company and saw a shift in emphasis for its passenger operations from the Indian subcontinent to East Africa. There was also a great sense of optimism in the post-war era about the opportunities offered by the burgeoning British East African territories. In 1948 BI announced that it had ordered a pair of 14,400gt passenger-cargo liners from Barclay, Curle for the London to East Africa service. These twin-screw, turbine-driven, 16-knot ships, *Kenya* (shown here) and *Uganda*, were without doubt the finest passenger ships owned by the company. They were nicely proportioned ships and with the original black hull and white band, looked very smart. The hull colours were changed to white in 1955. *Kenya* was the first to be completed in July 1951. Her cargo capacity was 390,000ft^3 and she could accommodate 297 passengers, 194 in first and 103 in tourist. However, unlike her streamlined Lloyd Triestino competitors *Africa* and *Europa*, she only had partial air-conditioning. Despite this, she and *Uganda*, delivered in 1952, were popular ships during the 1950s boom years for East Africa. In the following decade passenger numbers started to fall after the granting of independence to the former British colonies in the region and the arrival of jet airliners which meant that London could be reached in less than a day compared with three weeks by sea. *Uganda* was withdrawn in 1967 to start a new and successful career as a cruise and school ship. *Kenya* remained on the route for another two years when she was sold to Italian breakers after a career spanning only

eighteen years. One hundred and four years of BI services to Africa came to an end in May 1976 when *Karanja* made the final sailing from Durban to Bombay.

Between 1951 and 1952 Union-Castle Line took delivery of three 17,000gt, twin-screw, steam turbine, cabin class-only liners for the round-Africa service. These ships, *Rhodesia Castle*, *Kenya Castle* and *Braemar Castle* were designed as replacements for the oldest and smallest intermediate ships and were smaller versions of the pre-war motor ships *Durban Castle* (1938/17,388gt) and *Warwick Castle* (1939/17,392gt). Their reduced size was prompted by the realisation that the earlier ships were slightly too large for comfortable manoeuvring in some of the East African ports. It was also hoped at the time of the order that they would benefit from the Tanganyika Groundnuts Scheme which was introduced in 1947. This was an elaborate plan to develop three million acres of land for the production of peanuts. Heavily financed by the British Government, the Groundnuts Scheme also included the building of a railway in southern Tanganyika. However, the programme was a failure because of poor initial planning and was subsequently abandoned in 1951, with the almost inevitable outcome that all three ships struggled throughout their careers to show profits. Despite being steamships their funnels were about the same height as the pre-war motor ships. This caused problems with soot on deck and the funnels were later raised, spoiling their handsome profiles. The passenger capacity of *Rhodesia Castle*, the first in the trio, was similar to the two-class *Durban Castle* and *Warwick Castle* with the passenger accommodation for 530 passengers spread over five decks. The principal public rooms were on the promenade deck with the main lounge forward linked with the ubiquitous long gallery and library on the port side leading to a spacious smoking room. At the after end of the bridge deck overlooking the swimming pool was a covered veranda area with wicker chairs and tables. As the swimming pool had no windbreaks, it was exposed to the elements and suffered with soot problems from the low funnel. The 280-capacity dining saloon was situated just forward of amidships on the upper deck. It was air-conditioned as was the hairdressing salon and hospital. Although only 28 cabins had private baths or showers, many had portholes using the Bibby-style of cabin layout and also electric heaters. With five holds, the cargo capacity included 131,300ft^3 of refrigerated space. The Parsons-type double-reduction turbines made by the shipbuilder produced an output of 14,400shp enabling the ship to do a service speed of 18 knots. *Rhodesia Castle* entered service in 1952. Unfortunately the timing of the three new liners was not good. Not only did the Groundnuts Scheme come to nought, but also the first sign of the winds of change which would sweep through Africa started to show. The 1950s also saw the stability of Kenya seriously disrupted after the outbreak of the Mau Mau Rebellion. In 1960, to meet the increasing needs of the tourist trade, she was withdrawn for a major refit which included more air-conditioning and, to reduce problems with soot, her funnel was also raised by 12ft and given a domed top. Despite these changes, the writing was on the wall for the East African trade. After the independence of Tanganyika and Kenya in 1961 and 1963 respectively, there was no longer any need for colonial administrators, the mainstay of the East African passenger service. Also, air travel was now a serious alternative to the long sea journey, and following the introduction of *Transvaal Castle* in 1962, the company abandoned the round-Africa service and only operated from London to Durban via Suez. This was the beginning of the end especially as the round-Africa trio seldom made a profit. In 1965 *Braemar Castle* was withdrawn, leaving only *Rhodesia Castle* and *Kenya Castle* in service. A brief arrangement was made with the British India Steam Navigation Company for these two ships to operate a schedule with British India's *Uganda* and *Kenya*, but two years later when *Rhodesia Castle* arrived in London in April 1967 she brought the intermediate service to a close. She was sold to Taiwanese breakers later that year at the age of only sixteen.

Orient Line and P&O war replacements

Between 1948 and 1954 Orient Line also took delivery of three 28,000gt, geared steam-turbine liners built to replace ships lost in the war. The first of these was the second *Orcades*. Not only was she the largest and fastest ship (20 knots) on the Australian run to that date, she had a striking profile which again showed the forward-thinking ethos of Orient Line. She was followed nine months later by P&O's *Himalaya*, which was also built at Barrow using the same hull form. Whilst *Himalaya* was a traditional-looking ship with a foremast and a large single funnel, *Orcades* had no tall masts and a bridge and signal mast set back which almost merged with the funnel. The second in the trio, *Oronsay*, arrived in 1951 and was similar to *Orcades* except that she had a large signal mast in place of the tripod mast. The final ship, the 1954 *Orsova*, was the first large all-welded liner and the first to dispense with masts except for kingposts. Her bow had more flare than *Orcades* and *Oronsay* and, because of soot problems on her sisters, her funnel was fitted with a 'Welsh Hat'. She carried 685 first and 813 tourist class passenger This handsome ship had a career spanning only twenty years, however, and in 1974 she arrived at Kaohsiung for demolition.

P&O post-war liners

P&O's quartet of liners built between 1949 and 1954 were developments of arguably the first truly modern Orient and P&O liners, *Orion* and *Strathmore* of 1934 and 1935. They shared the same hull shape, engine machinery and dimensions. Because of the expense of building turbo-electric machinery, P&O reverted to tried and tested geared turbine engines. The same basic design was used for another pair of *Straths* and *Orion*'s sister *Orcades* and the immediate post-war P&O and Orient liners. The 29,734gt *Arcadia* of 1954 (seen here at New York) was the third of P&O's post-war ships and the first to be built on the Clyde by John Brown & Co. (Clydebank) Ltd. All the earlier ships had been constructed at Barrow-in-Furness by Vickers-Armstrongs Ltd. She had a tall, dome-top funnel, was designed for the London to Australia service and carried 699 first and 704 second class passengers. With a decline in the Australian market and cruising in the United States on the rise *Arcadia* was converted in 1970 into a 1,350-capacity, single-class cruise ship based in San Francisco. She was then the largest ship cruising on the west coast. After P&O's purchase in 1974 of Princess Cruises and the introduction of purpose-built cruise ships, *Arcadia* was sold to Taiwanese breakers in 1979.

ARCADIA

New African liners for Fraissinet

In 1951 Compagnie de Navigation Fraissinet took delivery of the 9,505gt, 17-knot *Foch*, the first of three motor ships for its Marseilles passenger, cargo and mail service to French West Africa. Founded in 1836 the Marseilles-based Fraissinet was one of the oldest French shipping lines and in 1955 it merged with Cyprien Fabre to form Compagnie de Navigation Fraissinet & Cyprien Fabre. The Fabre family had taken control of Chargeurs Réunis in 1927. *Foch* was followed by two enlarged, 12,450gt sisters, *General Mangin* in 1953 and *Jean Mermoz* in 1957. This trio were superior to the Chargeurs Réunis liners, not only in terms of appearance but also in the quality of the passenger accommodation which by the 1960s was fully air-conditioned. On *Foch*, seen here in Fraissinet colours, the best first class cabins were situated at the forward end of the bridge and promenade decks and, unusually, the dining saloons for both first and cabin class were on the bridge deck. There was also space for 406 troops in the lower forward decks. In 1964 Fraissinet & Cyprien Fabre was bought by Chargeurs Réunis and a new company, Nouvelle Compagnie de Paquebots (NCP), was formed with Compagnie de Navigation Paquet to operate the nine West Africa liners of all three companies. NCP was short-lived and following the independence of the French African colonies trade declined rapidly. By the end of the decade all three Fraissinet ships had been sold. *Foch* was bought by the People's Republic of China in 1967 and renamed *Jian Hua*. She was broken up at Shanghai in 1985.

Elder Dempster's largest liner

The Second World War devastated Elder Dempster's passenger liner fleet. The first replacements were the twin-screw, 11,600gt motor ships *Accra* and *Apapa* which were delivered by Vickers-Armstrongs Ltd., Barrow-in-Furness in 1947 and 1948 respectively. These rather old-fashioned ships took the names and profiles of two sisters which were lost during the war. In order to offer fortnightly sailings to and from West Africa a third larger motor ship was ordered, this time from Alexander Stephen & Sons Ltd., Glasgow. Completed in 1951, the 14,083gt *Aureol* was Elder Dempster's largest and last passenger liner. She was also their finest ship with an almost yacht-like profile, especially as she was painted white with green boot-topping and a gold hull band. She had kingposts instead of masts, a raked stem, overhanging stern and a tripod mast just ahead of a wide buff-coloured funnel. She had fine accommodation for 269 first class and 76 cabin passengers. All the first class cabins had toilets and in many cases a bathroom as well. There were four suites forward on the upper promenade deck, two of which also had a private veranda. The swimming pool aft was large whilst on the boat deck there was a children's playroom, play deck and paddling pool. Although the décor of the first class public rooms was relatively conservative and typical of British colonial liners of the day, it had comfortable furniture and panelled bulkheads. However, despite operating to one of the world's most humid regions, it was extraordinary that the first class dining saloon and hairdressing salon were the only air-conditioned rooms on the ship. Full air-conditioning was only installed in 1960, nine years after she entered service. In the late 1960s, following the withdrawal of *Accra* and *Apapa*, *Aureol* was the sole Elder Dempster passenger liner on the West Africa route which was transferred from Liverpool to Southampton in 1972. Two years later she brought the service to an end after 203 round-trips to West Africa. With a four-fold increase in the price of fuel oil and declining passenger numbers her costs were too high to continue operating at a profit. In 1974 she was bought by a company owned by John Latsis, the Greek shipping magnate with close connections to the Saudi royal family. Renamed *Marianna VI*, she was used as an accommodation vessel at Jeddah for the construction company Petrola International S.A. until her replacement by *Margarita L* (ex-*Windsor Castle*) in 1979. For most of the 1980s, she was moored at Rabegh in a similar role and in 1989 was laid up at Eleusis Bay where she remained, her original accommodation hardly altered, until 2001 when she was towed to Alang for breaking up.

The renewal of the Lloyd Triestino fleet

Between 1951 and 1953 Lloyd Triestino took delivery of seven fast, twin-screw, passenger-cargo motor ships. Three, the 18-knot, 12,839gt *Australia*, *Oceania*, shown here, and *Neptunia* were built for the Australian service. The other four were slightly smaller but faster, 19.5 knots, with the 11,427gt *Africa* and *Europa* serving the routes to East and Southern Africa whilst the final pair, the 11,695gt *Victoria* and *Asia*, operated in the Far East. The ships were funded by Italian Economic Recovery Programme money put at the disposal of the Allied Military Government in Trieste. Striking-looking ships painted white with light blue boot-topping and hull band, they also had kingposts instead of masts, a sharply raked bow, tripod mast abaft the bridge and a streamlined superstructure and tapered funnel. The profile of the final four ships differed from the Australian trio in that they had two sets of kingposts instead of three with No 3 hatch worked by cranes. The superstructure was also further forward with no well deck and also acted as the tourist class sports deck. The Australian liners were originally designed to carry around 800 passengers in two classes, first and tourist. All first class cabins were outboard with en-suite facilities whilst many of the ones in tourist class accommodation also had a shower fitted. There were also tourist class dormitory cabins and temporary berths in the cargo spaces for emigrants. The dining rooms in first and tourist were air-conditioned with each class having its own open-air swimming pool. As to be expected in an Italian liner of that era, the public rooms were beautifully fitted-out with distinctive furniture and original artwork. With five holds, they had space for 280,000ft^3 of cargo. Constructed at Trieste by Cantieri Riuniti dell'Adriatico they were delivered in 1951. *Africa* and *Europa* which were built at Monfalcone and La Spezia respectively entered service on the Genoa to Cape Town express route via Suez and East African ports in 1952. They carried 148 first and 336 tourist class passengers, 84 of the latter in dormitories. Not only were their passenger facilities far superior to anything offered by the Union-Castle Line intermediate liners, all dining saloons and public rooms were also air conditioned. The final pair, *Victoria* and *Asia*, built at Trieste, entered service in 1953 on the express route between Italy, Pakistan, India and the Far East. They were fully air-conditioned and carried 286 first class, 141 tourist class and 40 in dormitories. Because this was a prestigious route for the company, which had been operated before the war by the magnificent *Victoria* (1931/13,062gt), this pair had the finest décor of all the seven new liners. Named in honour of the earlier ship which had been lost in the war, the stylish public rooms on the new *Victoria* were designed by Gustavo Pulitzer Finali who had been responsible for the designs of the public rooms of the 1931 ship. In a 1959 refit the Australian trio had the well deck filled in and were given full air-conditioning. However, following the arrival of Lloyd Triestino's largest and last liners, the 28,000gt *Galileo Galilei* (left) and *Guglielmo Marconi* in 1963, the 1951 liners were transferred to Italia's Genoa to Central America and Valparaiso route and renamed *Donizetti* (ex-*Australia*), *Verdi* (ex-*Oceania*) and *Rossini* (ex-*Neptunia*). In the early 1970s the Italian Government decided that it could no longer provide financial support for Italian passenger services. The Far East route was the first to go in 1975 whilst the former Australian liners were withdrawn in 1976 and scrapped the following year. *Asia* became a sheep carrier and was sold for demolition in 1985 whilst *Victoria* had a long career until 2007 as the missionary ship *Anastasis*. The two African liners also ceased services in 1976 at around the same time *Galileo Galilei* and *Guglielmo Marconi* finished operating to Australia. *Europa* which had been sold and renamed *Persia* caught fire and sank in the Red Sea in 1976 whilst *Africa* was scrapped in 1980.

The largest French liners on the routes between Europe and South America

With *Pasteur* not returning to South America after the Second World War, and to replace war losses, Sud-Atlantique's Marseilles-based rival Société Générale de Transports Maritimes (SGTM), which had been operating to South America since 1867, ordered a pair of twin-screw, 20-knot steam turbine liners for the route. The 15,889gt *Provence*, shown here, and the slightly larger 16,355gt *Bretagne* were delivered in 1951 and 1952 respectively. In the years after the end of the war, emigration to South America boomed, especially from Italy, and both ships were designed to carry over 1,000 third class passengers in either dormitories or multiple-berth cabins. There was also accommodation for around 130 in first and less than 100 in second class. Unusually, all the main first class public rooms were situated at the aft end of 'B' deck and above the air-conditioned first class dining room. The décor was reminiscent of pre-war French transatlantic liners with decorative paintings and polished wood panels. They had a rounded raked stem, cruiser stern and a streamlined funnel with large vents fore and aft which was designed by Emile Lascroux to keep decks clear of smoke. The Lascroux-funnel was also used on a number of other well-known 1950s liners. At the time *Bretagne* and *Provence* were the largest French liners plying between Europe and South America and whilst the former was built at St-Nazaire, *Provence* was the tenth SGTM ship constructed on the Tyne by Swan, Hunter, & Wigham Richardson. Unfortunately, they proved to be too expensive to run and, with the emigrant trade significantly reduced, *Bretagne* was sold to Chandris Line and renamed *Brittany*. She was destroyed by fire in 1963. Meanwhile *Provence*, now painted white, operated to South America on a joint service with Costa Armatori, Genoa. She was bought by Costa in 1965 and renamed *Enrico C.*, she later became a successful full-time cruise ship. Her name was changed to *Enrico Costa* in 1984 and in 1990 she became a motor ship. Four years later she was sold to the Mediterranean Shipping and renamed *Symphony*. She went to the breakers in 2001.

Independence and *Constitution*'s 'Sun Lane' service to the Mediterranean

American Export Lines' 24,000gt, 22.5-knot *Independence* and *Constitution* with their two large tall funnels, raked bow and counter stern were among the most recognisable of all US liners of the twentieth century. Designed for the 'Sun Lane' service from New York to Gibraltar, Cannes, Genoa and Naples they were, in 1951, the largest and fastest liners operating between the US and the Mediterranean. The interiors were the work of Henry Dreyfuss, an American designer who had a very practical approach to his designs which included telephones, vacuum cleaners and trains. The theme of the décor was 'Modern American living at sea'. With few wall decorations the public rooms and cabins had rich but muted colours with soft indirect lighting. This created a stylish, unpretentious and informal atmosphere which was popular with American passengers. The forward first class observation lounge was completely circular and offered a 270° panoramic view of the sea whilst further aft, peninsula wings extended on either side of the tiled pool and pool café which was decorated with humorous mosaics of fish. There were also two 600ft^2 penthouse suites both of which had a veranda, living room, bedroom and two bathrooms. The ships were the first large passenger liners to be fully air-conditioned and the first to offer American hotel-style 24-hour room service. The outdoor decks for the 1,000 passengers, in three classes, were spacious and ideal for travel in the Mediterranean. Completed by Bethlehem Steel, they were heavily subsidised and like other US liners, were designed for conversion into troopships. In 1959 the passenger capacity was increased by 110 with an extraordinary rebuilding which involved the forward superstructure being raised up a deck and forward by 22ft. Unfortunately this spoiled their well-balanced profiles. Ten years later they were both laid up. Sold to C Y Tung in 1974, after refits they were based from 1980 in Hawaii as single class cruise ships. *Constitution* sank under tow for scrap in 1997 whilst *Independence* was broken up at Alang in 2009.

Royal Interocean Lines *Tjiwangi* and *Tjiluwah*

The only passenger liners built for Royal Interocean Lines were the twin-screw, 16.5-knot, motor ships *Tjiwangi* (1951/8,627gt) and *Tjiluwah* (1952/8,630gt). Constructed in Holland by C. Van der Giessen and Zonen's Scheepswerven N.V., they were designed for the Japan and Indonesia service via Singapore and Hong Kong and given traditional Java-China-Japan-Lijn names beginning with 'Tji'. They were attractive ships with two tall masts and a low raked funnel. As built they carried 98 first, 160 second and 1,700 deck passengers. All first class cabins were outboard whilst the forward lounge had a partially enclosed veranda. The dining saloon was entered from the deck above via a curved central staircase. At first these ships were very successful but with increasing tension between Indonesia and Holland in the mid-1950s passenger numbers started to fall. Calls at Indonesian ports ceased after the seizure of Dutch businesses in 1958 and in 1960 they were placed on the 12,000-mile route between Hong Kong, Japan and Australia. In the early 1960s both ships were given full air-conditioning and two swimming pools with their passenger accommodation altered to 104 first, 118 second and 202 third class. They were also painted white which greatly enhanced their appearance. Although they became very popular with Australian travellers, by the end of the 1960s, like most liners of that time, they suffered from the encroachment of jet air travel and were sold to the Singapore-based Pacific International Lines. In 1972 and 1974 *Tjiluwah* and *Tjiwangi* became *Kota Singapura* and *Kota Bali* respectively. They were placed on the Singapore to Fremantle route and were used as a cheaper means of travelling between the UK and Australia using a charter flight to Singapore and then by sea to Australia. *Kota Singapura* was withdrawn in 1979 and was scrapped whilst her sister continued in service until 1984 when she too went to the breakers.

Holland America Line's new concept in tourist travel

Because of the demand for cheap travel from Europe to America, Holland America Line decided in 1950 to convert the cargo liner *Dinteldijk*, which was on the stocks at the Wilton-Fijenoord yard, into a 15,015gt tourist class passenger liner for the Rotterdam to New York route. The new liner *Ryndam* (right) completed in 1951 was followed by a sister, *Maasdam*, in 1952. This pair of single-screw, 16.5-knot, geared turbine, fully air-conditioned ships had a profound impact on transatlantic travel as they offered not only far more comfortable surroundings but also more space for 842 tourist class passengers than existing ships in the trade. They also carried thirty-nine first class passengers because of Atlantic Passenger Conference requirements that liners had to include first class in the accommodation. However, these few passengers were housed in an exclusive 'penthouse' section on the boat deck which had its own dining room and lounge. All first class cabins were outboard with private facilities. The rest of the ship was solely for the use of those in tourist. The main stylishly-designed public rooms were on the enclosed promenade deck. They consisted of a large palm court forward with sea views on three sides, a library, card room, main lounge with a cocktail bar and smoking room at the after end of the deck. There was also an open-air tiled pool and a large sports deck. Three-quarters of the tourist class cabins were for two persons and each cabin had combination vanity table-desks, individual reading lights and ample wardrobe space. Externally, the ships had a distinctive profile mainly because of the unusual narrow, curved-top funnel design which was shaped like an aeroplane wing standing on end. The pair also introduced a new grey hull colour scheme for Holland America Line. However, because of problems with rolling due to their original design as cargo ships, they were fitted with stabilisers in the mid-1950s. The success of the tourist concept led to the order for a larger liner which would also feature mainly tourist class passengers. The handsome 24,294gt *Statendam* (below) delivered in 1957 carried 867 tourist and 84 first class passengers. *Maasdam* remained in the fleet until 1968 when she was sold to Polish Ocean Lines and renamed *Stefan Batory*. Four years later, *Ryndam* was bought by the Greek company Epirotiki Lines and was transformed into the cruise ship *Atlas*. Her end came in 2003 when she sank on the way to the breakers in Alang. Three years earlier her sister was broken up in Turkey. Meanwhile the former *Statendam* was sent to Indian breakers in 2004 after nine years of layup in Greece.

Greek Line's revolutionary *Olympia*

In 1951, the General Steam Navigation Company of Greece, better known as Greek Line, ordered its first new passenger liner from Alexander Stephen and Sons. Up to that time, the company's fleet consisted of second-hand ships. Designed for the Bremen to New York service via Cherbourg and Southampton, the 22,979gt, twin-screw, turbine-driven, 21-knot *Olympia* was a revolutionary liner. Not only was she the largest Greek-owned liner but she also introduced standards in tourist class travel which were far superior to any other liner on the North Atlantic. A two-class ship, she carried 138 first and 1,307 tourist class passengers. An unusual aspect of *Olympia*'s twenty-one public rooms was that instead of having an overall style of décor for the entire ship each room had its individual name and theme. For example the Zebra Room, which was the main tourist class lounge, had zebra-pattered chairs and patterned flooring whereas the Mycenaean Room in first class was a contemporary rendering of the Palace of Minos at Knossos. Colourful floor patterning was another feature of the ship's design. First class passengers had the use of two small dining rooms with all cabins having private facilities. About half the tourist class cabins were also equipped with a toilet and shower. As *Olympia* was also conceived to do winter cruising, each class had its own pool. The 300-capacity air-conditioned cinema was at that time the only two-storey cinema at sea whilst the ship also featured another first, a floating art gallery showing contemporary art. The air-conditioned dining rooms were situated on the main deck, above the galleys, so that passengers could enjoy clear views of the sea through large windows. The 580-capacity tourist class dining room was at that time the largest of any transatlantic liner. Completed in 1954, the all-white *Olympia* had a curved stem with a pronounced knuckle, glassed-in superstructure, a large tapered, dome funnel and two tripod masts. In 1955, because of competition from Home Lines on the Mediterranean to New York route, she was transferred to Greek Line's Piraeus-New York service. In 1961 she was fitted with full air-conditioning. By then, she also had stabilisers. Nine years later, she was transformed into a 1,032-single class ship. Her main mast was removed and her after decks extended to form a lido area with two pools. In 1974 because of rising costs she was laid up. In 1975 Greek Line was declared bankrupt. After seven years of layup *Olympia* was bought in 1981 and was later converted into the cruise ship *Caribe I* and given diesel engines. She subsequently had a successful second career as *Regal Empress* and was only sent to the breakers in 2009.

The mighty *United States*

The heavily-subsidised 53,329gt *United States* was constructed in a special dry-dock at Newport News and cost almost $77 million. Designed by William Francis Gibbs this extraordinary vessel was primarily a passenger liner but had to be readily available as a 14,000-capacity US Navy troopship in times of conflict. The Navy also insisted on stringent safety requirements which were incorporated into her design. For example, she had two engine rooms, a virtually-enclosed forward superstructure and the most comprehensive fireproofing ever seen on a passenger ship. All her fittings were made from fireproof materials, including 500,000ft^2 of carcinogenic Marinite asbestos! It was claimed that the only wooden items aboard were the butcher's chopping block and the grand piano. She was fully air-conditioned and although her interiors were considered to be rather stark she was very popular with the rich and famous. The most impressive aspect of the ship was undoubtedly her engine power which propelled the ship at almost 40 knots. Her quadruple screws were driven by powerful steam turbines similar to those used on US Navy aircraft carriers. On her maiden voyage from New York on 3 July 1952 she crossed the Atlantic in three days, ten hours and forty minutes at an average speed of over 36 knots, which was ten hours less than *Queen Mary*'s fourteen-year record crossing. She carried 871 first, 508 cabin and 549 tourist class passengers. The costs of operating under the US flag and constant labour problems were a major headache for United States Lines and *United States* was taken out of service in 1969. For the past forty-eight years she has not carried a single passenger and is laid up at Philadelphia.

The Ellerman quartet

Among the most exclusive British liners of the 1950s were the four 13,300gt, twin-screw, 16-knot passenger-cargo motor ships built for Ellerman Lines at Newcastle by Vickers-Armstrongs. Delivered between 1952 and 1954 they were designed to undertake the voyage between London and Cape Town in sixteen days. *City of Port Elizabeth* (below), *City of Exeter*, *City of York* and *City of Durban* carried only 107 passengers in outstanding accommodation. These handsome ships had a curved, raked bow, rounded cruiser stern, a tall foremast and a large elliptical funnel. Comfort rather than lavish ornamentation was the keynote of their accommodation. Unlike the moderne-style *City of Benares* of 1936, the décor of the post-war Ellerman quartet was distinctly old-fashioned with period-style furniture used in a number of the public rooms. This 'Home Counties' look also appeared on the post-war Union-Castle liners of the day and appealed to the relatively conservative tastes of the premium class passengers on the route. All cabins were outboard and most also had en-suite facilities. The restaurant, which had tables for six, four or two persons, could accommodate all passengers at one sitting. However, the ships had no air-conditioning so passengers had to contend with mechanical ventilation. With over 600,000ft^3 of cargo space, the Ellerman quartet were primarily cargo ships and after loading at Middlesbrough, Rotterdam and Antwerp sailed once a month from London to South Africa. Because they carried passengers, they also had priority over other cargo ships and this meant they were able to offer a reliable and fast service for shippers. Their home-from-home style made them very popular with travellers and it was a great shock when they were suddenly withdrawn in 1971. Their premature end happened because they were expensive to operate and Ellerman felt that it would be more profitable to run cargo-only ships. They were sold to the Greek shipowner Michail Karageorgis who planned to rebuild them as passenger-car ferries. *City of Exeter* emerged unrecognisable as *Mediterranean Sea* in 1972. *City of York* followed as *Mediterranean Sky* in 1974. The other pair were never converted and were sold for scrap in Taiwan. *Mediterranean Sea* was demolished in 1998 whilst her sister was laid up at Eleusis Bay, near Athens. In 2003 she keeled over in shallow waters where she remains to this day.

French Indo-China in the 1950s

Many of Messageries Maritimes' (MM's) liners were lost during the Second World War and because of the strategic importance of this state-subsidised company in serving the French colonies in Indo-China, the Indian Ocean (Madagascar and Réunion) and the Pacific (Polynesia and New Caledonia), nine new liners were built in the early 1950s. Although six were motor ships, the company ordered a trio of fast, 21-knot passenger-cargo liners with steam turbine machinery for the monthly service between Marseilles and the Far East. With Lascroux-type funnels and named after the three countries in French Indo-China, *Viet-Nam*, *Cambodge* and *Laos* were beautifully-proportioned liners and a far cry from the ugly square-funnelled pre-war MM motor ships. Their stylish interiors, each designed by a different architect, were also the antithesis of the early ships. They were much simpler and feature lighter colour-schemes. In first class there was a large swimming pool and thirty-four cabins with private balconies – these can be seen below the promenade deck in this view of *Cambodge*. In the 1960s the MM's Far Eastern routes suffered a double blow with the closure of the Suez Canal and the war in Vietnam and by 1970 all had been sold along with the four liners built for the Indian Ocean service.

Messageries Maritimes' last passenger-cargo liner

Although Messageries Maritimes's passenger services from Marseilles to the French Pacific territories and Australia, which started in 1882, ceased in 1971, MM's last passenger-cargo ship was the 14-knot yacht-like, motor ship *Polynésie* (1955/3,950gt). This handsome ship operated on the Sydney–Noumea–New Hebrides feeder service and carried thirty-six passengers in outboard cabins and had a cargo capacity of 140,400ft^3. She offered passengers comfortable surroundings with a separate dining room, lounge and cocktail bar. In 1975 she was withdrawn and sold to Guan Guan Shipping of Singapore. After spending much time laid up as *Golden Glory*, she was sold to Taiwanese breakers in 1979.

Matson Line's final liners

At the end of the war Matson Line faced a serious dilemma about the future of its four passenger liners. Stringent safety and health regulations required the ships to be extensively renovated, whilst the market conditions had also changed with the increased threat from air competition to Hawaii and a reduction in traffic to Australia. *Matsonia* and *Lurline* were sold to Home Lines whilst the remaining pair were eventually placed on the Hawaii run. Regular passenger services to New Zealand and Australia recommenced in 1956 when a new 14,812gt *Mariposa* (illustrated) was delivered. She was followed in 1957 by the 14,799gt *Montery*. Both ships had been converted from Mariner-class fast cargo liners and although not as luxurious as their 1930s namesakes, they had stabilisers and were fully air-conditioned. They also carried 365 passengers in a single class whilst all cabins had private facilities and they were the first liners on the Pacific to employ only waitresses in the dining saloon. Popular ships, they operated 42-day round-trip voyages across the Pacific until 1971 when Matson ceased its passenger services and both ships were sold. Although *Mariposa* ended her career in Chinese waters in 1995, *Montery* only went to the breakers in 2007.

Navigation Mixte's unique engines-aft liner

The extraordinary *El Djezair* (1952/7,608gt) was Europe's first engines-aft passenger ship and preceded Shaw Savill's *Southern Cross* (1955/2,204gt) by three years. Her geared steam turbines were salved from the sunken *El Djezair* of 1934 and with the boiler room immediately below the small F.C.M./Valenci-type funnel, the layout of her passenger accommodation was compromised. Although air-conditioned, the first class dining saloon and small bar and smoking room were situated on either side of the boiler casing on the promenade deck. Most of the superstructure was enclosed and access to the main forward cargo holds was by cranes on the long foredeck. Once in service on the Marseilles to North African routes, it was apparent that the ship had serious stability problems. She was not only stern-heavy but also top-heavy despite the use of lightweight alloys in her superstructure. These problems were sorted by the addition of ballast. However, her engines were found to be in good order and she managed over 23 knots on trials. She was sold to Sovereign Cruises in 1969 but was never used and four years later she was sold to Spanish breakers.

A thousand miles up the Amazon

The Liverpool-based Booth Line had been operating services from Liverpool to Brazil and the Amazon River since 1866. In 1951 it took delivery of its first post-war passenger-cargo liner, the 7,734gt *Hildebrand* which had been constructed at Birkenhead by Cammell, Laird and Company Ltd. Designed to operate on Booth Line's unique 1,000-mile voyage up the Amazon to Manaus, she was a rather functional-looking ship with a single foremast abaft the forecastle and two centreline derrick posts. Her superstructure consisted of a topgallant forecastle, poop and long deckhouses amidships surmounted

by a large funnel with a Thorneycroft top. She carried 50 first and 118 tourist class passengers. Although all first class cabins were outboard, the ship had no air-conditioning and in tourist class the rooms were fitted with cold running water only. Even more extraordinary, *Hildebrand* had no radar, a factor which played a major role in her loss whilst in thick fog off the coast of Portugal in 1957. In 1955 she was joined by an improved, slightly larger sister, the 7,905gt *Hubert*. She was designed to carry more refrigerated cargo than *Hildebrand* and had 359,000ft^3 of non-reefer cargo worked in five holds. She also carried more first class, seventy-four, and fewer, ninety-six, tourist class passengers. The first class dining saloon was forward on the upper deck with a rather old-fashioned style main lounge situated on the deck above. Tourist class was aft on the poop decks. Once again, there was no air-conditioning whilst the only swimming pool was a portable one forward of the main superstructure. The return voyage to Manaus, which usually took two months, was popular among those who wished to escape from Britain in the midst of winter. In 1964, with dwindling passenger numbers on the route, *Hubert* made the final Booth Line passenger sailing to the Amazon. Since 1946 the company had been part of the Vestey Group which also owned Blue Star Line and Lamport and Holt. *Hubert* was transferred in 1965 to an associate company, Austasia Line which operated passenger-cargo services between Singapore, Malaysia and Australia. Renamed *Malaysia* she remained on the route until 1976 when she was sold to Singaporean owners. She was converted into the sheep carrier *Khalij Express* and was eventually scrapped in 1984.

Paquet's new flagship

In 1949 Paquet placed an order with the La Seyne yard of Forges et Chantiers de la Méditerranée, builders of *Chella*, for another fast West African passenger-cargo liner. The twin-screwed, turbine-driven, 11,900gt *Lyautey*, completed in 1952 had a top speed of over 24 knots. She also had an unusual appearance for that time with a single mast and a large streamlined F.C.M./Valenci-type funnel two-thirds aft. Designed by a French scientist, Jacques Valenti, and often called a Strombos funnel, it was shaped like a short half-wing of an aircraft. The position of the funnel was achieved by placing the main engines forward of the boilers. Her passenger capacity was 634 in two classes with four categories of first class cabins including two grand luxe suites with verandas. The main first class public rooms were on the promenade deck and included a large cinema/chapel. She was only partially air-conditioned and, unusually for a hot-weather ship she only had a swimming pool installed in 1963. She was transferred to the Paquet subsidiary Cie Française de Navigation in 1965 and, renamed *Galilée*, operated cruises between Marseilles and Haifa. In 1967 she was sold to Constantine Efthymiades and as *Lindos* she was used on the Piraeus– Limassol route. After the collapse of Efthymiades Line she was sent to Spanish breakers in 1974.

Portugal's ships of state

Companhia Colonial de Navegação started operating passenger services between Lisbon and South America in 1940. Since Portugal was a neutral country, these continued throughout the war. In 1949 and 1950, as part of its fleet revitalisation programme, the company ordered two large liners from the Belgium shipyard S.A. Cockerill. Designed for the express Lisbon to Rio de Janeiro and River Plate service the turbine-driven, twin-screw, 20-knot *Vera Cruz* (1952/21,765gt), shown here, and *Santa Maria* (1953/20,906gt) were at that time the largest Portuguese passenger liners and the first over 20,000gt. They certainly were the most luxurious of all Portuguese liners and were often seen as Portugal's 'ships of state'. However, not only were their overall dimensions restricted by the constraints of the port of Recife but also they had to cater for a variety of passengers from seasonal workers to wealthy business travellers. There were four classes – 148 first, 250 second, 228 third and 616 emigrants in dormitories. These factors meant that the liners required a larger-than-normal superstructure and to save weight aluminium was used for the top two decks, the boats, davits and funnel. The main public rooms for the two top classes were on the promenade deck. The first class lounge and smoking room were forward of amidships whilst those for second class were further aft. Both classes had separate open-air swimming pools and dining rooms which could accommodate all in a single sitting. There were also four deluxe suites forward on 'B' deck. These were situated around a common entrance hall which was very unusual for that time. The quality of the contemporary décor was of a very high standard with rich tapestries, interesting wood carvings and large colourful decorative paintings. The first class staircase on *Vera Cruz* was marble whilst the two-deck-high dining saloon on *Santa Maria* was entered via a two-sided, sweeping staircase. In the late 1950s they were fitted with full air-conditioning. By then they were also operating to Central America and did many cruises. In 1961 *Santa Maria* hit the headlines after she was hijacked by a band of armed Portuguese opponents of the head of state António Salazar. In the same year, *Vera Cruz* was requisitioned by the Portuguese Government as a troopship for the Portuguese Colonial War (1961–74) whilst *Santa Maria* continued to operate to Central America and Port Everglades. Both ships were scrapped in 1973.

The last of the banana boats

In the 1950s Elders and Fyffes was a major importer and distributor of bananas in Britain, mainly from the West Indies. It had been formed in 1901 and a year later it acquired its first ship. Although it became part of the giant US company United Fruit in 1913, it remained essentially a British concern. During the Second World War the company lost fourteen ships and among the post-war replacement ships built by Alexander Stephen and Sons was the 8,730gt *Golfito*. A twin-screw, turbine-driven, 17.5-knot passenger-cargo liner, she was completed in 1949. At the time she was the largest and fastest ship in the fleet. Flushed-decked with a tall domed funnel she carried ninety-nine first class passengers. Seven years later she was joined by a sister-ship, the 8,735gt *Camito*, shown here, which also came from the Alexander Stephen yard. Although they looked similar, the 1956 ship featured a number of major differences including extensive use of welding in her construction. *Camito* was also the first British-built ship carrying over 100 passengers to use the highest standard of fire protection which involved all bulkheads and ceilings being lined with Marinite, a type of asbestos which was incombustible. She carried 103 first class passengers in single or two berth cabins, most of which had private facilities. There were also two suites, forward on the bridge deck, each with its own private entrance. The decorative style of the public rooms was relaxing and stylish without many decorative features. For example, the lounge and ballroom which overlooked the swimming pool at the aft end of the promenade deck, had mirrors, birch and cherry-panelled bulkheads and a parquet dance floor. She was of course principally a banana boat and cleverly designed 'tween-deck cargo spaces ensured that a full load of 140,000 stems of bananas, stored at 53°F, reached its destination in the best possible condition. *Camito* and *Golfito* operated a regular service, mainly from Southampton, to Jamaica with calls at Barbados and Trinidad. In 1966 both ships were fitted with air-conditioning but in 1972, faced with falling passenger numbers and rising costs, the company, now known as the Fyffes Group, decided to cease its passenger operation. Both ships were sold to breakers soon afterwards.

French Line's Caribbean twins

Not long after the end of the war, French Line prepared plans for a pair of French-built liners designed to operate on its routes to the West Indies. The first to be laid down in 1948 at the Dunkirk yard of Ateliers et Chantiers de France was the 20,469gt *Flandre*. However, during construction, she was modified so that she could run alongside *Ile de France* and *Liberte* on the Le Havre to New York service. Completed in 1952 as the largest post-war ship from a French yard, her virtually-identical sister, the 19,828gt *Antilles*, was delivered the following year. *Flandre* had a black hull whereas *Antilles*'s hull was white. They were distinctive-looking ships with a massive, curved bulbous bow and large circular anchor recesses. They also had a very wide funnel and a long clear fore deck which contained three holds worked by cranes. On trials, *Flandre*'s twin-screw geared-turbines produced an average speed of 25 knots, three more than the required service speed. As built, she carried 403 first, 285 cabin and 97 tourist class passengers in dormitory cabins. All first class cabins were air-conditioned and had private facilities. Two suites-de-luxe were situated at the after end of the boat deck. The first class public rooms were fitted out to a very high standard with light-coloured veneers and leather-covered chairs. The library had 2,000 books whilst the glass dance floor in the smoking room was illuminated from below by frequently-changing coloured lights. In the two-deck air-conditioned dining room, there was a separate dining area for children. Unfortunately, *Flandre*'s maiden voyage was marred by breakdowns and she was temporarily withdrawn until the spring of 1953. In 1962, following the introduction of *France* on the New York service, she was painted white and joined her sister on the West Indies run. In 1968 she was sold to Costa Armatori and converted into the single-class, 748-capacity cruise ship *Carla C*. Six years later her turbine engines, which had caused endless problems, were replaced with diesels. In the meantime, *Antilles* which remained in the French Line fleet was lost in a fire in 1971. By a strange twist of fate her sister, which had been sold by Costa in 1992, was also destroyed by fire in 1994 at Piraeus as Epirotiki Line's *Pallas Athena*.

The last of the Congo boats

Having lost most of its passenger ships during the war, Compagnie Belge Maritime ordered a quartet of replacement passenger-cargo motor ships which were delivered between 1948 and 1951. These 10,900gt, single-screw ships had more cargo space than the pre-war *Baudouinville* and carried fewer passengers, but had none of the style of the earlier liner. However, despite increased competition for airlines, they were usually fully booked and in 1952 the final pair of CMB liners was ordered to meet the growth in passenger numbers. The 13,724gt *Jadotville*, shown here, and her slightly-larger sister *Baudouinville* were delivered in 1956 and 1957 respectively. Unlike the earlier ships, these single-class, 300-capacity liners were driven by steam turbines. They were handsome vessels with a tall streamlined Lascroux-type funnel and curved bow. Despite having limited air-conditioning, all cabins were outboard with many also having private facilities. They also had short careers with CMB and after the horrific upheavals on the Congo following independence in 1960, they were sold to P&O and operated between the UK and the Far East as *Chitral* and *Cathay*. Although the former was scrapped in 1975, *Cathay* was bought by the Chinese state-owned China Ocean Shipping Company and as *Shanghai* was reported to have only been broken up in 2007.

Zim Line German-built reparation transatlantic liners

In 1952 the West Germany-Israel reparations pact was signed at Bonn. Under the agreement West Germany paid for the loss of property taken from Jews persecuted by the Nazis, and the cost of the resettlement in Israel. Part of the funds was loaned to Zim Line so that it could modernise its fleet. Between 1954 and 1961 thirty-five new ships were built in West Germany for the line, including four passenger liners: *Israel*, *Zion* (below), *Jerusalem* and *Theodor Herzl*. Two were placed on the Atlantic run and two on the Mediterranean service. The first passenger ships ordered under the reparations agreement were the 9,855gt transatlantic passenger-cargo liners, *Israel* and *Zion*, which were delivered in 1955 and 1956 respectively. These handsome, turbine-driven, single-screw steamships had attractive lines with a raked stem and cruiser stern. Built by Deutsche Werft, Hamburg they had accommodation for 312 passengers in two classes. All cabins had sea views and in first class there was a lift, a most unusual feature on ships of this size. The interior decoration was modern and reflected the egalitarian style of the new nation of Israel. Cargo was carried in five holds with a total capacity of 280,000ft^3 and ample refrigerated space. There was also a garage for thirty cars, which were loaded through side doors. With a service speed of 19 knots *Israel* and *Zion* provided a year round, three weekly service between Haifa and New York with a fourteen-day crossing time, including stops at Naples and Gibraltar. In 1966 they were sold to Portuguese buyers. *Zion* went to Empresa Insulana de Navegação and was renamed *Angra do Heroísmo* whilst *Israel* became *Amélia de Mello* for the Sociedade Geral de Commércio of Lisbon. This period was at the height of the Portuguese colonial war and soon afterwards Portuguese passenger shipping suffered a major decline. Whilst *Angra do Heroísmo* was scrapped in 1974, *Amélia de Mello* outlasted her sister by almost thirty years. Sold in 1972 to Greece, she was converted into the popular 750-capacity cruise ship *Ithaca*, which was chartered by Thomson Holidays. In 1979 she moved to Florida, was renamed *Dolphin IV* and spent most of the remainder of her career on short cruises to the Bahamas. After a period of lay-up, she was demolished at Alang in 2003.

The revolutionary *Southern Cross*

Shaw Savill Line's 20,203gt *Southern Cross* of 1955 was one of the most successful passenger liners of the second half of the twentieth century. Not only was she the first liner to be launched by a reigning British monarch but also she introduced a new engines-aft layout which has become commonplace in passenger ships of today. Because on-going waterfront strikes in Australia and New Zealand were causing havoc with sailing schedules of large passenger-cargo liners such as *Dominion Monarch* it was decided to order from Harland and Wolff a single class passenger-only liner. With her engine machinery and boiler room as far aft as possible, the 1,437 passengers could enjoy unrestricted access to all parts of the ship as well as 42,000ft^2 of deck space. Because she did not carry cargo she was also able to make four round-the-world voyages instead of three in the passenger-cargo ships. All cabins were air-conditioned as were the cinema lounge and the two main restaurants. Although Matson Line's *Lurline* (1908/6,572gt) was the world's first ocean-going passenger ship with engines aft, *Southern Cross* was the first large passenger-only engines-aft ocean liner. Her contemporary-design public rooms were of a high standard and were in some ways better than first class on the first post-war Union-Castle mailships. Her fares were also lower than P&O, Orient, New Zealand Line and Union-Castle with passengers able to use the whole ship instead of being confined to the stern area. Unlike *Dominion Monarch* she was a commercial success for Shaw Savill and in the first years of her career she was often fully booked. This led to an order for a similarly-designed running mate, *Northern Star*, which was delivered in 1962.

Unfortunately this ship had a short life of only thirteen years because of engine problems. With passenger number declining *Southern Cross* was sold in 1974 to a Greek company. She was converted into a 950-capacity cruise ship and renamed *Calypso*. Six years later she was again sold, this time to the Miami-based Eastern Cruise Line and renamed *Azure Seas*. Despite numerous owners and another name change to *OceanBreeze* she remained a popular cruise ship in Caribbean waters until her sale to Bangladeshi breakers in 2003.

Cunard's Canadian quartet

Between 1954 and 1957, four 22,000g intermediate passenger-cargo liners were built on the Clyde by John Brown for Cunard Line's Liverpool to Canada service. Built in pairs, *Saxonia*, *Ivernia*, *Carinthia* and *Sylvania* were handsome, 20-knot, twin-screw steamships with a distinctive domed-top funnel and a tall signal mast with a crow's nest abaft the bridge. Fitted with stabilisers they also had a large cargo capacity of 300,000ft^3 and carried around 900 passengers, mainly in tourist class. The interior décor of the first two liners, *Saxonia* (below) and *Ivernia*, reflected the optimistic colours and designs of the 1950s. Many of the designs were also based on Canadian decorative themes. For example, the Mounties Bar on *Ivernia* featured chequered furniture fabrics whilst the floor pattern included a sergeant's stripes. The colours of the public rooms were unlike anything seen previously on a Cunard liner. With its windows overlooking the bow, *Saxonia*'s first class 'Chintz Lounge' had a pink sheet-plastic wall panel studded with painted mirrors and fan-shaped ceiling lighting. The tourist class cabins also featured bright colours schemes for the carpets, curtains and bed covers. For the second pair of Canadian liners, *Carinthia* and *Sylvania*, Cunard returned to more traditional designs. The result was a mishmash of styles, clearly illustrated by the classical columns and pilasters and eighteenth century-style chairs in *Sylvania*'s first class restaurant. On *Carinthia*, the dining room chairs came from *Aquitania*. Although the quartet had ample deck space, a modern cinema and partial air-conditioning most tourist class passengers had to use shared bathroom facilities. Initially used on the Liverpool service, *Saxonia* and *Ivernia* were transferred to the Southampton–Le Havre–Quebec–Montreal route in 1957 whilst the second pair remained at Liverpool. In 1967, *Sylvania* sailed for Halifax and New York on the last transatlantic voyage for Cunard from Liverpool. This was also the last Cunard intermediate sailing. The following year, she and *Carinthia* were sold to Sitmar Line. Meanwhile their elder sisters, having been converted in 1963 into dual-purpose cruise and transatlantic liners, had been renamed *Carmania* (ex-*Saxonia*) and *Franconia* (ex-*Ivernia*). Painted in 'cruising green' they were fitted with a large lido deck, heated pool, sports deck and four sixty-passenger launches. Later in the decade they became full time cruise ships but with high operating costs were laid up in 1971. Sold to the Soviet Government in 1973 they were renamed respectively, *Leonid Sobinov* and *Fyodor Shalyapin*. Whilst the Russian pair had limited success, especially after the fall of the Soviet Union, the younger sisters operated as cruise ships until the early part of the twenty-first century with the former *Carinthia* the last to be sent for demolition in 2005.

The final 'Empress'

In the early 1950s air travel across the Atlantic was still in its infancy and many leading shipping lines believed that there would still be a demand for sea travel. Despite owning an airline, Canadian Pacific decided to order two new liners for its Liverpool to Montreal service especially as its main competitor on the route, Cunard Line, was about to introduce the 21,637gt *Saxonia*, the first of four new liners built for the market to Canada. The 25,526gt *Empress of Britain*, the first completely air-conditioned passenger liner to be built in Britain, and the 25,585gt *Empress of England* were delivered in 1956 and 1957 respectively. The main emphasis of these new liners was on tourist class and in 1958 an order was placed with the Tyne shipbuilder Vickers-Armstrongs for a slightly larger liner of the same type, the 27,300gt *Empress of Canada* (right). Completed in 1960 she was designed as a two-class 1,048-capacity North Atlantic cargo-passenger liner and for winter cruising, mainly out of New York, with 750 one-class passengers. She had two more top decks than the earlier pair and the main passenger areas were given an easier-to-understand layout. She was the first 'Empress' to dispense with alphabetical passenger deck names. Decks were given functional names with the main public rooms situated on the Empress and Promenade Decks. These rooms were designed in a relatively simple modern style devoid of much artwork and could be described as rather bland. However, all first class cabins and 70 per cent of the tourist class cabins had private facilities. Fitted with stabilisers, she was also the first Canadian Pacific liner to be given a bulbous bow. She also had a new design of funnel. Twin-screwed and turbine-driven *Empress of Canada*'s design speed was 20 knots. By the mid-1960s air travel had made huge inroads into the Europe to Canada passenger market with over 350,000 arriving by air compared with only 26,000 by sea. *Empress of Britain* was sold to Greek Line in 1964, followed by *Empress of England* which was withdrawn in 1970. A year later Canadian Pacific decided to leave the ocean-going passenger shipping business. *Empress of Canada* brought to a close eighty years of Canadian Pacific passenger liners when she arrived for the final time at Liverpool in November 1971. She was sold to the newly-formed Carnival Cruise Lines as its first cruise ship. Renamed *Mardi Gras*, she remained in the Carnival fleet until 1993 when she was bought by Epirotiki Lines and renamed *Olympic*. In 2003 she arrived at Alang for demolition.

PSNC's Queen of the Seas

In 1956, Royal Mail's associate company Pacific Steam Navigation Company took delivery of its first new passenger liner for twenty five years. The 20,234gt, twin-screw, 18-knot *Reina del Mar*, 'Queen of the Seas', was designed as a replacement for the iconic *Reina del Pacifico* and also as a single-class cruise ship in the off-season. However unlike her older consort she was powered by geared turbines instead of diesel engines. She was also fully air-conditioned, fitted with stabilisers and carried 207 first, 216 cabin and 343 tourist class passengers. A handsome ship, she had a slightly curved rounded stem, tall foremast and a single streamlined funnel. Internally, she was very different from *Reina del Pacifico* with much use of modern materials such as Formica. Designed by a series of decorators, her décor was rather bland and included an extraordinary period-style first class card room with a pair of antique columns. All first class cabins had private facilities whilst children in first enjoyed a separate area with a large paddling pool and separate dining room. Hard hit by increased use of air travel and the cessation of Cuban calls after Fidel Castro's revolution in 1959, *Reina del Mar* proved to be an expensive ship to operate. At the time of her final line voyage to South America in 1963 she was running at an annual loss of around £250,000. Her place on the fortnightly service from Liverpool was taken by twelve-passenger capacity freighters. In 1964 she was transformed into a 1,047-capacity cruise ship. The conversion work, which included a cinema forward of her funnel and extended promenade deck, ruined her fine lines. She was subsequently operated by Union-Castle Line and painted in its colours. Union-Castle bought the ship in 1973 but because, of sharp increases in the price of oil, she was sold to Taiwanese breakers two years later. Aged only nineteen, this was an early end to PSNC's final liner.

The fastest Cape mailship

Pendennis Castle was ordered from Harland and Wolff in March 1955 as a replacement for the elderly *Arundel Castle* (1921/19,206gt). Designed as the third in the *Pretoria Castle* class of mail ships her keel was laid in November 1955 five weeks before the takeover of Union-Castle Line by the British and Commonwealth Shipping Company Ltd. The new owners decided to change her design and engine specifications to provide for greater speed. Not only was her forward hull shape modified but she was also lengthened by 16ft and Denny-Brown stabilisers were installed, a first for a Union-Castle mailship. This was a major undertaking as work at Belfast was well advanced by then. Her profile was also different from the earlier mailships. The first without a mainmast, she was a very distinctive liner with a reduced foremast, a signal mast abaft the bridge and a tall streamlined funnel. She was also the first mailship to have her name illuminated at the base of the funnel. Unfortunately, because of a last-minute strike by shipyard workers, the naming ceremony in December 1957 was performed without a launch and as a result British and Commonwealth vowed that it would never again have a ship built in Belfast. Handed over in November 1958, *Pendennis Castle*'s passenger capacity was 167 in first and 475 in tourist class. Her cruising speed was 22.5 knots whilst her cargo capacity was 581,979ft^3 in seven holds, of which 339,309ft^3 was available for refrigerated cargo. The layout of the main first class public rooms on the promenade deck was radically different from earlier mailships. It was less formal, especially as it did not have a long gallery connecting the first class lounge and the smoking room. For the first time there was also an open-air pool in first class whilst the tourist class pool was a permanent feature and not one fitted into a hatch opening. The company employed as their 'decorative consultant' the well-known English country house-style designer Jean Monro to oversee some of the new ship's designs which were more colourful than the earlier mail ships. The first class lido and sheltered pool area aft of the promenade deck had been a feature of Orient Line and P&O ships since the 1930s. For years the old-fashioned Union-Castle Line had condemned first class swimmers aboard the mailships to a pool in the bowels of the ship. All this changed with *Pendennis Castle* which is one of the reasons she was often referred to as a 'fun ship'. The light blue and turquoise glass mosaic pool was surrounded by a crescent shaped, raised terrace with tables and striped umbrellas. By the late 1950s air-conditioning had become the norm in many liners travelling through tropical waters. Once again, Union-Castle Line had been slow to modernise and *Pendennis Castle* was built with only partial air-conditioning. This was restricted to the dining rooms, hair-dressing saloons, hospital, shops and some first class cabins. First class cabins also had telephones and port-holes, albeit using the Bibby system. The new ship heralded a break with the past for Union-Castle Line and set the scene for the final pair of mailships. She was also a record-breaker for the company. In August 1969 she arrived at Cape Town, after setting the final southbound record for the company: ten days, eleven hours and forty-six minutes. For seventeen years she continued to serve her owners with a minimum of mishaps and earned herself the reputation of being the most efficient mailship the company had ever built, fully answering the best definition of a Union-Castle mailship which was 'a very large, fast cargo carrier married to extensive passenger accommodation'. In March 1974 the South African Conference lines announced plans to containerise the South Africa–Europe trade. Without cargo, the passenger-mail ships were no longer viable. Union-Castle struggled to maintain its new ships in service. Now losing £1 million a year, *Pendennis Castle* was the first of the new mailships to go. She was withdrawn in June 1976 and sold to a Hong Kong company. Renamed *Ocean Queen* she was laid up on arrival at Hong Kong. The following year she was resold and renamed first *Sinbad* and later that year, *Sinbad I*. In April 1980, after almost four years of inactivity, she was sold to Taiwanese breakers for scrap at Kaohsiung.

The final KNSM passenger-cargo liners

In 1957, a year after it celebrated its centenary, Koninklijke Nederlandse Stoomboot-Maatschappij (KNSM) took delivery of its final two passenger-cargo liners. The handsome 7,200gt, single-screw, 15.5-knot motor ships *Prins der Nederlanden* and *Oranje Nassua* were designed for the four weekly sailings from Amsterdam to the Caribbean and carried 116 passengers and 218,000ft^3 of cargo. There was also group accommodation for sixty-eight emigrants, soldiers and students. With Amsterdam as its hub, KNSM provided a unique, integrated cargo transhipment network using its fleet of small Mediterranean traders and Rhine vessels and barges which were owned by its subsidiary the Nieuwe Rijnvaart Maatschappij. *Prins der Nederlanden*, shown here, had a raked stem and a long forecastle separated by a well from the main superstructure which extended aft. This contained the comfortable, partially air-conditioned passenger accommodation which included a large dining room, lounge and smoking room. Like most Dutch ships, there was a special area for children who were cared for by a qualified nurse. Although there was no swimming pool, passengers had the use of a large open promenade deck for games and relaxation. Following the advent of containerisation on the route, *Prins der Nederlanden* and *Oranje Nassua* were laid up in 1972 and sold the following year to the Cuban government, renamed respectively *Vietnam Heroico* and *XX Aniversario*. The former *Prins der Nederlanden* capsized alongside at Havana in 1984 whilst her sister was broken up by 1990.

The Moore-McCormack twins

Moore-McCormack Lines also took delivery of two new passenger-cargo liners in 1958 to replace its pre-war 'Good Neighbor Fleet' ships on the New York to South America service. The construction and operation of these two liners were, like those built for Grace Line, heavily subsidised by the United States Federal Maritime Board. However, the major difference between the ships was that the Moore-McCormack pair were also designed to operate as cruise ships. The fully air-conditioned and stabilised 14,984gt *Brasil* (right) and *Argentina* were constructed by the Ingalls Shipbuilding Corporation, Pascagoula, Mississippi. Twin-screwed with geared turbines, they had sufficient power to produce a service speed of 23.5 knots. Like *Rotterdam*, which entered service a year later, they had two tall smoke exhausts aft but with an unusual dummy funnel with an enclosed passenger observation bridge forward. Within the dummy funnel was a sheltered solarium for all-over sun bathing. Superb accommodation was provided for 553 passengers, all in first class. The exceptionally large cabins, including four de-luxe suites, were all outboard with private facilities. The well-known designers Raymond Loewy Associates designed not only the cabins but also the spacious interiors. The décor of the main public rooms on the promenade deck was typical of the rather stark designs of the late 1950s. However, what was unusual was the open-plan nature of the main rooms which meant that from the entrance to the main lounge one could look aft some 230ft to the swimming pool area. Another unique feature was the Deck Café overlooking the pool and sport deck. Not only did it have a two-deck-high windowed wall but it also had, at its centre, a shaped smorgasbord for casual dining. There was also cinema and a special sports deck for children with a full-size pool. The teenager area had a soft drinks bar and a jukebox. Served by waitresses, the dining room could seat all passengers at a sitting. Interestingly, the galley on the deck below was accessed by escalators. The pair also had very efficient gear to handle the 335,350ft^3 of dry cargo. Whilst access to three of the seven holds were via weather-deck hatches, the remaining holds were served by side ports, conveyors and elevators. Also designed for cruising, *Brasil* and *Argentina* undertook a number of cruises during their first years of operation including a 62-day round-Africa 'Sea Safari' and a 35-day cruise to Northern Europe. In 1963 two new decks were added which increased their passenger capacity to 670 but made them look rather top-heavy. However, by the mid-1960s, despite annual subsidies, they were losing $2.7 million each year and in 1969 were laid up at Baltimore. In 1971 they were bought by Holland America Line. Converted into 693-capacity cruise ships, they were renamed *Volendam* (ex-*Brasil*) and *Veendam* (ex-*Argentina*). The former spent her final years as the school ship *Universe Explorer* and was beached at Alang in 2004. Her sister met a similar end a year earlier as *Enchanted Isle*.

Two new 'Santas'

In 1958 Grace Line replaced the 24-year-old *Santa Rosa* and *Santa Paula* with a pair of twin-screw 15,400gt passenger-cargo liners bearing the same names. Constructed at Newport News and designed by William Francis Gibbs' firm of naval architects, Gibbs and Cox, the new, 300-capacity, first class-only, geared turbine, 20-knot *Santa Rosa* (below) and *Santa Paula* were striking ships with a signal mast above the bridge and a large stream-lined funnel with flat smoke deflectors. The hull colour was now grey instead of the black of the earlier 'Santas', although the internal layout was broadly similar to the 1930s ships. Once again, all public rooms were on the Promenade Deck including the amidships dining room with musician's gallery, but without the roll back roof. The dining room itself could accommodate all passengers in a single sitting, whilst the pre-war practice of using wait-resses instead of waiters was continued. Forward was the Caribbean Lounge with panoramic windows on three sides, whilst at the after end of the promenade deck was the Club Tropicana with its bar and substantial dance floor. On the sun deck there were three large suites, each with a private balcony facing aft. On the top La Playa deck was a 34ft by 22ft kidney-shaped pool said to be the largest open-air pool afloat. A contemporary brochure claimed that 'indoors and out, they offer more living space per passenger than any other ship afloat'. The décor of the public rooms was a sharp contrast to the Georgian style of their pre-war namesakes. Although among the most luxurious liners of the day, the furnishings and fittings were typical of the stark design of the 1950s, with little use of wood because of stringent US fire regulations. The colour scheme was, however, bright and cheerful, and reflected the Caribbean and South American destinations of the ships. They were fully air-conditioned, and were also the first American liners with Sperry Gyrofin stabilisers. Cargo was very important and each vessel had six holds with a dry cargo capacity of 337,000ft^3, and refrigerated space for a further 81,450ft^3. The new Grace sisters were very popular, and one of them sailed from New York every Friday on a thirteen-day trip round the Caribbean. In 1969 the Grace Line fleet was sold to the Prudential Lines Inc. of New York and two years later both ships were laid up. *Santa Paula* was bought by the Greek cruise company, Sun Line. However, plans to convert her into a full-time cruise ship came to naught and she was sold in 1976 as a static hotel in Kuwait. In 1980, she opened as the Kuwait Marriott Hotel. A popular venue for weddings, she became the Ramada Al Salaam Hotel in 1989 but, like most of Kuwait, she was destroyed by fleeing Iraqi soldiers in 1990. Meanwhile, her sister *Santa Rosa*, after lying aban-doned for almost twenty years at Baltimore, was bought by Regency Cruises and was hideously converted into a 1,198-capacity cruise ship. Eventually owned by Louis Cruises, she was sold for scrap as *Emerald* in 2012.

Russian revival

At the end of the Second World War the USSR's shipbuilding industry and merchant shipping fleet lay in ruins with the loss of some 1,400 ships. As war reparations, it was allocated 154 German ships including most of the surviving large ocean liners. The successful work undertaken by East German yards in transforming the pre-war German liners led to an order with VEB Mathias-Thesen-Werft, Wismar for a series of twin-screw, 4,722gt passenger-cargo motor ships intended for the Leningrad-London, Black Sea and Far Eastern services. The first of these attractive small liners, *Michael Kalinin*, was delivered in September 1958. She was designed to carry 68 first, 78 second and 185 third class passengers and had a service speed of 18 knots. Despite her size, most cabins were outboard and included a de-luxe suite with a separate living room, bedroom and bath. First class on the upper deck included an elegant wood-panelled lounge forward with a dance floor. Between 1958 and 1964, nineteen of these ships were completed, making them the largest ever group of similar-size passenger liners. When she was new *Michael Kalinin* became the first modern passenger liner to visit the Antarctic when she carried members of the USSR Antarctic expedition to the Soviet base in late 1958. She was later modernised and during the 1970s and 1980s became a popular 250-passenger cruise ship. A regular visitor to Tilbury, she was sold to the breakers in 1994. After the fall of the Soviet Union in 1991, most of the remaining *Michael Kalinin*-class ships were broken up.

The last Holland-Afrika '-fontein'

In 1953 Holland-Afrika Lijn's passenger-cargo liner *Klipfontein* (1939/10,544gt) hit uncharted rocks five miles from the coast of Mozambique whilst racing Union-Castle Line's *Bloemfontein Castle* (1949/18,400gt) for the sole berth at Beira. Her loss was a major blow to Holland-Afrika Lijn but led to a replacement order in 1956 for the finest of all the '-fontein' ships, the 13,694gt *Randfontein*. This beautifully proportioned, twin-screw motor ship was built in Holland by the Wilton-Fijenoord yard at Schiedam. With a service speed of 18.5 knots, she was not only the fastest-ever Holland-Afrika liner, but also the first to carry more tourist class (166) passengers than first (123). Most of the first class cabins were outboard with hinged windows so that passengers, when seated, could overlook the sea. The overall design of the main public rooms was cheerfully simplistic but with occasional works of art. All cabins and dining rooms were air-conditioned whilst each class had its own swimming pool. Although she carried passengers *Randfontein* was very much a cargo ship with over half a million cubic feet of cargo space including refrigerated space for fruit and deep tanks for edible oils. Her cargo-handling equipment included cranes, derricks and a 50-ton heavy-lift derrick on the foremast. She entered service in 1959 and replaced *Bloemfontein* (1934/10,081gt) which was sold to the breakers. The 1960s were a period of great change on the Europe–South Africa run with increased competition from the new Union-Castle Line mailships and the gradual move away from sea to travel by air. In 1967 both *Oranjefontein* (1945/10,547gt) and *Jagersfontein* (1950/10,547gt) were withdrawn leaving *Randfontein* as the sole Holland-Afrika Lijn passenger liner. Three years later, on 1 July 1970, most of the major Dutch shipping lines including Holland-Afrika Lijn became part of a new Dutch shipping giant, Koninklijke Nedlloyd N.V. In the inevitable rationalisation which followed, it was announced that *Randfontein* would be transferred from the South African service to the Hong Kong–Australia route of Koninklijke Java-China Paketvaart Lijnen N.V. *Randfontein* brought to a close over fifty years of '-fontein' ships when she arrived at Rotterdam from South Africa in September 1971. Renamed *Nieuw Holland* she was only on the Hong Kong run for two years before her sale to China Ocean Shipping Company Ltd, Shanghai in 1974. Renamed *Yu Hai* she carried Chinese workers to East Africa and was subsequently used on the Chinese coastal trade as *Hai Xing*. In 1996 she was sent to Alang for demolition.

Rotterdam, the 'Grande dame'

After the invasion of Holland in 1940 plans for a running mate for *Nieuw Amsterdam*, Holland's great 'ship of state', were put on hold. It was only in 1955 that Holland-America Line was able to confirm an order with the Rotterdam Drydock Company for a new, two-class, 38,645-ton transatlantic liner which was the largest-ever Dutch-built passenger ship. Launched by Queen Juliana of The Netherlands, *Rotterdam* was delivered in August 1959. Her outward appearance caused quite a stir. Although she had the hull shape of a classic transatlantic liner, the customary large funnels amidships with the company colours were replaced by two tall smoke exhausts two thirds aft. The reason for this was the situation of the engine room towards the stern, allowing greater use of the internal and deck space for passengers. It also meant less soot on deck, which was a major problem on older ships. The Dutch naval architects used the advantages of this layout to the full and came up with an ingenious arrangement for the passenger accommodation which allowed both first and second class passengers the impression of the full run of the ship but without meeting. Traditionally on transatlantic liners, classes were separated vertically with first class taking up most of the amidships space. On *Rotterdam*, complete decks were allocated to each class, including separate promenade decks with public rooms. These were linked by a trick double staircase based on the one in the sixteenth-century French Château de Chambord. This combined with dividers and lifts set to stop at specific decks, allowed passengers in each class to move about freely without mingling. More importantly, *Rotterdam* was also designed to be used as a cruise ship during the winter months and this flexibility enabled her to be easily transformed into a single-class ship. This forward-thinking design was the key reason for *Rotterdam*'s longevity and why the ship's interior layout remained virtually intact. Like *Nieuw Amsterdam*, most of the public rooms were situated on the two promenade decks and whilst the first class areas in the upper promenade were slightly more formal, those in tourist class on the promenade deck were brighter with a more open feeling. Great use was made of wood, concealed lighting and beautiful artwork from Holland's leading artists, no more so than in one of the most stylish rooms afloat, the two-level Ritz-Carlton lounge overlooking the stern of the ship. At the forward end of the promenade decks was a two deck high, 600-seater theatre, then the largest of its kind. It had a huge movie screen with equipment able to project the latest widescreen films. The two main restaurants on 'B' deck were two decks high with impressive domed ceilings. They were connected by a vestibule and could accommodate 894 passengers in a single sitting. *Rotterdam*'s passenger capacity was 1,456 in flexible first and tourist class. The ship was also fully air-conditioned and fitted with stabilisers. She had twin screws with double reduction geared triple-expansion engines which produced a service speed of 20.5 knots. Her maiden voyage from Rotterdam to New York via Le Havre and Southampton took place in September 1959. The first of twenty-eight around-the-world cruises commenced from New York in January 1961 and she soon attracted a dedicated following with one of the highest repeat rates in the business. At that time she was the world's largest cruise liner. However, during the 1960s, increasing operational costs spelt the end of the transatlantic liner and in 1969 *Rotterdam* became a single class, full-time cruise ship. In 1973 the company was renamed Holland America Cruises. For the next twenty years *Rotterdam* remained the flagship of the line. In 1997, with new safety requirements impending, the company decided to retire the ship. She was sold to Premier Cruises and became *Rembrandt* but after the collapse of Premier in 2000, she was laid up at Freeport where she languished for the next four years. Rescue came when the Port of Rotterdam bought her for use as a visitor attraction in Rotterdam, where she arrived in 2008 repainted in her 1959 dove-grey colours. Over a million passengers travelled aboard Holland-America's former flagship which was undoubtedly the most successful cruise-liner of the twentieth century.

Chapter 9
The Last Hurrah of the Liner

Despite increasing numbers of travellers choosing to fly rather than travel by sea, the 1960s saw a final burst of liner building. Unfortunately this was often a case of too little too late and in many cases the ships had shorter lives than planned.

Orient Line and P&O's largest and fastest liners

The last liners built for Orient Line and P&O, the 41,915gt *Oriana* and 45,733gt *Canberra*, were delivered in 1960 and 1961 respectively. They were not only fast ships but also the largest liners built for a non-Atlantic service. Their size meant that they were too big to operate out of London and although registered there, their home port was Southampton. Whilst *Oriana*'s design followed the basic format of earlier Orient and P&O ships, *Canberra* was radically different and was inspired by another iconic British liner, Shaw Savill's engines-aft *Southern Cross* of 1955. The decision to fit her with turbo-electric engines enabled the space taken by the engines to be fitted as far aft as possible. Like modern cruise ships this offered large inter-connecting passenger spaces free of engine uptakes. However, this also caused her stern to be overweight and with additional ballast amidships her draft was deeper than planned for. As built, she carried 538 first class and 1,560 tourist class passengers. Although her profile was not as modern-looking as other liners of the time, her interiors, like *Oriana*, featured the best of modern contemporary British design and she was always a popular ship among Australian and British travellers. In 1971 charter flight rules to Australia and the Far East were relaxed, making it cheaper to fly than to go by sea. This had a major impact on the profitability of liners to Australia. In 1973, after a disastrous cruise season operating out of New York, it was announced that *Canberra* would be withdrawn from service. With so many cabins lacking private facilities, she was not popular with American travellers. However, it was decided to place *Canberra* on a round-the-world cruise in 1974 and she was converted into a single-class, 1,737-capacity full-time cruise ship. She remained in the fleet for another twenty-three years and despite numerous efforts to save the ship, in October 1997 she sailed on her last voyage to Pakistani breakers.

The revolutionary *Oriana*

With a service speed of over 27 knots, Orient Line's final liner was the 41,916gt *Oriana*. Delivered in 1960, she was designed for a fast service to Australia, New Zealand and across the Pacific to San Francisco and Vancouver. Unlike any passenger liner built before or since, she was a revolutionary vessel and arguably Britain's only truly modern liner, both inside and out. Her controversial exterior design with two small funnels (the aft one was a dummy) and rather boxy shape generated much negative and positive comment. A two-class ship, *Oriana* carried 685 first and 1,496 tourist class passengers. The upper part of her superstructure was made from aluminium and this enabled an extra deck to be added, which in turn significantly increased the spaciousness of the accommodation in both classes. Not only were there vast areas of open deck space for outdoor activities, passengers were also offered many innovative facilities including a 350-seater cinema. On her trials, *Oriana* managed over 30 knots and sailed from Southampton for Australia on her maiden voyage in December 1960. When she reached Sydney twenty-seven days later she became the largest and fastest on the Australian run, clipping four days off the record. After the integration of Orient Line into P&O in 1966, her hull was painted white and in 1974 she was converted into a single-class, 1,677-capacity cruise ship under the P&O Cruises banner. Between 1981 and 1986 she was based in Sydney and, a few months after her twenty-fifth birthday, she was withdrawn from service. Until she was broken up in 2005, she spent the last years as a static floating hotel and tourist attraction, firstly in Japan and finally at Dalian in north-east China.

Royal Mail's 'Three Graces'

Although the unfortunate *Magdalena* was not replaced, in 1956 Royal Mail Line ordered a trio of 20,350gt, twin-screw, 17.5-knot passenger-cargo motor ships from Harland and Wolff for delivery in 1960. Painted white, they were designed as replacements for the ageing 'Highland' ships on the all-important London–River Plate route. Known as the 'Three Graces', *Amazon*, *Aragon* and *Arlanza* were probably the most attractive of all Royal Mail liners. They had the usual split-superstructure feature but with a raked stem, cruiser stern, a tripod mast above the bridge and a streamlined funnel to ensure maximum smoke abatement. Each had 435,000ft^3 of insulated cargo space and carried 107 first, 82 cabin and 275 third class passengers in attractive but not ostentatious accommodation. Not only did they have Denny-Brown stabilisers, they were also full air-conditioned. All first class staterooms had either a private bath or shower, whilst each class had its own open-air swimming pool. They were also the first British ships to have galley escalators. These attractive ships had relatively short careers because of falling passenger numbers and a downturn in beef imports from Argentina following an outbreak of foot and mouth disease in Britain. They were also expensive to operate and in 1969 the Furness Withy Group, which had taken over Royal Mail Line in 1965, decided to bring to an end to Royal Mail Line's South American passenger service after 118 years. The 'Three Graces' were transferred to Shaw Savill Line, another Furness Withy subsidiary. Changed into single-class ships they were sold in 1971 to Norwegian owners following a major review of the company's costs. Transformed beyond recognition into car carriers, they were sent to the breakers in 1983.

Replacement for *Andrea Doria*

In 1952 Italia Line took delivery of one of its finest transatlantic ships, the 29,083gt *Andrea Doria*. She and her sister *Christoforo Colombo*, completed in 1954, were at the time Italy's largest liners. Unfortunately *Andrea Doria* sank in 1956 after she was hit by the Swedish American liner *Stockholm* (1948/11,700gt) and a replacement ship was ordered soon afterwards. The 33,340gt, 25-knot *Leonardo da Vinci*, completed at Genoa-Sestri by Cantiere Navale Ansaldo in 1960, is often thought of as the most attractive of all the Italian transatlantic liners. Although she had a similar profile to *Andrea Doria* and *Christoforo Colombo*, her lines were finer, especially her after decks which had no cargo-handling gear. She also had a raked bow with a bulbous forefoot, an elegant spoon-shaped stern and a superstructure dominated by a massive funnel and a streamlined mast above the bridge. A twin-screw turbine ship, her engine room machinery layout was most unusual. In order to provide maximum protection against flooding she had two complete machine rooms, one for each propeller shaft. Her engine room spaces were also designed for conversion into possible nuclear propulsion. With one deck more than the earlier ships she suffered initially from stability problems and had to have 500 tons of extra ballast added which significantly increased her fuel consumption. She was also the first Italian liner to be fitted with two sets of Denny Brown stabilisers. She carried 413 first, 342 cabin and 571 tourist class passengers in fully air-conditioned accommodation. All first and cabins class cabins had private facilities as did 80 per cent of those in tourist, whilst the majority of the first class cabins were outboard and many had windows instead of portholes. The outdoor areas on *Leonardo da Vinci* were vast and covered an area of 32,000ft^2 with much of the space given to lidos. There were five swimming pools, one for each class and two for children. As to be expected on a prestigious Italian liner of that time, the modern interior design of the public rooms was outstanding. Many well-known designers were involved with her décor including Gustavo Pulitzer Finali and Nino Zoncada. The main first class foyer was panelled in rosewood and featured a silver relief of Leonardo da Vinci's head at the side of a golden staircase. Interesting sculptures were attached to the walls of the main restaurant whilst the Tapestry Lounge with its large wooden dance floor was lined with sets of modern Italian tapestries. Although she operated mainly on the Genoa to New York service *Leonardo da Vinci* was also used extensively for cruises. However, like all Italian liners she was heavily subsidised and, faced with rising fuel prices, in 1973 the Italian Government announced that it would withdraw support for all long-distance passenger liners by 1978. *Leonardo da Vinci* took the final North Atlantic crossing by an Italian liner in March 1977. After a series of cruises she was laid up at La Spezia in September 1978 where she was destroyed by fire two years later.

The beautiful *France*

Launched in 1960 by Madame de Gaulle, the 66,348gt *France* was seen as a symbol of the resurgence of French pride and prestige after the shame of the Second World War. She was also heavily subsidised by the French Government and built at a time when the writing was already on the wall for the transatlantic liner. Airlines now carried three times more passengers than those who went by sea. However, French Line needed a replacement for the ageing *Ile de France* and *Liberté* and four years earlier the company had signed a contract with the shipyard Chantiers de L'Atlantique for a 31-knot, quadruple-screw, turbine-driven ship able to cross between Le Havre and New York in five days. *France* was completed in 1961 and during her trials reached a speed of over 35 knots. Although smaller in tonnage than her predecessor *Normandie* she was the longest liner in the world and remained so for over forty years. Beautifully proportioned, she had two large red, black-topped funnels with wings either side for smoke dispersal. At the time she was the largest two-class liner in the world with 407 first and 1,637 tourist class passengers. She was also the first large liner to have two enclosed promenade decks and at the forward end of these promenade decks was the largest theatre-cinema (700-seater) afloat where both first and tourist class passengers could enjoy the same entertainment. However, *France*'s interiors were a disappointment for those who had been used to the decorative splendour of earlier liners. She was all metal, plastic and glass and the epitome of 1960s design. Despite this, she had many redeeming features, including great cuisine with a wide choice on the menu and complimentary wine with each meal. In February 1962 she sailed from Le Havre on her maiden Atlantic crossing, arriving in New York five days later. Ten years later the former *Queen Elizabeth* was destroyed by fire at Hong Kong and *France* became the largest passenger ship in the world. Despite her popularity and numerous cruises during the winter months, rising fuel costs forced the French Government to withdraw its subsidy in 1974. Her short career under the French flag came to a premature end in September of that year when disgruntled crewmembers seized the ship and she was laid up at Le Havre. Sold initially in 1977 to Saudi interests, in 1979 she was sold again, this time to the Norwegian shipowner Knut Kloster. Kloster, seen by many as the father of modern cruising, formed Norwegian Caribbean Lines in 1966. He was the first to build a fleet of purpose-built ships for cruising in the Caribbean and his purchase of the world's largest passenger ship, soon to become *Norway*, changed the industry forever. Up to then, the optimum size for a cruise ship was about 20,000 tons but with the introduction of the 70,000-ton *Norway*, increasingly larger ships were ordered. The transformation from *France* to *Norway* took place in Germany and was one of the most impressive conversions ever undertaken. The naval architects managed to change her from a two-class transatlantic liner into a single-class, 1,944-capacity cruise ship operating in tropical waters, with relatively little change to her beautiful exterior lines. Her decks were extended aft to provide more open deck space than any other cruise ship. With a multitude of passenger facilities, she was also the first cruise ship to be marketed as a floating resort. As she no longer needed great speed, her forward engine room was shut down and her two outer propellers removed. She entered service as *Norway* in June 1980 and, although she lost her top spot as the world's largest cruise ship to Royal Caribbean's *Sovereign of the Seas* in 1987, she remained the longest until the advent of Cunard Line's *Queen Mary 2* in 2003. *Norway* became one of the most successful cruise ships of all time and remained in the NCL fleet until 2004. In 2006 she arrived at Alang for demolition.

The last Cape mailships

In 1960 and 1961 respectively Union-Castle Line took delivery of its final passenger-cargo, turbine-driven mail-ships, the 37,640gt *Windsor Castle* and the 32,697gt *Transvaal Castle* (below). Whilst *Windsor Castle* was the company's largest mailship and last two-class liner, her younger sister was the only single-class mailship built. She certainly was a revolutionary ship. With first class passenger numbers falling and the ever-present threat of more people travelling by air, the company decided to build a ship in which all passengers shared the same public facilities but had a choice as to what type of cabin they wished to travel in. Dubbed a hotel ship, there were eleven grades of cabins ranging from an inner three- or four-berth cabin to a suite with a bedroom and sitting room. She was delivered not long after Orient Line's iconic *Oriana* (1960/41,915gt) and P&O's *Canberra* (1961/45,720gt). Although all three ships used a number of well-known designers for the interiors, the two Australian service liners were showcases for contemporary art and design whereas the new Union-Castle ship was the usual mixture of old fashioned and modern design with floral chintz material much in evidence in cabins. The positioning of the eight hatches on *Transvaal Castle* was also a major challenge for the naval architects. On the two-class mail ships the task was relatively easy because of the divided accommodation. However, on a single class ship with public rooms and deck areas taking up entire decks, more unusual methods had to be used including the opening for No 6 hatch which was situated in the Golden Room lounge where a large section of the floor was a hydraulically-operated, flush-with-the-deck hatch cover. A major dining innovation on *Transvaal Castle* was the introduction of waitresses. This was the first time female staff had been employed by a British ocean-going company for this kind of service. With a more compact superstructure and tall, detached funnel, *Transvaal Castle* was different from *Windsor Castle* and arguably had a more distinctive profile. She also had a beautiful clipper bow and was among the first British passenger liners to be fitted with a bulbous bow. Overall she presented a very attractive and symmetrical profile. Her cargo capacity consisted of 635,500ft^3 of cargo space, 363,600ft^3 of which was refrigerated, and she carried 728 passengers. Although she managed 24.7 knots on her trials, her service speed was 23 knots. After only four years in Union-Castle colours in January 1966 she was sold to the South African Marine Corporation Limited's British subsidiary. Painted white, she was renamed *S.A. Vaal* although her crew and management remained with Union-Castle Line. In February 1969 her ownership was transferred from the British subsidiary to the parent company South African Marine Corporation Limited and she was registered at Cape Town. In October 1977, following the decision to cease the UK–South Africa passenger-mail service, she took the final passenger-mail ship departure and brought to an end 120 years of the passenger-mail service to South Africa. Sold to the six-year-old Carnival Cruise Lines she was sent to Japan for a major transformation into a 1,750-capacity cruise ship. Renamed *Festivale*, she started weekly cruises to the Caribbean from Miami in October 1978. At the time she was the largest and fastest cruise ship sailing from Miami to the Caribbean. In 1998, after twenty years with Carnival she became part of the Premier Cruise Lines' fleet as *IslandBreeze* and then *The Big Red Boat III*. Unfortunately Premier collapsed in 2000 and after three years laid up at Freeport, Bahamas she was sold to Indian breakers. Meanwhile *Windsor Castle*, renamed *Margarita L.*, had been sold to John S. Latsis the Greek oil and shipping tycoon in 1977 and converted into a 852-berth floating accommodation ship. In 2005 she too went to India for demolition.

The last Portuguese liners

1961 saw the final flurry of Portuguese liners with each of the leading shipping lines taking delivery of a new flagship. These were Empresa Insulana de Navegação's 9,824gt *Funchal* designed for service to the Portuguese-owned Madeira and the Azores and two African liners, Companhia Nacional de Navegação's 19,393gt *Principe Perfeito* and Companhia Colonial de Navegação's 23,306gt *Infante Dom Henrique*. The most significant of the three was undoubtedly the 20-knot, turbine-driven, twin-screw *Infante Dom Henrique*. Constructed by S.A. Cockerill, the Belgium yard which built *Vera Cruz* and *Santa Maria*, she was Portugal's largest liner. She had a very attractive profile with a raked bow, streamlined superstructure, tall signal mast and a distinctive Lascroux-type funnel which sloped aft. Her overall appearance was further enhanced by a new grey hull colour scheme. She was fully air-conditioned and carried 156 first and 862 tourist class passengers. All first class cabins were outboard with private facilities. There were also four deluxe suites which were situated just below the navigating bridge. The main public rooms for first, forward, and tourist, aft, were situated on the lower promenade deck. The up-to-date modern interiors were devoid of classical features or wood panels and made great use of concealed lighting. The décor was themed around the early Portuguese explorers and Prince Henry the Navigator (Infante Dom Henrique) in particular. In the 164-seater first class dining room, there was large multi-coloured enamelled panel on this theme whilst in the first class hall on the lower promenade deck was a large bronze statue of Infante Dom Henrique. Throughout the ship there were many fine artworks including a series of murals in the hall for the deluxe suites depicting the life of Prince Henry and his brothers. The interior style in first class was also reflected in tourist class which had similar facilities to those in first including a swimming pool and a single-sitting dining room. *Infante Dom Henrique* ran on the Lisbon to Beira route for fourteen years but in 1976, two years after independence was declared in Angola and Mozambique, she was withdrawn from service and joined *Principe Perfeito* which had been laid up in Lisbon in 1975. *Infante Dom Henrique* was converted into a floating hotel and accommodation ship based in Sines from 1977 to 1986. She later had a chequered career as cruise ship, first as *Vasco de Gama* and then *SeaWind Crown* before being scrapped in 2004. Meanwhile, *Principe Perfeito* became an accommodation ship and was sold to breakers in 2001. This leaves *Funchal* (right) as the sole surviving Portuguese liner.

The nuclear ship *Savannah*

In 1955 President Eisenhower proposed that the United States build the world's first atomic-powered merchant vessel to demonstrate to the world America's peaceful use of the atom. This would be the ultimate advance in marine engineering and a far cry from the direct-acting, single-expansion engines in regular use 100 years earlier. The 13,599gt, passenger-cargo liner *Savannah* was completed in 1961 by the New York Shipbuilding Corporation at Camden, New Jersey. Designed by George G Sharp Inc. she was a beautiful ship with a flared bow, streamlined superstructure and modified cruiser stern. The nuclear reactor was situated forward of the bridge with the steam turbines which drove her single screw slightly further aft. At a cruising speed of 21 knots she could travel 336,000 nautical miles on a single fuel load. Her 746,200ft^3 of cargo was also handled by unusual rigged booms in lieu of normal king-posts. The air-conditioned accommodation for her sixty passengers was ultra-modern with an elegant carpeted lounge forward on the promenade deck. At the after end were the swimming pool and a veranda with large windows, cocktail bar and dance floor. All cabins had either a bath or shower. After extensive trials and testing *Savannah*'s maiden voyage via the Panama Canal took place in 1962 when she visited US West Coast ports and Hawaii. In 1964, managed by American Export Isbrandtsen Lines, she made her first transatlantic crossing which included a series of goodwill visits. Although she was generally well received, many people, especially in Australia, New Zealand and Japan, were concerned about the safety of such a ship and this constrained the extent of her operations. Her principal route therefore was between the USA and the Mediterranean ports but in 1965 it was decided that she should operate without passengers. She continued on the route until 1971 when she was laid up at her home port of Savannah. Saved from the breakers *Savannah* was designated a National Historic Landmark in 1991 and is now moored at Baltimore.

The last large French Africa liner

Paquet's twin-screw, 22.5-knot, 14,224gt *Ancreville* of 1962 was the last large French Africa liner. Unlike her predecessors she had diesel engines and was built at St-Nazaire by Chantiers de l'Atlantique. Named after the birthplace of the company's founder, she was painted white and had a distinctive profile with a split-funnel amidships. A three-class, fully air-conditioned liner with stabilisers, she was also designed to be used as a one-class cruise ship. She carried 171 in first, 342 in tourist and 243 in standard. Every cabin had a window or porthole whilst each class had its own swimming pool. The standard class pool was on the fore deck. The layout of first class was unusual with the main public rooms, apart from the cinema, situated aft. The modern stylish décor of *Ancreville*'s interiors was typical of the early 1960s and was rather stark by today's standards. In 1964 Paquet ordered a smaller 11,723gt version of for its Marseilles–Israel service. *Renaissance* was completed in 1966 and became a full-time cruise ship. *Ancreville* meanwhile continued to operate on the Marseilles–Casablanca–Dakar service until 1973 when she was sold to the People's Republic of China and renamed *Minghua*. Used for a while as a passenger ship to Australia, in 1983 she became a static leisure centre at Shekou, southern China. Renamed *Shekou Sea World* she remains in existence whilst *Renaissance* had a successful career as a cruise ship and was only broken up in 2010.

Russia's poet class

The early 1960s was a great period for the Soviet Union as it re-emerged from behind the Iron Curtain in the post-Stalin era, onto the world's stage. Not only did it put the first man in space but also socialism was on the rise after the Cuban revolution in 1959. Soviet influence and trade was spreading in Africa, South America and Asia and by the mid-1960s it is estimated that Soviet merchant ships were calling at over 800 ports in 90 different countries. To deal with this expansion, the USSR started a huge rebuilding programme for its merchant fleet and this included large passenger liners. In 1960 a further order was placed with Mathias-Thesen Werft, the East German yard which had built the *Michael Kalinin*-class ships, this time for a large single-class, 19,861gt passenger ship, *Ivan Franko*, which could be used for cruising and for liner services. In fact, five of these impressive 750-capacity ships were built between 1964 and 1972. They were named after famous Russian, Georgian and Ukrainian poets and writers. Three, *Ivan Franko*, *Taras Shevchenko* and *Shota Rustaveli*, shown here, were registered at Odessa under the ownership of the Black Sea Steamship Company whilst two, *Aleksandr Pushkin* and *Mikhail Lermontov*, were registered at Leningrad under the ownership of the Baltic Steamship Company. *Ivan Franko* was the first to be delivered in 1963. Like the others in her class she was a twin-screw motor ship with an average speed of 20 knots. She had a raked bow, ice-strengthened hull, rounded stern and pronounced sheer whilst her superstructure was tiered with a single mast and a streamlined funnel which gave her a striking and distinctive profile. Although many cabins did not have private facilities all were outboard. She also had a shop, cinema and a heated indoor swimming pool with a sliding roof. In 1974 her passenger accommodation was improved when her boat and saloon decks were extended forward, slightly spoiling her well-balanced superstructure. Meanwhile, in 1966 *Aleksandr Pushkin* inaugurated the first regular Russian transatlantic service since 1909 and the first to Canada. She was also required by the Atlantic Conference to operate as a two-class ship and was very popular with younger passengers and tourists to Europe. After the 1979 Russian invasion of Afghanistan she ceased her Canadian operations in 1980. All five ships were used not only as cruise ships but also by the Russian military as they had additional space for a large number of troops. In 1986 *Mikhail Lermontov* was wrecked off the coast of New Zealand whilst the three Odessa liners were sold to the breakers between 1997 and 2005. The sole survivor of the class is *Aleksandr Pushkin* which was converted into the popular cruise ship *Marco Polo* in 1993.

The unique passenger-livestock carrier *Centaur*

Blue Funnel's 8,262gt, twin-screw *Centaur* was a highly unusual ship. Not only did she carry 190 passengers but she also had space for 4,500 sheep and 50 dairy cows, for producing the ship's cream and butter, or alternatively 700 cattle. The livestock was loaded through side doors in the ship's hull. Designed for the service between Fremantle and Singapore she replaced two elderly ships on the route, *Gorgon* (1933/3,533gt) and *Charon* (1936/3,703gt). Constructed on the Clyde by John Brown, she was delivered in 1964. Her engines and superstructure were well aft to give clear space forward for her holds and sports deck. The whole of her bottom was also specially strengthened to withstand the stresses incurred when she went aground for a few hours at the ports of Derby and Broome, North-west Australia to load cattle for Fremantle. In addition to conventional derricks, she also had cranes, which was a first for Blue Funnel. Powered by Burmeister and Wain diesels, her service speed was 20 knots. The passenger accommodation on *Centaur* was unpretentious and functional with relatively small public rooms and very basic seating in the dining room. Although she was fitted with stabilisers and was fully air-conditioned, a surprising number of cabins did not have private facilities. A Blue Funnel spokesperson rather arrogantly summed up the accommodation as follows. 'Great luxury is not wanted in passenger ships today. Passengers look for clean lines and simplicity.' In 1979 her route changed when she starting making round trips from Fremantle to Hong Kong via Manila and Singapore.

With declining cargo and passengers, she made her final voyage from Fremantle in 1982. She was then chartered to St. Helena Shipping for a year on the St. Helena service which operated between Avonmouth and Cape Town followed by a year in layup. She was sold to a Shanghai-based company in 1985. As *Hai Da* she sailed between Hong Kong and Shanghai and was reportedly broken up in 2006.

The unlucky *Shalom*

Zim Line's largest liner *Shalom* was an unlucky ship. She also had one of the shortest careers of any 'ship of state'. Ordered in 1960 from Chantiers de l'Atlantique, St-Nazaire, the 24,500gt, 21-knot liner was designed to reduce the sailing time between Haifa and New York by two days. Zim wanted to operate her as a single-class liner but the Atlantic Passenger Conference required a two-class system, which is why she originally carried 1,018 tourist-class passengers and only 72 in first. Her original name was to be *King David*. This was later changed to *King Solomon* and eventually *Shalom*. Shalom means peace, which is not the word used to describe the furore that broke out over the ship's kosher-only kitchens. The requirement by the religious authorities in Israel for kosher catering limited the appeal of the ship, especially among American Jewish and non-Jewish travellers. Delayed by the shipyard, *Shalom* sailed from Haifa on her maiden voyage to New York in April 1964. In October, she had a refit to double the number in first class and the following month, leaving New York in fog, she sliced a Norwegian tanker in two. Nineteen of the tanker's crew were killed and *Shalom* was out of service for almost two months. The following year, despite a winter cruising programme, the ship made large losses, exacerbated by expensive Israeli crew. In May 1967, the three-year-old pride of Israel was sold to the Deutsche Atlantik Linie of Hamburg and renamed *Hanseatic*. For a while during her brief German career she was the largest German-owned liner. In 1973, with German Atlantic in financial difficulties, she was sold to Home Line and operated as *Doric* until 1981 when she was bought by Royal Cruise Line. Renamed *Royal Odyssey* she was given an extensive refit, which included the replacement of her twin funnels with a single larger one. She was soon rated among the top cruise ships in the world and in 1988 was again sold, this time to Regency Cruises as *Regent Sun*. In 1995 Regency Cruises folded and she was laid up at Nassau where she languished until her sale six years later to Indian breakers. In July 2001 she sank under tow off the coast of South Africa.

The biggest and fastest ships on the Sunny Southern Atlantic Route

Italia's largest and fastest liners, the 45,900gt *Michelangelo* and *Raffaello*, should never have been built. They were originally conceived in 1956 as sisters to *Leonardo da Vinci* but with changing trends in Atlantic travel it was decided that larger and faster vessels were required. They were also part of an Italian state-subsidised building programme and as such became, like *France* and *United States*, a national prestige project. Completed in 1965 they took almost five years to build mainly because of Italian Government requirements that a large proportion of the furnishings had to be supplied by Italian firms. They were unique-looking ships with an extreme flared bow, old-fashioned squared-off bridge front and a pair of lattice-work funnels, the likes of which have been never seen before or since. Designed by the Turin Politecnico they were very effective at dispersing smoke high over the stern. Fitted with two sets of Denny Brown stabilisers, the sisters had twin screws driven by powerful geared turbine engines which gave the liners a maximum speed of 29 knots and a cruising speed of 27 knots. They also had two separate machine rooms like *Leonardo da Vinci* and provision was made for conversion to nuclear power. Fully air-conditioned and carrying 535 first, 550 cabin and 742 tourist class passengers, they were the first transatlantic liners to offer private facilities in all classes. One oddity of their design was the lack of portholes for cabins on the three lowest decks which was a major problem when the ships were used on cruises. There were also six open-air swimming pools, three of which were for children. The first class lido and pool area was situated forward of the funnels. The thirty public rooms included a 425-capacity cinemascope theatre with balcony seating. Once again, some of Italy's finest designers worked on the decor of the public rooms, the most magnificent being the first class ballroom on *Michelangelo* with its domed ceiling and large chandeliers. However, the interiors of the pair came in for criticism as it was felt that with their vastness some of the public rooms had lost something of the cosy, intimate atmosphere of early ships. When *Michelangelo* and *Raffaello* entered service in 1965 Italia Line confidently expected load factors of 80 per cent in a market which was not only experiencing falling passenger numbers but also faced increased competition from Greek Line and Zim Line. Unfortunately, these targets were seldom met with the number of passengers crossing the Atlantic down by 50 per cent three years after they entered service. By 1975 suffering large losses, they were withdrawn after only ten years on their intended route. They were laid up together at La Spezia before being sold in 1976 to Iran as floating barracks for the Imperial Iranian Navy. During the Iran-Iraq War *Raffaello* was destroyed in 1982 whilst her sister eventually went to Pakistani breakers in 1991.

Oceanic, the ship of tomorrow

Home Lines 27,645gt *Oceanic* is regarded by many as one of the most significant passenger ships of the twentieth century and more akin to a modern cruise ship than a liner built in 1965. She was originally ordered in 1961 from Cantieri Riuniti dell'Adriatico, Trieste as a two-class (220 first and 1,370 tourist) transatlantic liner for Home Lines service between Germany and Canada. However, the arrival of cheap air travel had such a devastating impact on Home Lines transatlantic business that it decided to withdraw from the Europe–Canada business in 1963 and operate exclusively in the cruising market. *Oceanic*, then under construction, was modified into a single class, fully air-conditioned and stabilised cruise ship. As the first engines-aft transatlantic liner, she was Italy's answer to the 1961-built, *Canberra* but with a more attractive and streamlined profile. Designed by the naval architect Nicolò Costanzi, her lifeboats were situated, like *Canberra*, low down on the hull. Her ice-strengthened hull had a flared, bulbous bow whilst her stern had a transom stern for the underwater portion and a cruiser stern for the part above. Turbine-driven and twin-screwed, she was also a fast ship with a top speed of 27 knots and a service speed of 25.5 knots. Her passenger facilities and accommodation for 1,601 passengers were outstanding and included private facilities in all cabins. Not only did she have eight suites with private balconies, but she was also the first ship to have a large lido area (10,350ft^2) with two shaped pools between the funnel and signal mast and the first to be fitted with a Magrodome sliding roof. Her main public rooms were situated on two decks and included the Escoffier Grill at the forward end of the Lido Deck. This 182-seater restaurant was originally designed as the first class dining room. The former tourist class dining room on 'B' deck, the 656-capacity Oceanic Restaurant was immense and was one of the largest rooms afloat. There were 17 public rooms including a 420-seater cinema and a central lounge, the Aegean Room, with seating for 574. The same group of famous Italian designers who were involved in the décor of Italia's final liners also worked on *Oceanic*. The public areas included some great art. Among these were thirty-two carved aluminium panels by Nino Zoncada which decorated the staircase halls. *Oceanic* was delivered in March 1965 and the following month was placed on the Home Lines seven-day cruise service between New York and the Bahamas. After twenty years based in New York, she was sold in 1985 to become one of Premier Cruises 'Big Red Boats' operating out of Port Canaveral, Florida as *StarShip Oceanic*. She was renamed *Red Boat I* not long after Premier went bankrupt in 2000 and was sold to the Spanish-based Pullmantur Cruises, reverting to her original name. In 2009 she was bought by the Japanese Peace Boat organisation and was sold to Chinese breakers in 2012.

Costa's final passenger liner

In the immediate post-war years Linea C or Costa Line, as it was known in the English-speaking world, converted a number of former American ships for a new service between Italy and South America aimed at the thousands of Italians leaving Italy in search of a better life abroad. New routes opened to Central America and the company gained an excellent reputation for reliability and quality of service so much so that in 1958, it took delivery of its first newly-built passenger liner. *Federico C.*, a handsome 20,416gt liner with a large funnel, was the first liner on the Europe-South America run with stabilisers. The design of her public rooms by the naval architect Nino Zoncada was also of a very high standard and she remained on the River Plate route until 1966 when she was replaced by the 30,567gt *Eugenio C.* Built at the same yard as *Oceanic*, she was one of the finest liners to operate to South America. Designed as a dual-purpose ship for the liner trade to South America and for cruising, her interiors were mainly the work of Nino Zoncada. He produced a series of public rooms which were both comfortable and modern looking without the starkness usually associated with 1960s design. The first class ballroom, for example, had orange and white seating and an elliptical shaped metal-coloured ceiling. The last passenger liner built in Italy, the hull of *Eugenio C.* was similar to *Oceanic*, i.e. a clipper-type forward-sloping bulbous bow with a wave guide and a cruiser stern combined with a transom stern. She was also designed to proceed up the Rio de Plata as far as Buenos Aires. Her streamlined superstructure and passenger layout were further influenced by the Home Line ship including a lido area amidships with a sliding roof. However, unlike *Oceanic*, only half her 1,666 passengers (208 first and 1,458 tourist) enjoyed cabins with private facilities. The most distinctive aspect of *Eugenio C.* was the unusual shape of her funnels. Designed by Turin Politecnico, creators of *Michelangelo* and *Raffaello*'s lattice-work funnels, the slightly divaricated twin funnels were mounted side by side, each with a fin at the crown to ensure maximum smoke dispersal away from the passenger decks. Driven by twin-screws and geared turbines, the 28-knot *Eugenio C.* was the fastest liner operating to South America. The six and a half days she took to steam from Lisbon to Rio de Janeiro in 1966, at an average speed of 27.5 knots, remains the record liner crossing for the route. For the next thirty years she was used increasingly as a cruise ship with occasional voyages to South America. In 1996 she was sold to the shipyard Bremer Vulkan after which time her career went steadily downhill. A brief spell in the UK market as *Edinburgh Castle* was followed by a charter to Premier Cruises as *The Big Red Boat II*. After the collapse of Premier in 2000 she was laid up at Freeport and sold to Alang breakers five years later.

The last Swedish liner

Although Swedish American Line only owned a few passenger ships, the company had an outstanding reputation for the quality of its accommodation and the service provided for passengers. This was especially true in the 1950s when it took delivery of two new 22,000-ton twin-funnelled liners, *Kungsholm* and *Gripsholm*. These liners were among the most exclusive of their day. Although built for the North Atlantic, they were also used extensively for cruising. The decline in the North Atlantic passenger trade in the early 1960s caused Swedish American to shift away from the North Atlantic and focus more on upmarket cruising. In 1962 it placed an order with the Clydebank yard, John Brown and Company for a 26,678gt, 23-knot, twin-screw replacement for *Kungsholm* which was sold in 1965 to Norddeutscher Lloyd. Completed in 1966 the new *Kungsholm* was an evolution of the earlier pair of Swedish American liners with two raked funnels with fins, the forward funnel was a dummy. She also had a beautifully-shaped clipper bow, bulbous forepart, cruiser stern, a steel hull strengthened fore and aft for North Atlantic service and was fitted with special anti-creak girders to reduce movement noise whilst underway. On the North Atlantic run she was a 750-capacity two-class ship, but on cruises only carried 450 passengers in a single class. There was also a garage in the forward hatch trunk with space for fifteen cars and dog kennels on the sun deck. The design of her public rooms was undertaken by a number of British and Swedish designers co-ordinated by the Swedish marine interior designer Robert Tillberg. The main public rooms were situated on the promenade and veranda decks whilst the dining room was in the traditional position lower down in the ship. The forward observation lounge was a most attractive room with its raised deck and verandas on either side overlooking the bow. On the deck below was a 307-seater auditorium, which was designed to serve as a cinema, theatre, lecture hall and church. However, the *pièce de résistance* was the cherry wood-panelled dining room which had seating for more than 500 people and was able to accommodate all passengers whilst on cruises. When she was completed it was boasted that no bed in the 304 cabins was less than 6ft 7ins in length and 2ft 10ins in width. The majority of cabins also had a bath. *Kungsholm* soon gained a reputation as not only one of the finest cruise ships in the world but also as being among the most attractive-looking passenger ships of the day. Known as the 'White Viking Fleet', for the next nine years *Kungsholm* and *Gripsholm* travelled the globe with only the occasional transatlantic voyage. By the mid-1970s, the two liners operated at a loss because of rocketing fuel prices and the high cost of using an all-Swedish crew. In September 1975, *Kungsholm* was taken out of service, bringing to an end almost sixty years of Swedish American Line passenger services. After a brief spell with Flagship Cruises, she was bought by P&O Cruises. She was given a refit, which saw her transformed almost beyond recognition. The major external change to the ship was the removal of her forward dummy funnel and the heightening of the remaining one. In March 1979 she entered service as *Sea Princess*. This was later changed to *Victoria* to fit in with the UK market branding of the other two ships in the P&O Cruises' fleet, *Canberra* and *Oriana*. By 2002 following the arrival of increasingly larger ships, *Victoria* no longer fitted into the P&O fleet and was sold. Renamed *Mona Lisa*, she had a chequered career and was sold to Indian breakers in Alang in 2015.

Cunard's new 'Queen'

Although its main threat in the 1950s and 1960s was from air travel, Cunard Line also faced serious competition from its transatlantic rivals. In 1952, United States Lines' *United States* had broken *Queen Mary*'s fourteen-year-old record westbound crossing whilst later in the decade French Line, Holland America Line and Italia were building and planning beautiful streamlined flagships such as *France*, *Rotterdam*, *Michelangelo* and *Raffaello*. The Cunard pre-war liners on the New York run were looking decidedly old-fashioned and out of date. In 1959 Cunard announced that it intended to replace *Queen Mary* with a new ship. A year later, the British Government-sponsored Chandos Report was published and recommended that the *Queen Mary* replacement should be a 75,000gt, 29.5-knot, 2,270-capacity liner at a cost estimated to be up to £28 million. However, the '*Q3*' project, as it became known, evoked mixed reactions because of a continuing decline in transatlantic traffic. A concept proposal was produced for a smaller, twin-screw liner described by Cunard as 'a top flight cruise ship and a revolutionary North Atlantic unit'. In 1964, the contract was awarded to John Brown for the new liner, which was due for delivery in 1968. After a spectacular launch by Her Majesty Queen Elizabeth in 1967, the completion of the 67,139gt, 28.5-knot *Queen Elizabeth 2* in late 1968 was an embarrassment not just for Britain but British shipbuilding in particular. During her final acceptance trials and shakedown cruise, she developed a major technical problem with her starboard turbine. On her arrival back at Southampton in January 1969, Cunard refused to accept the ship and there was a five-month delay before her maiden voyage. Despite these teething problems, *Queen Elizabeth 2* went on to become one of the best-loved passenger ships of the twentieth century. As built her passenger capacity was 564 first and 1,441 tourist. Whilst cruising she carried 1,400 in a single class. However, unlike *Rotterdam*, many of her public rooms were altered over the years and although she was designed for cruising, her two-class configuration was often confusing for passengers finding their way around the ship. Her interiors were conceived by a team of Britain's most talented designers. The most successful public room was undoubtedly the Queen's Room, which was designed by Michael Inchbald. With its space-age ceiling and columns reminiscent of Stanley Kubrick's 1968 film *2001: A Space Odyssey*, the Queen's Room remained virtually unchanged throughout her 39-year career with Cunard. The quality of *Queen Elizabeth 2*'s cabins was superior to most British liners in 1969 and all had en-suite toilets and showers or baths. In 1972 she had a refit which included the addition of ten penthouse suites on the Sports Deck and replacement of her stabilisers. Three years later she left Southampton on the first of many world cruises. *Queen Elizabeth 2* was in the news again in 1982 when she was requisitioned by the British Government as a troopship during the Falklands War. On her return her funnel was repainted in traditional Cunard colours and in 1983 her hull reverted to traditional Cunard charcoal grey. In 1987 her steam turbines were replaced by diesel engines which extended her life but were noisier than the turbines especially for those in amidships cabins. Her funnel was also replaced with a wider and more substantial one. In 1998 Cunard was acquired by the Carnival Corporation and ten years later she was sold to QE2 Enterprises, Dubai for use as a floating hotel.

The German 'Space Ship'

One of the last large passenger liners ever built was the 23-knot, twin-screw, turbine-driven, 25,022gt *Hamburg* which was completed for Deutsche Atlantik Linie in 1969. She had been conceived as a consort to *Hanseatic* (ex-*Empress of Scotland* 1930/30,030gt) which operated Hamburg Atlantik Linie's service between Cuxhaven and New York. After *Hanseatic* was lost in a fire in 1966 Hamburg Atlantik Linie was wound up and a new company Deutsche Atlantik Linie formed. It placed an order the same year with Deutsche Werft, Hamburg for the new liner and in 1967 it acquired Zim Line's *Shalom* as a new *Hanseatic*. In 1968 Deutsche Atlantik Linie decided to discontinue the North Atlantic service and concentrate on cruising. Thus, the new ship under construction was completed as a cruise ship with occasional transatlantic positioning voyages. She was designed as a consort to the similar-sized second *Hanseatic* and therefore also had a funnel two-thirds aft. It was this unique saucer-shape funnel top funnel which gave *Hamburg* her distinctive appearance. She carried only 652 passengers, was fully air-conditioned and equipped with Denny Brown stabilisers. At the time she was referred to 'The Space Ship' because the greatest possible area was devoted to passenger comfort. She had two decks of contemporary-designed public rooms including a theatre, two ballrooms and a chapel. There were also two pools, one outdoor and another indoors with sauna and massage rooms. Another unusual aspect of *Hamburg* was that she had three restaurants including a grill room so that passengers chose where they wished to dine according to their mood. Almost all her cabins had a bath although many were inboard because the company felt that it was better to offer an ample-size cabin rather than a small one with a porthole. At the time of her completion *Hamburg* was the largest liner to be built in Germany for thirty years. In 1973 after *Hanseatic* was sold, *Hamburg* was renamed *Hanseatic*. Unfortunately, at the end of the year Deutsche Atlantik Linie ceased operations and she was laid up. Meanwhile, around the same time the USSR decided to become a major player in the cruise market mainly because it produced badly needed hard foreign currency. In 1974 *Hanseatic* was sold to the Russian state-owned Black Sea Steamship Company. Renamed *Maksim Gorki* she became the largest Russian passenger ship. For twenty-years from 1988 to 2008 she was chartered to the German tour operator Phoenix Reisen and became a very popular ship in the German market. However, as a steam turbine ship her operating costs became too high and in 2009 she was sold to Indian breakers.

The passenger-cargo liner today

Although the days of the large passenger liner have long since gone, apart from *Queen Mary 2* which does cruises across the Atlantic, passenger-cargo liners continue to operate to the more remote parts of the world. These include *St Helena* (1990/6,767gt) which sails between Cape Town and St Helena and *Aranui 5* (2015/7,500gt) which runs between Tahiti and the Marquesas Islands. The Shipping Corporation of India also operates a fleet of passenger ships in Indian waters. In the 1970s it bought the British India liners *Santhia* (1950/8,908gt) and *Karanja* (1948/10,294gt) and renamed them respectively *State of Haryana* and *Nancowry*. In 1974, the company took delivery of *Harsha Vardhana*, the first air-conditioned passenger-cargo liner designed and built in India. Named after the Indian emperor who ruled northern India during the seventh century, this 9,450gt ship was built by Mazagon Dock Ltd. in Mumbai. She was designed for the routes between India and East Africa and the Persian Gulf. With a service speed of 17.4 knots she has accommodation for 153 passengers in cabins and 600 bunk-berthed. She also had a distinctive saucer-shaped funnel top which was also a feature on the German liner *Hamburg*. *Harsha Vardhana* was later transferred to the Andaman and Nicobar Islands service where she runs between Kolkata (Calcutta) and Port Blair (Andaman Islands) as one of the world's oldest regularly-operating large passenger vessels. She continues to operate but in a poor state of maintenance.

Index

IVERNIA
LIVERPOOL